PLANNING AND PRODUCTIVITY IN SWEDEN

Planning and Productivity in Sweden

H. G. JONES

CROOM HELM LONDON
ROWMAN AND LITTLEFIELD TOTOWA N.J.

First published 1976

Croom Helm Ltd, 2-10 St John's Road London SW 11

ISBN 0–85664–214–2

First published in the United States 1976
by ROWMAN AND LITTLEFIELD, Totowa, New Jersey

Library of Congress Cataloging in Publication Data

Jones, H G
Planning and Productivity in Sweden

1. Sweden - - Economic conditions - - 1945 - 2. Labor policy - - Sweden. 3. Industrial relations - - Sweden. 4. Employees' representation in management - - Sweden. I. Title.
HC375.J62 330.9'485'05 75 - 19088
ISBN 0-87471-758-2

Printed and bound in Great Britain by
Redwood Burn Limited, Trowbridge & Esher

CONTENTS

ACKNOWLEDGEMENTS

This book arose out of an investigation into the criteria for successful capital investment sponsored by the Esmée Fairbairn Charitable Trust, to whom thanks are due for financial support. During the work, it was apparent that Sweden has dealt so successfully with many of the factors influencing the outcome of industrial development, that the analysis seemed worthy of wide appreciation.

I would express my gratitude to the very many Swedes who, through discussion and the ready supply of information, have made the work both viable and enjoyable. The permission to reproduce certain illustrations is acknowledged in the text.

My thanks are also due to the several colleagues in the Operational Research Department of the University of Strathclyde, Scotland, who have read the manuscript critically and have made constructive comments.

PART 1: SWEDEN'S ECONOMIC SUCCESS

1 THE SWEDISH ECONOMIC BACKGROUND

Introduction

This book does not pretend to be be an impartial survey of all that is good or bad in Swedish life. It is quite frankly partisan, deliberately seeking to identify the many good points in which the Swedish economy and working arrangements are ahead of most of the industrialised countries of the world. The object is not to denigrate other nations but to show how benefit might be derived from Sweden's experience.

Subsequent chapters examine why a country like Sweden, relatively poor in natural resources, has attained one of the highest living standards in the world judged by any yardstick. The growth in prosperity is not the result of an accident. It has involved conscious acts of policy by management, by unions and occasionally by government. It has involved a professional approach to many problems and dedication to ensure success. It would be naive to hope the transference of an idea or system from one national culture to another would produce the same result: but the idea should at least colour thinking elsewhere and perhaps form the basis for homegrown developments aiming in time for a similar degree of success.

A selection of Swedish aims and activities are discussed in an objective manner and in sufficient detail to enable the reader to appreciate the background against which events have occurred. This book is concerned with attitudes, but to analyse a mental process can be highly subjective and can lead to a morass of jargon: instead the text discusses actions which are the outward signs of the inner attitudes.

Although not written with political intent, it would be gratifying if a wider knowledge of Sweden's experience did lead to material changes in the economy of other countries, including the UK, and so help industry to deal with the problems of the 1980s and beyond. All the available help will certainly be needed if the developed countries are to enjoy the continually rising standards of personal life which in the final analysis can only be paid for through an industrial revival in a flagging economy. It may also help the developing countries to avoid some of the pitfalls of industrialisation.

The rate of exchange at the time of writing is 9.5 Swedish Kroner to the £ sterling, or 4.0 Swedish Kroner to the US Dollar. Generally speaking, figures in the tables are quoted in S. kr. while the text cites figures in £s converted at the approximate rate of 10 S. kr to the £1, with some rounding off.

The background

The first thing that impresses about Sweden is its location. Most people are surprised to find that it is so far north. The most southerly tip, around Malmö, is at the same latitude as Glasgow in the UK, or Winnipeg in Canada. The capital and largest city of Stockholm, situated about 'a quarter of the way up' the country, is further north than the Orkney Isles or Goose Bay in Labrador, while the northern part of the country is well within the Arctic Circle.

It is claimed the Gulf Stream protects Sweden from the full rigours of its situation but in spite of this the northern parts on the Baltic Sea are icebound for several months of the year. Even in Stockholm, the frost is not out of the ground until late April. The winters by temperate standards are long, dark and hard for much of the country. In compensation, for a few weeks in high summer the sun shines brightly and scarcely sets. There is a long and often beautiful coast line, flat in the southern region, more hilly elsewhere, but the boundary with Norway, and much of northern Sweden also, consists largely of rugged mountain ranges. The distance from north to south of about 1,500 road miles is roughly twice the distance from John o' Groats to Lands End, yet the population of 8.1 million is only a seventh of that of the UK. The density of population at 18 per sq. km is very sparse in contrast to a figure in excess of 200 for many industrialised countries of comparable area, as Table 1.1 illustrates. The proportion of the population over 65 years of age, on the other hand, is greater than in many other countries. This is not really the kind of ideal specification one would choose for economic success.

What manner of people are the Swedes to triumph over this combination of circumstances? Possibly because of the winters and partly because of their upbringing, the Swedes tend to be rather serious, hard working folk prepared to attend classes in the winter for self-improvement, for leisure pursuits or to gain knowledge of union interests – 'canny' perhaps describes this aspect of the Swedish character. But for a few weeks in summer, life is to be enjoyed in outdoor activities of every kind: everyone gets four weeks holiday on full pay and many take even longer holidays by changing jobs if necessary to get the time off from work. Physical fitness is almost a national obsession. Like all generalisations, these descriptions are not wholly true for everyone, but it is not an unfair picture and certainly is not intended to be uncharitable.

Table 1.1 Comparative population figures

	Sweden	USA	UK	West Germany	Japan	Holland
Population per sq. km	18	22	229	247	289	326
Total population m (1972)	8.1	209	55.8	61.7	106	13.3
Relative area	2.8	39	1	1	1.5	0.2
% of population over 65	14.0	8.2	12.3	11.0	6.9	-

About a quarter of the total population is centered on the three large conurbations of Stockholm (1.3m), Götenborg or Gothenburg (0.7m), and Malmö (0.5m) in each of which much of the accommodation is in large blocks of flats. A further large percentage of the population lives in a belt of country stretching, fairly narrow at first, from Gothenburg on the west coast and fanning out to Stockholm on the east coast. It follows then that north of this belt, the country is very sparsely populated indeed; even within this belt and also south of it, there are long stretches of agricultural or forest lands. Because both of these industries are highly mechanised, in much of the countryside there is scant evidence of man.

Swedish agriculture obviously cannot compete with the exotic products of the Mediterranean countries. By a process of agricultural research followed by intensive use of fertilisers, the grain crop of 4.6m tons per annum now shows a yield comparable with the best in Europe, while the potato crop of 1.2m tons and 1.7m tons of sugar beet both make worthwhile contributions to the economy. Although these figures for crops are high, some 80 per cent of farm income is derived from animal products.

With the risk of war very much in mind, the aim is for Sweden to be 80 per cent self-sufficient in the production of foodstuffs. Encouragement is given to agriculture through flexible import duties designed to enable farmers to get a satisfactory price for their products. The farmers have helped themselves by uniting into cooperatives for the marketing of their products and the purchase of equipment: two such organisations, one for the sale of meat and the second for other products, rank ninth and tenth in turnover in the business league for the whole of Sweden and between them employ 18,000 workers. In spite of all this activity, only 7 per cent of the country's labour force is currently employed in agriculture and forestry, which are thus very efficient.

Natural resources

Forestry

More than half of the land area of Sweden is covered with magnificent forests; lumbering and the kindred industries are accordingly the most widely dispersed of all the country's industries, but even so the centre of gravity is well to the south. This is partly because of the easier access for labour and to markets, but also because the productivity per hectare is better in the south, the trees growing closer together and only requiring 80 years to mature compared with the 120 years in the north. Lumbering operations have been streamlined into efficient production units, and associated with them, usually in vertically integrated organisations, there is a thriving industry for the manufacture and export of quality furniture: a parallel industry exists for the production of prefabricated building sections. The output of these industries has grown rapidly in recent years and is expected to continue to grow at the rate of 7.4 per cent per annum in the five years leading up to 1977.

Production of wood pulp is on a massive scale and is increasing steadily at about 6 per cent per annum, the 9.5m tons produced in 1972 making Sweden the fourth largest producer of pulp in the world. Of this, nearly 3.8m tons was converted into newsprint, kraft paper or board in fully integrated mills. The combined production of all the timber related industries amounts by value to 14.5 per cent of the total manufacturing capacity of the country, and to about 25 per cent of the total exports of Sweden. In this respect at any rate, other countries lacking timber resources cannot emulate Sweden: they can only look with admiration at the growth rates achieved by a major sector of the economy, and achieved moreover with a diminishing labour force.

Iron and steel

Sweden has no reserves of fossil fuels, all of which have to be imported. The only other material resource of any magnitude is iron ore which is mined in two areas, one around Bergslagen in the centre of Sweden and the other around Gällivare in the far north. The latter is a high purity ore which finds favour in export markets. To export a raw material, such as iron ore from Sweden, coal from the UK, or cotton from the USA, is not necessarily the wisest economic policy: it is better to process the raw material and then export it, or a product made from it, at a higher value. The Swedes have been conscious of this and over the years have proceeded along three routes. The first is to process the ore through crushing, refining and pelletising: this has been followed in the north. Also in the north, a works has been built at Lulea to convert the iron ore into mild steel sections for use mostly in Sweden: this is the second route and is operated by the only state owned steel works in socialist Sweden and the one incidentally for which the direct economics are dubious.

The third route is followed by the remaining twenty-two steel works in Sweden: these are concerned to produce steel of the highest quality (and therefore the highest price) and often also to convert this steel into quality products. Three companies in this area are of interest. Sandvik, employing 19,000 on the manufacture of high grade specialty steels of which 88 per cent is exported, earned 5.8 per cent on total capital employed in 1972. Gränges, rather more diversified, employ 21,000 and produce amongst other products the heavy steel plate upon which the modernised shipbuilding industry of Sweden largely depends; return on working capital was 3.5 per cent. Lastly, the Domnarvet plant of the diversified company of Stora, with 14,000 workers has been in existence since the Middle Ages and claims to be the oldest joint stock company in the world: profit was only 2.1 per cent on working capital in 1972.

Energy

Lacking fossil fuels, Sweden has been forced to turn to other sources of energy. Fortunately water power is reasonably plentiful and currently 80 per cent of the electricity consumption of the country is supplied from hydro-electric stations – incidentally 52 per cent of the electrical system of the country is in private ownership. Nature has not been over cooperative since the sources of water power are almost invariably located well away from the centres of consumption: transmission costs are therefore considerable. Moreover the potential for further development is restricted and by 1980 is expected to be non-existent.

Although Sweden has been active in the nuclear energy field since 1954, only 0.1 per cent of the total energy of the country was derived in 1971 from nuclear fuels compared with 3 per cent in the UK, or about 0.4 per cent in the USA, Germany or Japan. Recognising the undesirability of a heavy dependence on imported oil, Sweden has planned a major expansion of nuclear power stations so that by 1990, nuclear capacity will have increased fifty-fold, whereas other nuclear capacity is expected to increase at a lower rate – thirty-five-fold for Germany, twelve-fold for the UK and sixteen-fold (to 1985) for USA.

Imported oil is largely used to generate the balance of 20 per cent of the electrical load through back pressure stations, the residual heat being used for district heating schemes – heating of one form or another consumes forty-three per cent of the total energy of the country, a reflection of the climate and of the standard of living in nearly universally centrally heated buildings. Transport (apart from the railways which are all electrified) is a heavy consumer of oil. In fact Sweden is more dependent on imported oils than most countries: in 1971, 74 per cent of the total energy was supplied from this source and was only narrowly exceeded by Japan at 75 per cent, compared with 45 per cent for the UK and the USA, or 61 per cent for the OECD as a whole. Since the Middle East oil troubles, Sweden has made some progress in changing the balance away from oil but this can only be a slow process.

Living standards

This then is the basic background to the Swedish economy. To a not overpromising picture should be added a somewhat isolated position for export trading, Sweden being hemmed in on the one hand by the giant neighbours of Russia and Germany and on the other by the Scandinavian countries of Norway, Finland and Denmark with not dissimiliar and therefore competing economies. Yet Table 1.2 shows that the Gross Domestic Product per capita is second only to that of the USA and almost twice that of the UK and Japan. There are per head of population more cars, more television sets, more doctors, nearly twice as many telephones and twice as many students in Sweden as compared with the UK. If that is not enough to demonstrate a higher standard of living, Swedes now spend three and a half times as much per head on foreign holidays as do Britons and when at home have very extensive municipal parks, sports stadia and swimming pools and so on for their enjoyment. Many of these comparisons hold with equal force for the other progressive countries of Table 1.2.

The Swedish standard of living in the early 1970s was thus rivalling that of the USA (the world's leaders) and is rising steadily. Japan has the fastest growing economy but the standard of living is well behind that of Sweden.

Table 1.2 Indicators of material prosperity for 1971 (GDP for 1972: Doctors for 1970)

	Sweden	USA	West Germany	UK	Japan
In S. kr per capita					
Gross Domestic Product	24,500	26,170	19,880	13,140	13,210
Foreign travel	319	100	253	92	24
Per 1,000 inhabitants					
No. of cars	291	446	240	219	101
No. of TV sets	322	449	299	298	222
No. of telephones	557	604	319	289	282
No. of students	14	39	7	6	16
No. of doctors	1.3	1.5	1.7	1.2	1.1

Swedish industry

The standard of living has not always been high. Apart from early iron making, industrialisation was late in arriving in Sweden. It was not until the opening decades of the twentieth century that industrial development led to the growth of urban communities by migration from the countryside. Thus while the worst excesses of the industrial revolution were avoided, life in the main was hard and comfort could only be at a level a struggling agricultural economy could sustain. How then was this transformation achieved in about half a century?

In part this has been due to a skilful management concentrating on the production of premium products that are in tune with world market requirements. Equally important has been the generation of an industrial climate that has enabled industry to modernise with so little fuss. Radical changes in working practices have been introduced for a high productivity to become the norm for the country – throughout the 1960s the output of manufacturing industry rose by about 7 per cent per annum, and at the same time the man-hours worked fell by about 1 per cent per annum. Neither is production interrupted by strikes which are believed in the long run to be harmful to the best interests of both sides of industry, and also damaging to the social fabric of the community. Later chapters discuss at some length the problems involved in reaching this enviable state. The development of union structure and of the corresponding employers' associations is also traced because there are many lessons to be observed: without appreciating these, the present status of the Swedish economy would resemble the accomplishment of a magician rather than the result of determined creative action by many people.

Swedish business has been very much alive to the changing pattern of demand in recent years. Where the change process has been accelerated by technological development, or where it has been desirable to restructure production in order to obtain economies of scale, the satisfactory labour relations have enabled Sweden to accommodate the changes rapidly and efficiently. If a high productivity is the norm for Sweden, so can change be described as a second norm. The result is that the Swedish manufacturing scene is dominated by a few advanced products which have gained an international reputation for excellence. Many of these are in engineering which currently accounts for more than a half of Swedish industry and exports the very high figure of 46 per cent of its output by value.

The manufacture of heavy electrical generators and electric motors was developed for the domestic market by ASEA but this has expanded into an export market of some size. The same can be said for telephonic equipment in which the firm of L. M. Ericsson has played a major part, while the AGA company has an international reputation for domestic appliances and in maritime circles for the acetylene lighthouse which it pioneered. The invention of the refrigerator without moving parts is due to Electrolux while in the engineering fields it is not possible to mention ball bearings without thinking of Skefco, nor of gauge blocks without C. E. Johansson. The common factor among all of these is the high quality, precision nature of the products, all with a high value added content and therefore eminently suitable for exporting.

Characteristically, the Swedes have developed well engineered equipment to deal effectively with their only raw materials in the shape of mobile mechanised units for the cutting, trimming and handling of timber, and specialised machines for the crushing, refining and other treatment of iron ore. This equipment is so good that an export market has also developed for the sale of the equipment on world markets.

With a typical emphasis on top class design features, cars have been produced for the upper middle band of the market by Volvo and by Saab. It is also typical that Volvo have diversified successfully into earth moving equipment and light marine engines, and also that Saab make more profit from the manufacture of aeroplanes than from cars.

The list of firms and accomplishments may be distinguished but it is not never-ending; because Sweden is a country with a small population, the same names are apt to recur repeatedly in the management literature. They have been introduced at this stage to give the flavour of the country's industry but the full significance of the progressive nature of Swedish thinking can be better appreciated from a brief examination of a particular sector such as shipbuilding which has a progressive outlook and is profitable in Sweden.

Shipbuilding

The shipbuilding industry in Sweden is dominated by Kockums, a yard located in Malmö and engaged in the production of large oil tankers of 250,000 and 350,000 ton capacity. The word 'production' is used advisedly since this is precisely what Kockums set out to do – to convert shipbuilding into a production line, and in so doing convert a loss of £5.4m in 1969 into a profit before tax of £13m in 1973.

When examining the spectacular changes in the fortunes of Kockums, it is easy to lose sight of the fact that Swedish shipbuilding as a whole constitutes a formidable modern industry employing directly or indirectly some 50,000 people. Of the fourteen shipbuilding yards, eight have been modernised, sometimes at considerable capital cost with the introduction of flow line methods of production: a further four yards have specialised to reach a high level of efficiency in the design and output of smaller vessels for particular markets. The result is that by 1971 and in subsequent years, the output of the Swedish yards is second only in world volume to that of Japan.

Some of the buyers are from shipbuilding countries such as the UK. Why do these companies go to Sweden to buy ships? The Swedish shipbuilders association claim it is because 'the Swedish shipyards have certain common characteristics: high quality products, advanced technical expertise, delivery dates that can be relied upon and competitive prices'. Surely a good formula for financial success. It is also a formula that requires much hard work and considerable capital investment. Having reached a high peak of efficiency, the industry is not standing still but has programmes for further investment and a strong commitment to research and development. The state owned yard at Uddevalla, for instance, claims that in order to remain competitive the yard 'must renew itself at least every ten to twelve years'. If, as a 1973 OECD report indicates, there is surplus shipbuilding capacity by the 1980s, it is the weak who will go to the wall – and Sweden obviously does not intend to be among the weak.

For the last three years, Kockums has spent an average of £1.18m per annum on research and development, 35 per cent of which is paid for by a government grant from the technical development board: the total is approximately 1.5 per cent of the annual turnover measured as invoiced sales and about £220 per annum per employee. During the same period, the turnover per employee in the shipyard division has been about £15,000 per annum.

Not all of the Kockums' story has been of unqualified success. In the 1960s, it was an organisation struggling to remain alive. Subsequent attempts to diversify were not altogether successful and culminated in the liquidation in 1972 of certain loss making subsidiaries mainly concerned with excavation and earth moving equipment: the outstanding exception has been the design and manufacture of heavy equipment and systems for the logging industry which presently is a growth area for capital investment. In fact, the non-shipbuilding division achieved an invoiced sales turnover of £2,400 per employee in 1973. Because of the earlier difficulties, Kockums embarked on the market research, planning and philosophy which have led to the present success.

There are very clear lessons in all of the above for shipbuilding economies. In particular, without adequate capital investment backed by the right kind of research and improved labour relations leading to a streamlining of production methods, the shipbuilding industry of the western world will have difficulty in withstanding the challenge from Sweden as well as from Japan.

Conclusion

It is obviously not part of the function of this book to dwell at length on the shortcomings of the Swedish economic-industrial-social system. It would be equally wrong to leave the impression that everything is perfect, or that everyone in Sweden is rapturously happy with the state influence on the economy. The high rate of taxation on higher incomes also has its critics. The socialist policy of equality too will not please everyone although at the same time the doctrine of social responsibility for the less able is widely accepted. Some may believe an overpowerful establishment has been created: powerful it certainly is but not inflexible.

Later chapters discuss how the Swedish system has developed a flexibility and a willingness first to analyse and then to deal with a new problem before it reached too intractable proportions. The flexibility did not come easily but it is now indeed a remarkable feature in the success of Sweden that as a result the economy is often better able to face the future than it was before the problems arose. Real, fundamental solutions are sought rather than expediencies. Moreover this kind of evolution is recognised in most quarters as a continuing process; it may be an uncomfortable process but it is inevitable, so why resist? The philosophy of acceptance after due reasoning is widespread in Sweden and makes for a continuation of the authority of the establishment. Peoples in other economies with different political backgrounds may not find it so easy to accept new ideas even though Sweden has demonstrated the utility of acceptance.

Whatever one thinks of this aspect of the Swedish system, there can be no doubting of the solid achievements described in this chapter. The next two chapters go in some detail into the interactive mechanism between state and industry which has fostered the material development of Swedish society. There follow three chapters tracing the changing relationship between employers and unions; early bitterness has been replaced by wise counsel from both sides of industry seeking, with considerable success, to create a situation wherein reason and discussion prevail, thus making possible the material progress in the standard of living. In spite of this advantageous position, shop floor dissatisfaction became apparent only to be met realistically and sympathetically with different forms of industrial democracy, as indicated in the next three chapters. This survey continues with two chapters examining how effective have been attempts to control the economy, the financial effects of investment and the functioning of the national pension funds. The survey concludes with an estimate of the future trends of controls and planning and the social pressures these trends are likely to generate.

Sweden continues to demonstrate how a small country with few natural advantages can, with determination, attain in the modern world a remarkable prosperity. Can other nations benefit from Sweden's experience? It is hoped this book will encourage them to try.

2 PLANNING THE ECONOMY: THE ROLE OF THE LABOUR MARKET BOARD

Political system

In order to appreciate the influence of central planning on the Swedish economy, it is necessary first to look briefly at the political structure of the country.

Unemployment in Sweden in 1931 was at the disastrously high level of 32 per cent with the result that the ruling Conservative party lost the election of the next year and have remained out of office ever since. The Social Democrats took over and, apart from 100 days in 1936, have remained in office either as the majority party or as the main party in a coalition government: since 1957, the socialists have formed a single party cabinet, usually with only a narrow majority. Although the socialists are still in office, the 1973 election resulted in a dead heat, the socialists and the anti-socialists bloc each having 175 seats in the Riksdag disposed as shown below:

Social Democrats	156 seats	Conservatives	51 seats
Communists	19	Liberals	34
		Centre Party	90
	175		175

To prevent the recurrence of a similar *impasse*, the size of the Riksdag has been reduced by one seat for the next election. Since 1971, there has only been one house consisting entirely of members elected for a term of three years.

Government has been possible because, broadly speaking, the Centre Party is not unsympathetic to many of the proposals advanced by a socialist cabinet. The continuity of power has merits in that it enables a stable policy to be enacted through the legislation and then to permeate through the economic life of the community. It is evident that these policies have found favour with sufficient of the electorate for the socialists to be re-elected time and time again. The continuity persists in part because the electoral system is based on proportional representation, one virtue of which is that the comparatively slow and minor changes in opinion (that is apart from the 'don't knows') of the majority do not result in a landslide of seats one way or the other. To avoid a proliferation of minority groups which would make the task of forming and running government difficult, to gain representation, a party must secure 12 per cent of the votes in a particular constituency (310 members represent constituencies) or 4 per cent of the national vote (by which the remaining forty members of the Riksdag are elected). Since 1966, each party receives a state grant proportional to its representation in the Riksdag.

Local government functions are discharged through twenty-three county councils (which look after medical care) and 278 municipal or local councils which, broadly speaking, look after other local functions. All of these councils, which are elected on the same day as the Riksdag, are supported by a proportion of the income tax, 9 per cent going to the county councils and 15 per cent going to the local councils, with some adjustment from the government to even out inequalities between resources and responsibilities. The importance of the bigger municipalities lies in the relatively large funds they have at their disposal and the way in which they have used these funds to promote social schemes, subject to the interests of the Directorate of National Planning.

The main administrative difference between Sweden and other western democracies appears in the way the central government operates. The government, or more especially the minister of a department such as Welfare or Labour, determines policy but is not directly responsible for the day-to-day implementation of the policy. The implementation is at two levels: the one, decentralised and at county level, carries out the government policy through administrative boards headed by governors, all government nominees; the other is a centralised function operating through a board consisting of members representing different interests and headed by a director general who is a government nominee – frequently a politician or trade union leader. The central board is permitted to operate very largely in an autonomous fashion within the guidelines of government policy. The central function will often have representatives working at county level.

Sweden has therefore a considerable bureaucracy concerned with the execution of government. The system has the very real advantage that officials can get on with the work without having to adjust to the vagaries of frequently changing ministers. Stability of departmental purpose is thus much enhanced in Sweden and has probably helped in maintaining the steady progress towards economic stability.

It is with the influence of one of the most powerful of these bureaucracies, the Labour Market Board, that this chapter is largely concerned, but before going further, it is only fair to say that some view the rise to power of the bureaucrats with disquiet. Roland Huntford in *The New Totalitarians* views with alarm the creeping danger of the state interfering with the right to self-determinism of the individual; he is equally alarmed at the potential influence of an efficient bureaucracy on the workings of democracy. In the same vein, a Swedish working party concerned with future trends declared in 1972 that 'planning harbours a danger of rule by experts and elites'. Without participating in this argument beyond recognising that it does have some validity, it must be said that the Labour Market Board is a powerful body, exercising a considerable influence both on the economy and on the lives of many workers, but this power has been exercised responsibly and with discretion by the present incumbents of its senior posts. It remains to be seen whether the next generation will be equally successful in avoiding the pitfalls of power. Time alone will show whether the Swedes as a whole will be prepared to continue to accept the remarkable influence of the bureaucrats, beneficial though it has been.

Objectives of a balanced economy

When the socialists came into power in 1932, they recognised the need to temper their ambitions to the reality of sober economics. Before new social benefits could be distributed, the very formidable economic troubles of high unemployment and lost production through strikes and lockouts had to be cured. Instead of chopping up the national cake, the politicians decided first to create a bigger cake. The chief 'chef' is generally believed to be Ernst Wigforss, the Minister of Finance, who laid down the principles of a planned economy with full employment as a major first objective, not only for social reasons but, through the capitalist system, to create the wealth on which future prosperity depended.

The planned economy has been seen to work so well that it is now accepted by all the political parties in Sweden. Its success has also been due in no small part to the recognition in recent years by the employers and the unions that they have a large measure of common interest in raising the level of the country's Gross Domestic Product. It is agreed on all sides that the only way to achieve real increases in the standard of living is through higher productivity and through avoiding interruptions to production.

The Labour Market Board (known in Sweden as the AMS) was established as a principal means of controlling the economy. It does this to a large degree through the Investment Funds, encouraging investment at the approach of a recession, restricting investment when the economy is buoyant. It encourages the redeployment of workers through training schemes and financial assistance. Its aim is to develop an active manpower planning policy which both encourages and anticipates change.

The unemployment figures are the first measure of the success of the policy: in the nine years to 1940, unemployment was reduced gradually from the peak of 32 per cent to a figure of 8.5 per cent. It had been the opinion expressed in a model of the economy advanced by the economist Güsta Rehn, and widely accepted in Sweden, that 100 per cent employment was impossible: a controlled situation with workers changing jobs in accordance with demand would be represented by 3 or 4 per cent unemployment. In fact, Sweden has done rather better than this, the fall in unemployment continuing steadily to a level of 1.5 per cent in 1950: apart from minor excursions due to recessions which were tackled vigorously, unemployment has since remained between 1.5 and 2 per cent.

Germany and Japan have also maintained high levels of productive employment. The exception perhaps is the UK, where the level of unemployment in recent years has also been about 1.5 per cent or less but at the cost of overmanning. In Sweden unemployment has been held at the low level at the same time as industry has been modernised to a high level of efficiency and the manning adjusted according to real requirements.

It has not been part of the Labour Market Board philosophy to maintain full employment at the expense of overmanning. The trade unions are entirely in sympathy with this philosophy, indeed to be otherwise would be in conflict with the double aim of increasing job satisfaction for their members, as described in chapter eight, and of raising living standards. Within this philosophy, there can be no place for state ownership of industry as a means of preserving the same number of jobs as a kind of sacred trust (or political dogma) regardless of economics.

It is agreed in Sweden that it is a mistake to tax the profitable and therefore efficient companies in order to support the inefficient by means of subsidies or to underwrite state ownership simply as a means of preserving jobs: to do so would have the effect of lowering the tempo of the economy. The Swedes look for an expanding and prosperous economy and so prefer to encourage the profitable, through tax concessions, to reinvest and become still more efficient. Taxes on profits are high at 54 per cent (made up of corporation tax at 40 per cent and local tax at an average of 14 per cent), so there is considerable incentive to use all the concessions available.

State ownership

In view of the foregoing, it is not surprising to find in socialist Sweden that only 4 per cent of the industry is in state ownership together with another 2 per cent owned by the large municipalities.

The state enterprises, some twenty-nine in all, operate on business lines through a company in which the state is the sole shareholder, with its own managing director and other officials totalling the remarkably low figure of thirty-six for a labour force of 35,000. The company, known as Statsföretag, was established in January 1970 by an act of parliament to take over some existing state enterprises; it is expected to compete on the open market and to make a profit. Table 2.1 shows that overall it did make a profit of approximately £29m in 1972 in spite of losses in some areas. With invoiced sales running at £12,300 per employee and 54 per cent of that in export markets, this is obviously no weakling requiring the support of the state.

The range of interests is very wide: it includes two shipbuilding yards, Uddevallavarvet and Karlskronavarvet, both of which made a profit in 1972, and of which the former, although already very modern, is preparing heavy investment programmes in order to enter the 1980s with modern and efficient installations. The group takes an aggressive interest in improving its efficiency through investment in key subsidiaries.

Table 2.1 Profits in m S. kr, before tax and allocations, of nationalised sectors of the Swedish economy in 1972

	Profit	No. of subsidiaries
Mines	262.9	2
Steelworks, etc.	−68.1	6
Forest products	−24.9	1
Tobacco	139.6	1
Pharmaceuticals	20.4	1
Hotels and restaurants	−26.7	1
Other activities	−18.3	17
Totals	284.9	29

A company is only taken over by Statsföretag either as a temporary measure while the workers find other employment or because there seems a reasonable chance of attaining profitability through rationalisation with other subsidiaries within the group. That there is no feather-bedding can be seen from SMT, a small group owned by Statsföretag and specialising in the design and manufacture of numerically controlled lathes and other semi-automatic machine tools. In order to concentrate production at Västerås, in 1972, two subsidiaries located at Ronneby and Karlskoga were sold and a branch in Eskilstuna was closed down, the numbers employed being reduced by 300. The loudest criticism against Statsföretag is that if it takes over a company, initially it only pays 60 per cent of the asset value until profitability is determined when further payments may be made: the balance sheet therefore shows an inflated return on total assets at 3.5 per cent before tax.

The exceptions to the generalisation on state takeover are in the far north of Sweden where the iron ore mines in the Arctic Circle are regarded as a national asset. These were taken over completely in 1957 when the government exercised an option existing since 1907 to buy out the 50 per cent holding of Gränges, the company which had developed and operated the mines. More than 90 per cent of the iron ore is exported after only limited treatment. The steelworks near Lulea is an attempt to increase the value added component of the product before export. A major expansion to increase the capacity of the steel making plant (as opposed to the rolling mills) from 1.4 million tons per annum in 1972 to 5.4 million tons was under intensive study in 1972 when it became an election issue to prevent depopulation of the far north: the scheme is now going ahead in stages as 'Project 80'.

This is very major expansion indeed which will be faced with immense difficulties because of its location. The Baltic Sea is frozen for many months of the year thus necessitating new ice breakers to bring in the coke and to ship out the ingots or blooms; an elaborate planning system will need to be devised to support this import-export complex. It is by no means certain this project will be economically successful. All of the coke has to be imported. The value added is limited because production is only to ingots or blooms and stops short of the more profitable, but capital intensive, finishing processes. Although sales are being negotiated with finishing plants in Germany and Holland, there are fears that the price may not be maintained. It can also be argued that to use the high grade ore found at Kiruna to make steel by the L-D process is wasting a national asset. If conserved, the ore might be sold in pelletised form at a very high price for use in the direct reduction plants forecast as means of utilising the by-product gases from the oil refining plants due to be erected around the North Sea.

A final criticism is that the effect on depopulation is largely illusionary: since a new town will need to be built to house a present non-urban population, the countryside will be depopulated anyway, so why build the town on the edge of the Arctic Circle? Faced with this kind of opposition expressed largely by the Employers' Federation and Professor Ingemar Stahl of Lund University, and the fact that the existing steelworks has made a loss for several years, one imagines there will be no major moves towards direct state intervention in the near future.

Organisation of the Labour Market Board

The Governing Body of the Labour Market Board is remarkable when seen through foreign eyes, because of its membership. It is headed by a Director General, Bertil Rehnberg, who is the chairman of the Governing Body, together with a Deputy Director General, Aksel Spendrup, who is also the Head of the Planning function: other members, totalling eleven, are nominated – three by the Confederation of Employers, three by the Confederation of Trade Unions, two by the salaried employees, and one by the professional staff association. Two other representatives, one for female workers, and one for agriculture complete the Governing Body. It represents a mix of interests which, fortunately for Sweden, have worked together in common cause to avoid unemployment through the application of sound planning principles. Since the government is also involved, although remotely and perhaps as a background partner, it means agreement can be reached at the early stage of a recession and the actions of the Board can be sure of general support. In Sweden, this is not the only point of contact between employers and labour, but it is an important contact and one that is seen to operate fairly on behalf of the community.

The representatives of the government, the employers and the unions are seen to discuss on a continuing and meaningful basis, measures for controlling the economy of the country. What is more, these representatives then work together to ensure the measures are successful. Is Sweden lucky, or do the Swedes work harder at collaboration?

Figure 2.1 shows the work of the Board is divided into three main functions – administration, planning and employment service, covering in all a wide range of activities. The central organisation is supported by a country wide system of County Labour Boards (chaired by the

Figure 2.1 Organisation of the Labour Market Board (reproduced by permission of the Board)

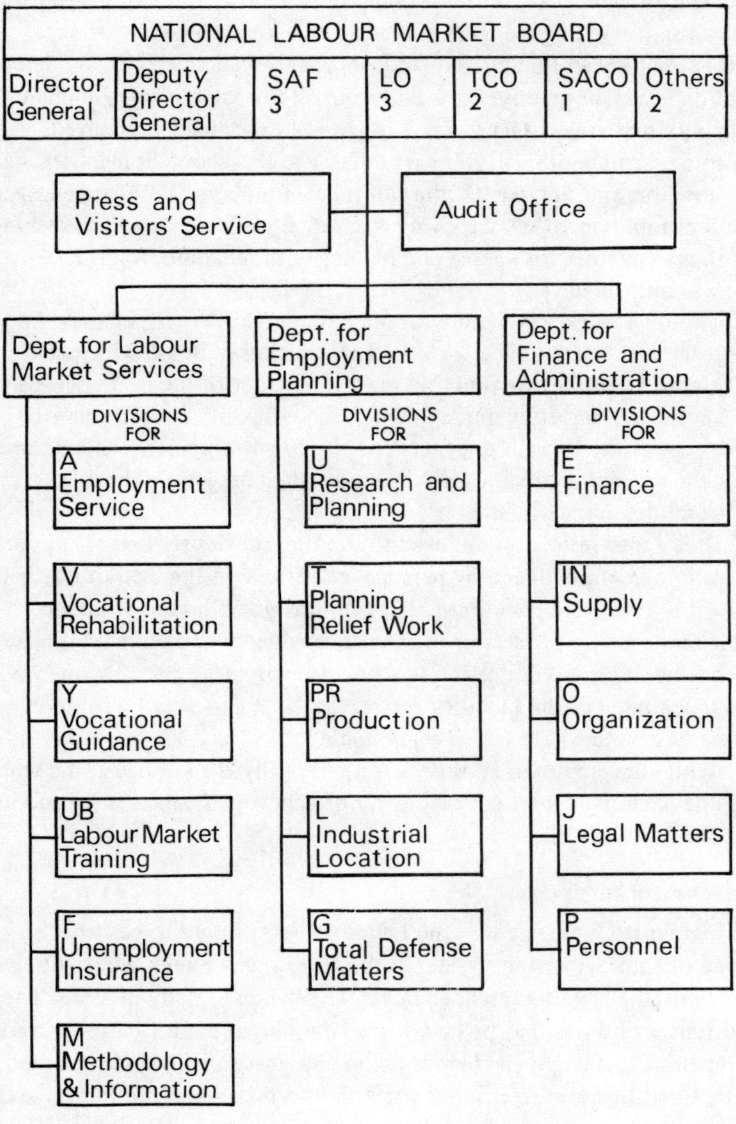

Governor of the County) and 220 district or local offices. At all levels there is a continuous cooperation between the Board, the employers and the unions, who jointly arrive at decisions and see the decisions into action.

The efficient operation of a manpower policy requires a dispersed organisation with good local contacts and a knowledge of the local labour market so that a rapid feedback can be generated. In fact delegation is widely practised, the Governing Body establishing guidelines for action at regional level. In all, some 6,200 people are involved, together with another 1,100 part-time officials – contact men, teacher counsellors and the like. Of the full-time employees, 3,390 are engaged in the employment service giving vocational guidance as well as seeking suitable openings for people and helping with rehabilitation if redeployment is involved.

Before a worker is eligible for unemployment benefit, he must be registered as unemployed with the Labour Market Board which also exercises an overseeing function on the activities of the insurance societies administering unemployment benefits. In addition some 18 per cent of the Board's budget is concerned with further cash assistance for the unemployed, although the emphasis is on getting the worker into gainful employment.

It is a nice reflection on Swedish life that previously registering for unemployment has been by personal call at one of the district offices, but it is now more common to leave a message with the automatic telephone answering service of the office which will then make a return call when it has a suitable job to offer. This procedure is welcomed as a streamlining of the facilities and leaves the Board's staff with more time to devote to the search for suitable jobs.

While the employment service is numerically the strongest, the work of the planning department is clearly of great significance in the success of the Board.

Investment funds

A main instrument used by the Labour Market Board to control the level of employment in Sweden is the Investment Funds. First initiated in 1938, the law was amended in 1947, 1955 and finally in 1963. The current position is that by law, every company is permitted to set aside 40 per cent of its profits before tax in any year to an investment fund. There are, however, restrictions attached to this concession. Forty-six per cent of this money must be deposited interest free in a blocked account in the Central Bank of Sweden and can only be spent on authorisation either by the Crown or by the Labour Market Board for specific projects concerned with investment – the only exception is that after five years a company can spend up to 30 per cent of the money set aside without authority from the Board provided this is on a capital project.

In principle, authorisation by the Labour Market Board can be of two kinds. In the first, the funds are released on the request of a company, usually in a general release period (of which more later) or sometimes against a specific release concerned with geographical factors or a particular sector of industry; the aim is to secure a proper timing of investment projects in the light of economic requirements. The second method, which has not yet been applied but none the less exists in the act, is that a company can be instructed by the Labour Market Board to spend its own money on a specific investment project at a specific time. As the law now stands, the Board also has powers to persuade companies to invest in development areas, on the one hand by the early release of funds, and often also by additional grants the government is prepared to make.

In addition to investments in buildings and plant, machinery and equipment, the Investment Funds can be used to finance temporary increases in inventories, phased to smooth trade cycles and so diminish this effect on production and employment levels. The funds released (equal in size to the value of the increase in inventory in any given year), are transferred to an 'inventory investment account', which can be drawn upon for a period of up to four years. In addition, 10 per cent of the money released from the Investment Funds for inventory or other projects can be claimed as a deduction in the following year's tax return. There are also conditions which are discussed later on the methods of calculating depreciation for tax purposes.*

Table 2.2 shows that the accumulated reserves in the Investment Funds are now massive at just under £400m, of which very approximately a half might be released in a year of recession in trade. The importance of the funds on the economy is therefore very considerable.

The published accounts for most Swedish companies now contain figures for the movement of finance in and out of the Investment

---

* For 1974 only, as a means of combating the recession, two additional tax free but compulsory funds were established. In the first, 20 per cent of all profits in excess of £10,000 *must* be set aside to improve working conditions. In the second, 15 per cent of profits in excess of £100,000 *must* be set aside for investment in plant and equipment.

Funds (shown as untaxed reserves), also for changes in the blocked account held by the Central Bank (shown as part of the company assets). Table 2.3 is constructed from the annual reports of three Swedish companies to show the amount of money available at the end of the financial year – Volvo, for instance, has £63m available for investment.

Table 2:2 Size of Investment Funds in m S. kr

Year	1955	1960	1965	1970	1971	1972
Accumulation	414	2046	3345	3991	3820	
No. of firms				3519	3768	

Immediately a release from the Funds is authorised, the money is transferred from the blocked account to the company, who then hold it in their investment fund account until a project is due for payment. The payment into the blocked account is due before 1 May, which may not be in the financial year of the company accounts, the value of the payment due being held meantime in the investment fund account. These two reasons explain why the blocked account, at any given time, is not 46 per cent of the investment account, as might be expected.

It will be seen that two of the companies are using the Investment Funds to finance part of their inventory – £5m for these two firms together – a factor which is becoming of greater interest as the cost of money increases. The third company, Sydkraft, generates and distributes electricity so that it cannot make for stock: this company is of great interest because of the way it plans its long term developments with the size of the Investment Fund and the depreciation for tax purposes very much in mind.

Asked if he found the restrictions on the spending of the company's money irksome, the vice president in charge of finance in one major company replied that the tax advantages far outweighed any inconvenience. Another financial director agreed, but added Sweden was a small country with an efficient 'old boy network' and the bigger companies at any rate had learnt how to trim their new projects to the prevailing

Table 2.3 Extracts from the annual accounts of three Swedish companies. Figures in m S. kr

	Volvo	Statsföretag	Sydkraft
Blocked account in Central Bank	127.6	15.6	12.0
Investment fund account	477.5	66.0	124.8
Inventory investment account	22.2	30.1	-
Year ending	Dec '73	Dec '72	Dec '73

climate. Moreover, the actions of the Labour Market Board did make sense because a major project might be difficult to get off the ground during a labour shortage.

In making application for the release of capital from the Investment Funds, a company must state in broad outline the reason for the project and its financial viability: the start and finish dates of the project and the labour required must be stated in precise detail. The Labour Market Board accepts no responsibility for the accuracy of the prepared case, but it can refuse to release funds if the project looks like being unprofitable. The Labour Market Board monitors very carefully the timing of the project if authorisation is granted, and in an extreme case of slippage without good reason, may even withhold the money.

The working of the authorisation system can clearly be seen from an examination of the history of recent recessions in Sweden – in 1958, 1962, 1967 and 1972 – and of a boom period in 1960, all of which are discussed in some detail in chapter ten.

Handicapped workers

The Swedes also go to extreme lengths to foster the integration of the handicapped into normal life by providing special training and financial assistance to industrial firms to adapt normal workplaces to suitable configurations for specific handicapped people. The Labour Market Board will provide grants to cover between 50 and 100 per cent of the conversion costs up to a maximum of £2,000 per person (the average in 1972 was £850 for 215 people): grants for special tools or appliances up to a maximum of £1,500 can also be paid (the average in 1972 was £125 for 312 people). There are also more than 12,000 people employed in special archive work. Thus the worthy aim of integration is converted into practice with the help of reasonable financial resources but it must be admitted that in times of recession the handicapped may be among the first to suffer unemployment and since it is more difficult for them to secure short term alternative employment, special relief work was set up during the recession of 1972 by the Labour Market Board for 7,400 handicapped workers.

33,200 places have been established in sheltered workshops and a further 4,100 places exist in semi-sheltered workshops. For some, the sheltered workshop represents the only hope for gainful employment. For others, it is hoped the sheltered workshop represents a stage in the progression to a special place in industry – for which the state pays 40 per cent of the salary. If the task of absorbing handicapped workers is fully costed, the economics are not attractive. Yet it is believed in Sweden this represents an area with great latent capacity which becomes more manifest as the facilities improve.

To assist in the development, 3,700 'adjustment groups' have been set up for the employers, workers and the employment service section of the Labour Market Board, to discuss ways and means of overcoming the problems of fitting handicapped people into productive life. Sweden is fully committed to this as a desirable social policy and is prepared to make available the not inconsiderable money shown in Table 2.4 for 1972, which is expected to rise in the future. When it is remembered the population of Sweden is less than one seventh of that of the UK, Germany or Japan, the figures quoted in this section are very significant.

Grants are also under consideration for handicapped people in self-employment or in partnership with others not handicapped. To all of these, it should be added that grants exist for the provision of suitably modified motor vehicles. In the kind of modern, highly efficient industrial and commercial society that Sweden is creating, the productive incapacity of the handicapped stands out so conspicuously as to make them appear at first sight to be unattractive candidates for employment. Yet the handicapped include a wide range of disabilities ranging from age to physical or mental, psychological or social disabilities. The first part of the Labour Market programme is aimed at mapping out the resources of the handicapped through psychological tests in some cases, aptitude tests in others, to find the work potential and also to assist in breaking down the mental barriers to employment. As a result, handicapped people who never dreamed of a job before, are now able to enter the labour market.

Table 2.4 Cost of creating employment for the hard-to-place in the financial year 1972-3 (in 1000's of S. kr)

	1000's S. kr	No. of people
Special aids for the handicapped	14,748	234,700
Industrial assistance	9,949	527
Special relief work	635,161	7,400
Archive work	241,383	12,000
Semi-sheltered employment	15,361	4,100
Sheltered employment	78,014	33,200
Work at home	1,667	
Administration	14,477	
Total	1,011,030	

Regional development

More than a quarter of the population of Sweden lives in the three large conurbations of Stockholm (1.3m), Gothenburg (0.7m), and Malmö (0.5m); this is in part a function of the fact that these localities are the most suitable for the development of modern industry, but the depopulation of the countryside has been accelerated by the policy of concentrating the population through the building of blocks of three or four storied flats. Writing in 1968, Huntford advances the theory that this has been a deliberate act on the part of the bureaucracies to breed a race of compliant, identical citizens. Contrary to this idea, the Labour Market Board has devoted much effort to encouraging economic prosperity outside the three main conurbations.

The area eligible for regional development aid does not consist solely of the counties in the far north: the southern boundary is in fact only a few miles north of the line from Gothenburg to Stockholm. There is also an area of the east coast of Stockholm (including Kalmar) eligible for regional aid. The total classified as development areas is in size about two thirds of the land area of Sweden, yet contains less than 20 per cent of the population. Traditionally these have been areas where the main industries have been mining and metal extraction, farming and forestry, all of which have undergone major mechanisation to give large increases in productivity without a natural inflow of alternative employment to absorb the displaced workers. In the twelve years preceding 1972 the forestry industry reduced its manpower from 114,000 to 70,000, while farming reduced its manpower from 468,000 to 244,000. Not all of these changes were in the present development areas but sufficient were for them now to account for about half of the total unemployment in Sweden.

The government has recognised the existence of this problem by making available, since 1965, financial assistance to firms going into the development areas. In order to qualify for aid, the enterprise must show promise of profitability and of being self-supporting after the initial aid. Before going into the area, the firm will be advised by the Labour Market Board on the social and cultural facilities, which it will supplement if necessary, as well as on the economic and labour situation. Firms wishing to establish or expand their activities in the main conurbations need to give notice of this intention to the Labour Market Board who may seek to persuade the firm to examine the possibilities of investing in the development areas: in 1972, 190 such notices were given and consultation took place in 163 cases, but the outcome is unknown.

Under the regional development scheme, a firm is entitled to claim a grant from the Labour Market Board of 35 per cent of approved building costs. In certain cases, combined grants and loans up to a total of 66 per cent can be made available for both building and equipment costs. These loans are interest free for the first three years, and the installation need not be amortised in the first three years.

The government will guarantee certain loans for 50 per cent of the working capital in development regions – it did so for thirty-one firms in 1972, and made direct loans to 112 firms, the total amounting to £30m.

Thus there is considerable activity on the regional front, as many as 4,550 people being placed in new employment in 1972 at a cost of roughly £8,600 per head.

The firms already operating in the development regions are not forgotten. For each increase in the annual labour force, they receive a subsidy, spread over three years, of £700 per worker for each of the first two years, reducing to half this amount for the third year, provided the increase is maintained. In 1973, first year subsidies covered 894 jobs, second year subsidies 845 jobs, and third year subsidies 849 jobs, i.e. an increase over the three years of 2,590 permanent jobs. This is one of the few inducements in Sweden to *increase* manning.

Table 2.5 Financial assistance provided to the Development Regions in 1972

	No. of firms	Amount in m S. kr
Regional grants	18	93 (grants and loans combined)
Regional loans	190	
Loan guarantees	112	301
New jobs in existing firms		14.9

One of the problems of introducing a new firm into a development area is the lack of an industrial tradition in the labour force. Training grants are accordingly paid to the firm at the rate of £0.5 per working hour for the first six months of employment, but in exchange for this the firm is expected to provide training up to the standard required by the Labour Market Board. Migration allowances are also payable, as will be discussed later under training and mobility.

In order to arrive at a uniform yet constructive basis for dealing with regional problems, in 1967 the government commissioned the county administrative boards to assess future growth of their provinces up to 1980. This was intended to be a continuing exercise, with a constant reappraisal of the growth prospects and the distribution of workers within the industrial pattern. It was established in principle that to correct the growing imbalance between the three major conurbations and the remainder of Sweden, there should exist in each province a centre with a wide range of services and employment opportunities. To achieve this balance, a locality classification has been drawn up, indicating which industry is suitable for expansion in that locality, and in future it is hoped to restrict capital expenditure to those industries. The object is clearly to increase government control by directing industry to the provincial centres. The declared aim is to satisfy, for each individual, the needs of employment, of satisfactory social services, and of a good environment: many would argue these could be achieved without the powers at present being invoked.

The early actions in the development regions of the Labour Market Board and the government might be described as a cleaning up after the event of changes brought about by economic forces. The post 1967 policy has seen the first signs of an altered political attitude in the attempt to create more robust industrial structures, insensitive to rapid change. At the same time, a working party (called an Expert Group for Regional Studies), established by the Riksdag in 1965, has been examining the fundamental causes of regional problems. This group is led by Ingvar Ohlsson, the Director General of the Central Bureau of Statistics, and is composed of officials from various ministries and bureaucracies interested in the regions, together with university representatives. The group is supported by a technical secretariat which in turn looks after a number of project groups, as well as undertaking investigations. In all, more than a hundred people have been involved in this research. This organisation is regarded as a useful model for similar research projects in different problems. The ministries, far from attempting to oversteer the research, have been willing to act as collaborative agents, seeing that the results get into the right hands as quickly as possible: the research is welcomed as opening up new interdisciplinary activities as well as providing an interface for workers from different geographical areas.

So far research has been broadly of two kinds. The first concerned with the problems arising from intense urbanisation and the resultant depopulation of other areas. The second has been to define the objectives of a balanced economy with particular reference to the conflicting demands of the 'outback'.

Depreciation and obsolescence

Closely associated with the Investment Funds is the method allowed by the government of offsetting depreciation against the assessment of tax. The effect, which is deliberate, is to provide a further incentive to modernisation.

Any tax free monies from the Investment Funds must be depreciated fully in the first twelve months – this applies even to buildings: an extra benefit is given in the form of a special investment deduction of 10 per cent of the amount released from the fund, which the firm can apply in the tax returns for the next financial year. All other investment must be depreciated fully over the first five years of its life, either in equal instalments or on an agreed scale (which includes 45 per cent depreciation in the first year). A further factor is that inventory, whether of in-process or finished goods form, can be written down to 40 per cent of its value or cost, which ever is the lower, and the other 60 per cent shown as an untaxed reserve.

The influence of these measures is apparent in five distinct forms:

(a) The after tax profit in the balance sheet can vary widely from year to year from these measures alone, and in an extreme case of only one major investment, the after tax profit would peak in the first year and then steadily decline.

(b) There is pressure on the companies to maintain a steady stream of investment, with a major installation at least every five years, both to obtain the depreciation tax allowance and to even after-tax profits.

(c) Many Swedish companies work with at least two sets of accounts, firstly as shown in the published accounts with the tax form of depreciation, and secondly with depreciation spread over a more realistic period, often taken as ten years, either spread evenly or on a sliding scale. The alternative set of accounts are used for internal control purposes and also for discussion and supporting evidence when trying to raise international finance.

Volvo summarised the position neatly in a note to the Annual Report for 1973. Depreciation for cost accounting purposes is determined on the basis of the calculated present purchase value of the fixed assets and their economic life. For financial accounting, the depreciation is calculated on historical cost, the depreciation rate for buildings being between 2 to 4 per cent per annum and plant and equipment 10 to 15 per cent per annum. The difference between depreciation permitted for taxation purposes and financial depreciation is known as extra depreciation – this is shown in the balance sheet under the untaxed reserves with the heading 'Accumulated extra depreciation'.

It will then come as no surprise to see an entry in the Volvo Annual Report which reads:

	m S. kr		
	Cost	According to the balance sheet	Fire Insurance value
Machinery and equipment	1,552	658	2,566

The annual reports of most Swedish companies are more informative than many of the counterparts in the UK.

Sydkraft employ all three of the above methods of estimating depreciation and for their twelve year forward projection, they include yet another calculation – that of a form of inflation accounting based on the replacement cost at the end of the expected useful life of the plant.

(d) The rate of return on capital either on equity or on total capital in a Swedish balance sheet is therefore misleading. After allowing for true depreciation and hidden assets, the return by UK standards is relatively low but that does not deter the investor provided the return is above the going rate for money. In fact, in at least two large companies, the minimum return before taxes for a project to proceed was between 15 and 16 per cent, yielding only 8 per cent after tax, but these are clearly the 'no-go minimum' figures with the goal much higher.

Sydkraft is much exercised to determine a realistic measure of its financial performance. For some years prior to 1973, the nett profit as a percentage of turnover was low at between 2 and 3 per cent: Tariff charges were increased in 1973 (apart from the increases tied to the price of oil), so that the nett profit was in excess of 6 per cent. To remain viable in the future, the company consider a profit of at least double this amount is required and so a programme of work is in hand to distribute tariff charges more realistically in line with real costs: this has involved the company in a fundamental look at tariffs and the way in which future demand will be met. In recent years, 44 per cent of the load of about 2,500 MW has been supplied from water power; the potential for further expansion of water power is diminishing, only 8 per cent of an investment of £60m in 1974 being on hydro-electric developments, while the proportion on water power is negligible by 1986 in a planned budget investment of £205m. The changing emphasis will obviously react on the tariff structure and also on the policy for obsolescence, since the life of a water scheme is clearly longer than a fuel fired station.

(e) Although it cannot be quantified, the last effect of the depreciation policy is probably the most important – it is the psychological effect the short term depreciation has on the Swedish executive. After a short time of five years for the accounts, or ten years for planned obsolescence, the assets will have no book value so there are no inhibitions to modernisation from that source. Major companies, such as shipbuilding, operating heavy capital equipment, can cheerfully talk about scrapping this after ten years in order to create more modern facilities, and to repeat the process every ten years or so. The contrast with less progressive economies is remarkable. After ten years heavy capital equipment (and not necessarily in shipbuilding only) can still be working very well: it may still be working well after twenty years, but how does the productivity compare with what might be achieved through newer technology? Equally, what is the effect on the rest of the production process when management has to think in terms of a twenty year concept for the life of heavy equipment and buildings?

Admittedly the Swedish executive has several positive forces working for him. He is conditioned to think in terms of modernisation. The unions welcome change as a means of raising the standard of living, and are aware that redeployment of workers may be part of that change. The Investment Funds help in providing a source for some of the capital. The stimulus given by the lack of book value of the assets, too, can help to break down any final psychological barrier there may be to modernisation.

The discussion on the strength of the Labour Market Board is continued in chapters three and ten, but sufficient has been said to demonstrate that it is truly a remarkable body, having a many sided effect on the Swedish economy. It has made a major contribution to the smooth development of Swedish prosperity.

There is much to be said in favour of the creation of a scheme to encourage capital investment through tax allowances for investment funds and for special depreciation allowances to foster the modernisation of industry. Sweden has indicated to the world how the controls can be applied without the growth of a new top-heavy administration.

3 MODERNISATION THROUGH INVESTMENT AND CHANGING PATTERNS OF EMPLOYMENT

Criteria for successful investment

The Swedish approach to industrial life is quite simple. Efficiency is essential to improve the standard of living, and greater efficiency (which is equated with modernisation) cannot be sustained without substantial and continuing investment. But investment of itself is of no virtue. To be successful, investment needs to be discriminating. Investment needs to be supported by in-depth studies directed to satisfying three essential criteria which may seem very obvious and for that reason perhaps their importance is underestimated. The criteria to be satisfied are:

(a) the concept must be correct;
(b) the capital must be available;
(c) the climate must be receptive.

The first criterion is that the concept or scope of the investment must be correct. To invest in the same old equipment as before is rarely the best policy in an age of advancing technology; but to install new technology just because it is new, can be equally disastrous. A careful evaluation of the potential is essential and it may be necessary to think fundamentally and imaginatively around the traditional methods in order to make the breakthrough. It is not profitable to produce the finest product in the world if there is an inadequate market for it; Concorde is an example of the need for in-depth market research. Having explored the market, a decision on policy needs to be made, followed by detailed planning in order to create a quality project.

Quality of the investment concept

The Swedes are very good at this kind of reasoning. To quote but a few examples, the management of Kockums were much concerned about their future, particularly because some activities were running at a loss. The then president of the company, a lawyer by training who had arrived at Kockums via the Employers' Federation, headed an investigation to survey world shipbuilding requirements of the future. In the light of the company's capabilities and resources, a decision was made on the most profitable area. Around 1965, reorganisation of the yard was started in order to capture a large share of the selected market, basing the attack on price and delivery competitiveness.

The Kockum's philosophy has been that profitability can only be obtained by mass production methods on standard ships – huge oil tankers in the first instance. Drawing office work has not seriously decreased because of the standardisation; considerable effort is required to win the benefits of standardisation, firstly through improved design and then in planning production in still better methods. There is clear evidence of a willingness on all sides to apply the necessary effort. Kockums have invested heavily in sheds and equipment to streamline the shipbuilding process. The latest addition has been the monster Goliath crane to lift 1,500 tons which was commissioned in 1974 with two main objectives: to build still bigger sections now and to be suitably poised for future developments if the 500,000 ton tanker becomes a commercial venture; to provide an insurance in meeting promised delivery dates.

This second objective is a dominant feature of Swedish thinking. Prior to 1974, the yard was dependent to a large degree on a smaller Goliath crane which would lift 800 tons and had been out of commission for one day in four years: so the monster crane, dominating the scene for miles, was added to straddle the first at a total annual cost for eleven years of between £1.8m and £2.0m. How many yards in other countries would be able and willing to invest this amount as an insurance to the customer?

Having obtained a strong position, Kockums do not relax: the annual report for 1973 contains the significant passage 'increased resources have been allocated to the evaluation of the future demand for tonnage in terms of both size and the distribution among various types of vessels'. They have faced up to the reality that their highly efficient production line for 250,000 ton and, more recently, 350,000 ton oil tankers might be dislocated by demands for still bigger tankers, even up to a million tons: they have also faced up to the fact that the tanker market is limited, so they have conducted very detailed studies of the problems encountered in the design of bigger carriers for LNG (Liquified Natural Gas) as a possible market of the future.

A further illustration from Kockums on the importance of being alive to the market requirements can be seen in the pioneering development and selling of computer installations for ships, both for loading sequences and for the automatic control of the boiler room. This is a spin-off, from the company knowledge of ships and the experience gained with computer systems in production control, which led to £3.5m worth of orders in 1973.

The one area in which industrial investment occurs in Sweden as a matter of faith is in improvements to the environment (encouraged by government grants to restrict pollution), both in the arrangement of working areas and in the reduction of noise levels. The improvements can often lead to dramatic changes in production methods. In forestry, safety was a prime consideration and as a result, the job of a lumberman is no longer work for 'real' men with cool nerves and muscles in all the right places, but is now that of a technical operator of complex equipment, seated in a safe, air conditioned and relatively quiet cab, in control of entire logging operations. At the same time, the productivity has increased enormously. The numbers employed in forestry and kindred industries fell from 114,000 to 70,000 in the twelve years preceding 1972, mostly in the primary sector of timber felling and handling, with a slight increase of 10 per cent in output.

The heavy labour involved in the handling of timber has almost disappeared as a result of investment for mechanisation. The changes in the saw mill sector have been so great as to justify the opinion that virtually a new industry has been created, and the profitability of many saw mills has been raised from the inadequate level of the early 1960s. Two new features are also apparent. Many of the companies concerned are vertically integrated and they operate in the more accessible area of southern Sweden. Through further investment, it is expected that the productivity per man will rise still higher in the 1970s until it reaches a level of ten-fold that of 1960. Thus a development that started as a safety project has grown to one of economic significance. Add to this a developing export market for the sale of equipment pioneered by the Swedish manufacturers, and the story is yet another one of success.

Another factor determining the suitability of the investment is that an ever watchful eye must be kept on the size of the market. The market volume of textiles in Sweden has not substantially altered between 1960 and 1973, so modernisation has taken place without expansion, the labour force falling from 145,000 to 73,000, a grim realisation that neither productivity nor the market can be ignored in a competitive age.

Not even a machine tool can be bought in one Swedish engineering company without an estimate of its effect on the market and *vice versa*. Before an investment is approved, a very clearly defined set of forms has to be completed in this company: these forms serve as a checklist to ensure that the necessary market research, for instance, has been carried out, and that several alternatives have been examined and costed. This work is the responsibility of the grass roots producing company in a conglomerate and includes estimates of the annual pay-off for one, two or five years, depending on the nature of the investment. There are also columns on the form for the follow up insertions of performance in costs, sales and profits. There is thus a very formal control mechanism. A criticism might be perhaps that too much of the initiative is left at the grass roots level, but is that necessarily a bad thing, provided the parent company functions intelligently?

Applied research

To increase the number of 'good' investments, there is a heavy burden of responsibility on management to undertake in-depth studies in fundamental terms of products, markets, prices and production methods. In the present economic climate, this could equally be a matter of survival. The largest companies have the resources in most instances, but how far are they prepared to commit these resources? Even with the biggest organisation, with a major project, a case can be made for an independent second opinion on the merits of a particular scheme.

The small one-boss outfit might, through the personal enthusiasm and skills of this one man – the personification of private enterprise – also be able to think sufficiently fundamentally to be successful. It is, however, doubtful if the medium size companies have the resources to undertake this work. This ought to be an area in which the universities have the width of understanding and the knowledge to see past the traditional, and the imagination to make a firm contribution. This kind of study cannot be research done in isolation: it requires close cooperation with and within a company probably over a period of time, and demands that patience be exercised on both sides. Economics, the logistics of production, new production techniques, computer thinking, are of the essence in this kind of applied research, and of these, operational research, by virtue of its discipline and its emphasis on management problems, would appear to occupy a unique position as a catalytic agent.

Having made this plea for joint research between industry and university, it must be confessed that this collaboration in Sweden does not appear to occur at any great depth. This is perhaps because there are only four major universities and five technological universities of a smaller size to embrace the whole range of intellectual activity for the country: it follows then that the coverage of particular fields may be limited. On the other hand, liaison between university and industry undoubtedly does occur at an advisory level and there is a reasonable interchange of staff in the technical fields – but very little interchange in economics and mathematics, except at high government level. Swedish management prides itself on its professionalism – 73 per cent of the graduates in Swedish industry are trained in a technical field as compared with 60 per cent in the rest of Europe – so this probably aids the quantification and analysis of problems at managerial level.

Pure research and development in Sweden is not unduly high at 1.2 per cent of the Gross Domestic Product (USA 2.7 per cent, UK 2.1 per cent, Germany, 1.9 per cent, Japan 1.7 per cent) but it does appear to have been successfully oriented to the growth of a sophisticated industry in which know-how and quality are determining ingredients. Many companies have been so successful at problem solving that there is an export market in soft ware.

To summarise the need for the right concept, the best investments are characterised by in-depth studies directed at ascertaining the real dimensions of the problem, followed by an all out attempt to think radically outside the constraints of tradition. Furthermore, the process is continuous. Plant should not be regarded as sacrosanct for twenty years.

Availability of capital

The second criterion to be satisfied for efficient investment is that capital must be available on time. One method of raising capital in Sweden is through the Investment Funds, which, coupled with the tax allowances, gives considerable incentive to invest. The retroverse system of loans, discussed in chapter eleven, whereby a firm is able to borrow 50 per cent of its contributions to the National Pension Funds also helps to keep finance in the productive sector of the economy. A high level of private saving in Sweden also helps to make money available for investment. If sufficient capital is not generated in this fashion, then the balance needs to be raised on the open market. The various financial criteria and the sources of funds are discussed in chapter eleven, the overall result being that Sweden is at the top of the league in gross investment per capita. The merits of the Swedish system would appeal to many businessmen in other countries: in time, the politicians, too, might appreciate the advantages.

The climate for modernisation

The third, and often overlooked, condition for successful investment is that the climate must be right. The controlling climate may be in the market place: a sudden change in ecological opinion, for instance, may wreck the marketing of an otherwise good project, or a bankrupt economy may not be able to afford a magnificent luxury product. More likely, the controlling climate will be on the shop floor if the investment involves a change in production methods. For all the good work Kockums did on the concept of modernisation, they could have floundered (and nearly did), because the shop floor climate was not receptive to new ideas without first getting rid of old problems. This action is discussed in later chapters, but meantime another aspect will be explored.

A change from a state of conflict to a collaborative climate, in which innovations are welcomed by management and men alike, is difficult to achieve and does not come by chance overnight. Honest and constructive discussions to explore the implications of modernisation well in advance of the event are essential for success. A move into twentieth-century methods may alter the product, increase the throughput or reduce the manning; it may involve a combination of all three factors, but it is unrealistic to expect workers to be quiescent in the face of redundancy. It is equally unrealistic to expect employers to invest in new equipment if they are unable to reap the benefits. The result is stalemate, and a general worsening of the competitive position unless a collaborative atmosphere can be generated.

What can be done? A long history of nearly four decades of collaboration in Sweden has been seen to work to the benefit of all. It is no accident that the Swedes have modernised their industry with so little disturbance: they have worked hard at collaboration. It is widely accepted that modernisation may mean a different kind of work. If the market cannot expand, it may mean fewer workers in a particular industry. This philosophy is only acceptable because of the steps taken, largely by the Labour Market Board, to retrain and relocate workers, with adequate financial support and almost as an ethical responsibility.

Redeployment

Dealing first with the financial side, if a worker is undergoing training the basic payment is at the rate of £75 per month, for married and unmarried alike, and is independent of the spouse's earnings. If it is necessary to live away from home during the training, an additional allowance of £45 per month is payable. For certain forms of training for which there is a shortage of skilled workers (currently in nursing and engineering), further incentive payments of £30 per month are made. Thus under certain circumstances, the payment during training can amount to £150 per month. Rental allowances can also sometimes be obtained.

There are 300 different types of course available, the number of places and the syllabi being largely determined by the Labour Market Board, so that student output is in phase with the anticipated demand. The career orientation is enhanced by the steps taken by the Board to ensure that the technology on the courses is fully in step with the needs and changing standards of the business community. A staggering 142,821 people (65,014 being women) took part in the courses during the year ending June 1973 – this would correspond to about a million people in the UK or Germany and 3.7 million in the USA.

Apart from the scarcity occupations, to be eligible for a course a worker must be over twenty years of age and either be unemployed or expect to be unemployed within a period of six months. Obviously there must be different types of course to suit different people, varying in length from a few weeks for a refresher course to two years for a specialised training. About 50 per cent of the students attended courses arranged in fifty training centres by the National Board of Education, while 20 per cent became students within the normal educational system. Some 19 per cent were trained on the job, for which the firm received the £0.5 per hour training allowance, while the trainee got the full rate for the job.

About 2,500 unemployed workers took part in two-year courses in which there is a marked supervisory bias in production technology, sales techniques, retailing and secretarial work, as well as for teaching. Finally, 33,000 people started courses of a general educational nature which would help them to adjust more easily to the community – this is particularly the case for immigrant workers. A special emphasis in all of the courses is that they are regarded as establishing a base for the worker to continue his or her education on return to employment in order to keep up with advancing technology.

It is thus recognised that modernisation will leave some people with outmoded skills. To help them adjust to the personal and financial problems, these officially sponsored courses must be seen to be an effective instrument of an active manpower policy which aims to give the individual free and well considered choice of work in line with the demand. Follow-up studies undertaken continuously by the Board indicate that 75 per cent of the students find work in the course area within three months of the completion of the course: a high success rate.

A last item of interest is that special courses are also arranged for workers in occupations which undergo seasonal changes, due to bad weather, for them to improve their working knowledge within their own trade, or indeed to learn new trades which might improve their long term prospects of employment. Training completed, the whole weight of the employment section of the Labour Market Board is thrown into the balance to fit the worker into a suitable job. The Board attaches great importance to labour market training as a means of channeling less competitive people into expanding sectors of the economy.

To complement the occupational mobility, a grant is paid to an unemployed worker to enable him or her to make an exploratory trip to a new town, if need be, to find out first hand about the new job and its environment; or if the new location happens to be in an area of labour shortage, financial assistance is given to the worker to visit more than one firm. The cost of removing the family and household goods up to a maximum of £300, and a settling in allowance equivalent to the first week's wages, are also paid. If the members of a family have to live apart for a period due to lack of accommodation, a separation allowance is paid to help in the expense of double housekeeping. Lastly, if a house owner cannot sell his house or flat on moving to a new job, the Labour Market Board can make the purchase. These moves give the blue collar worker the benefit of the best conditions pertaining for the white collar worker.

Two other factors assisting job mobility are that pension rights exist for all workers and are completely transferable, and that pay differentials are reducing year by year so that a mobile worker is less likely to be at a loss than if big pay differentials exist.

The worker's fears about the effect of modernisation on him personally are then largely allayed and so modernisation can be accepted as a progression towards higher living standards. This process is helped by the mental attitude of the Swedes who recognise better libraries, swimming pools and sports stadia as factors raising the standard of living almost as much as a bigger pay packet.

One disquieting note is apparent, however. Some two thirds of the relatively large number of 94,000 people seeking vocational rehabilitation within one year had been in touch with the system once or even several times before. While sixty per cent of these had bodily disabilities, possibly of a minor nature, the others had social or psychological problems in adjusting to their work; just under 4,000 of the latter were referred for psychological aptitude tests in 1972.

The budget of the Labour Market Board

From the foregoing it will be realised the Labour Market Board is a body with extensive interests which are reflected in the breakdown of its budget shown in Figure 3.1 (with no allowance for inflation). To an outside observer, it is perhaps remarkable that it exists in such detail for five years ahead, but this kind of forward planning is typical of Sweden.

The budget reflects the belief that effective control is based on information and that information can be costly – 6.5 per cent of the budget in 1979. The experimentation already in hand on computerised vacancy lists will continue in enhanced form and the next stage of experimentation, matching applicants and vacancies, will commence. Many manuals or brochures exist or are in preparation, ranging from the 'Swedish Occupational Dictionary' (which contains general information about working life and different industries in part 1, and will contain articles on different occupations in part 2), to the 130 brochures being prepared on particular occupations, with details of type of work, training and the labour market. The budget shows a growth in information activity from 1974 to 1975, followed by a steady level of expenditure.

The other activities of the Board are expected to continue in the same relative form up to 1979 but on an expanding basis. Training and resettlement then consumes 29 per cent of the budget, and as such, is more than the 26 per cent spent on the payment of unemployment benefits. If the 24.5 per cent spent on integrating the handicapped is included, the training far outweighs the cash benefits to the unemployed.

Relief work and the regions are expected to continue to absorb resources (19 per cent of the budget) from the Labour Market Board, although both are dependent on trade cycles.

Changing patterns of employment

With continued modernisation, even allowing for increased demand, inevitably there comes a time when the worker can no longer be gainfully employed in the production of goods or food. In Sweden in 1964, 47 per cent of the working population were thus employed. By 1972, the figure had fallen to 36 per cent and Figure 3.2 suggests the down-

Figure 3.1 LMB budget

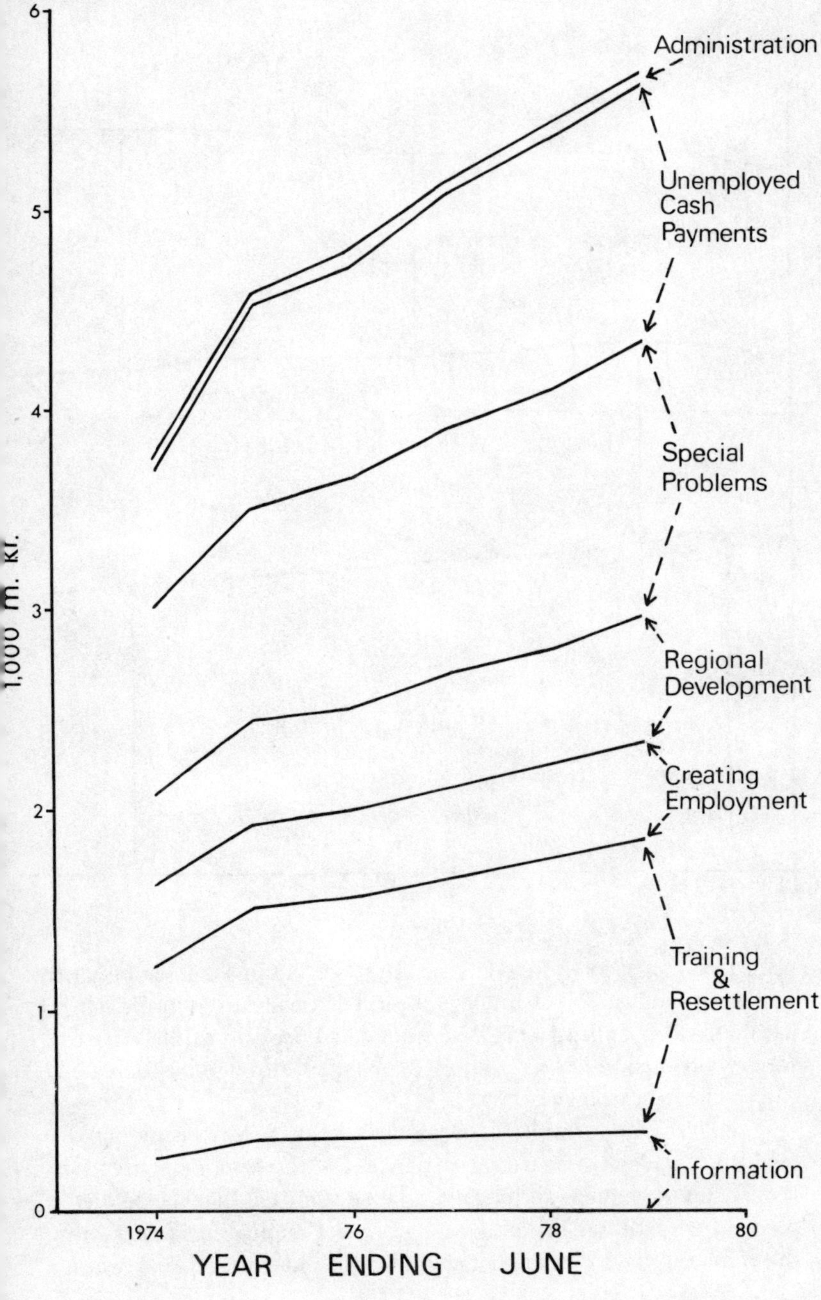

Figure 3.2 Million employed

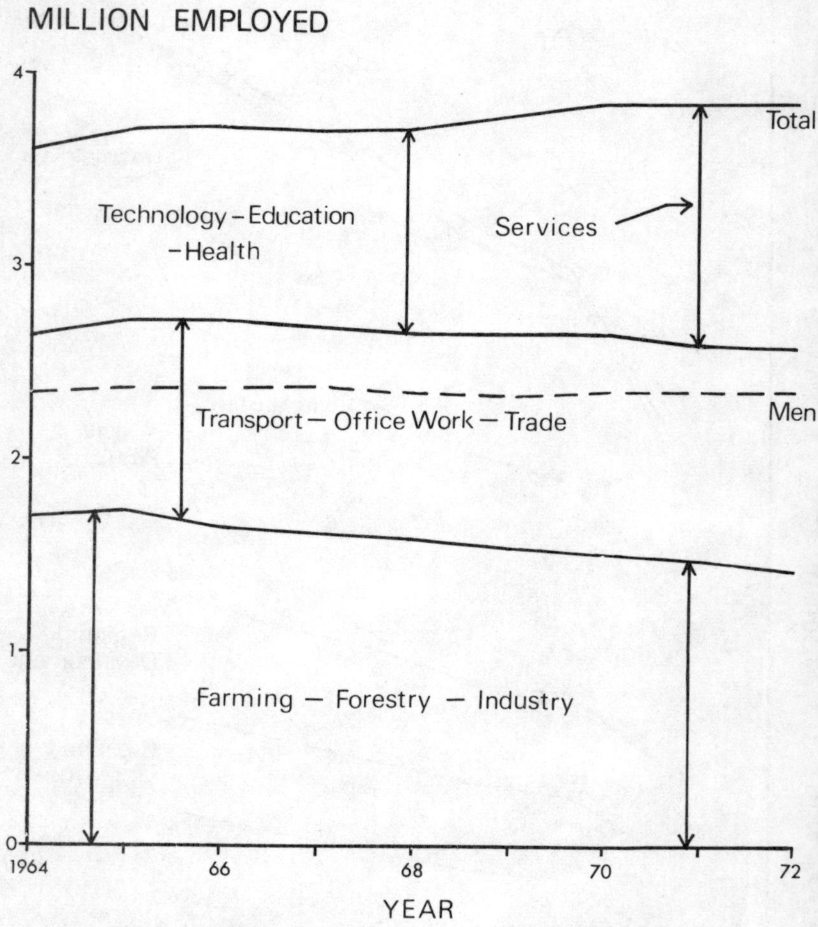

ward tendency is likely to continue. This does not mean unemployment. The service industries (technology, health and education) in the same period have expanded from 27 per cent to 33 per cent of the labour force which had itself increased by 6.8 per cent through the increased employment of women.

Equality of opportunity between the sexes is rapidly becoming a reality in Sweden where nearly 40 per cent of the working population is made up of women (although it must be admitted the women are predominantly in the lower income groups). Coupling this figure with the emphasis placed on obtaining useful work for the handicapped, it should be expected that a greater proportion of the total population would be at work in Sweden than other countries – it is, but the respective figures for Sweden and the UK, for instance, are 47 per cent and 45 per cent, less of a difference than would be expected.

A further factor influencing the size of the working population is that in the ten years preceding 1970, the immigrant population more than doubled and although it has remained static since 1972, at present about 5 per cent of the working population consists of foreigners. The Finns (200,000 immigrants) are about half the total – there is a reciprocal labour agreement among the four Scandinavian countries of Sweden, Norway, Finland and Denmark, whereby the nationals of one can work without formality and derive benefit from the educational system of any of the other three. In addition, there is a representation from other European countries, Yugoslavia at 40,000 being the largest, together with a number of Asiatics, often doing the less rewarding jobs. These numbers are sufficient to present the Labour Market Board with a language teaching problem.

Theoretically there is a limit to the amount of labour that can be transferred from the productive sectors of industry to the services but the saturation point does not seem imminent. According to the planning department of the Labour Market Board, there is currently no shortage of worthwhile schemes, and, as the standard of living rises, it is confidently expected that new concepts of service demands will appear. In the last resort, all services have to be paid for by the efforts of productive industry. Although the number of workers employed in productive industry is declining, the output is not declining.

Column 2 of Table 3.1 shows that the rate of growth per annum in the output of the primary producers (defined here to include agriculture, forestry, mining and manufacturing, electricity, gas, waterworks and sanitary services, building and construction), has always been increasing at a faster rate than the rest of the economy classified as 'all services' in column 3. All services will then include trading activities, transport and communication (which although essential to production do not increase the value of the commodity), letting of premises, private and public services. The very high growth rate of 6.8 per cent per annum of the production function in the early 1960s explains the high standard of living, and while it has decreased, at a projection of 4.9 per cent per annum for the five years up to 1977, it is still high enough to ensure rising standards of prosperity. It may be felt the growth rate only tells part of the story. Column 5 indicates that the productive sector within the same definition is steadily increasing

Table 3.1 Analysis of changes in the production of the Gross Domestic Product in Sweden

% Annual Growth Rate			% of Gross Domestic Product			
Years	Productive Industry	All Services	Year	Productive Industry	Mining and Manu-facturing	Public Services
(1)	(2)	(3)	(4)	(5)	(6)	(7)
1960-65	6.8	4.4	1960	41.8	24.5	15.8
1965-70	4.5	3.8	1965	44.6	27.8	15.0
1970-75	3.5	3.3	1970	45.4	29.8	16.2
1972-75	4.9	4.0	1972	44.8	29.4	16.8
			1975	45.7	31.2	16.5
			1977	45.9	32.7	16.5

The data in Table 3.1 can be examined from a number of viewpoints which together present a picture of a healthy and expanding economy.

(apart from a minor hesitation in 1972) its share of the Gross Domestic Product in spite of the reduction in the numbers employed therein.

It might still be argued that the definition of productive industries is not really satisfactory for this purpose since it includes house building and sanitary facilities which are only marginal (and in fact suffered a marked decline in the years 1970-75). So column 6 shows the percentage of the Gross Domestic Product derived from mining and engineering – an even more marked increase over the years is apparent, certainly rising much faster than the public services shown in column 7.

Two qualifications to the table are desirable. The first is the relatively small increase in the share of the GDP in the public services is compensated by an almost identical falling off in the share of the private services, although the absolute level of both is rising at about 3.8 and 2.8 per cent per annum respectively. The table also conceals the fact that the forestry and agricultural industries are declining in their share of the GDP although the output in forestry and kindred industries is showing a slight increase in volume. Agriculture is changing only little in volume in spite of the falling off in number of workers at the rate of 7 per cent per annum over two decades.

Swedish agricultural policy has two prime objectives: for the country to be 80 per cent self-sufficient in food production; and for the agriculture to be sufficiently efficient for the farmers and farm workers to earn an income comparable with their industrial counterparts. These aims have been achieved through intensive research into crop improvement, extensive mechanisation (often on fairly small farms) and efficient marketing. Organised cooperation between farmers is long standing and producer cooperatives now market farm products and in turn supply farmers with equipment.

In the manufacturing industry, recent years have seen a growing dominance of the more advanced technological products. The evolution of this new balance of products has been accompanied by a number of mergers (and consequent shutting down of small plants) in order to introduce specialisation and the advantages of scale both in production and in research, as well as in marketing and administration. The one exception is the textile industry which has reduced the labour force by about half in the thirteen years preceding 1973, and has suffered a loss in output of about 6 per cent per year in the same period. In spite of the decline, the Swedish textile industry is highly mechanised and capital intensive: output is expected to rise between 1975 and 1977, but it is also expected that the number employed will continue to fall.

Social services

It is the Swedish practice to include the contribution of the social services to the Gross Domestic Product at cost. In view of the progressive and extensive nature of the Swedish social services, and the analytical and quantitative approach to matters industrial, it would not be surprising to find sophisticated cost benefit analysis undertaken of new developments before authorisation, followed by further analysis after implementation. While there is considerable debate, the only formal cost benefit examination of substance appears to be that undertaken by Kurt Lekås and Nils-Erik Norén for the new town and steelworks to be constructed by the state owned company near Lulea in the far north. This model, too, is incomplete in the sense that useful numerical results do not seem yet to have been obtained, but it is an interesting examination of the complex interaction between the many variables which need to be embraced in any worthwhile cost benefit analysis.

It is, of course, a notoriously difficult area. How should the contribution to the community of a first class swimming pool be evaluated in numerical terms? Interesting ideas in this general field are being generated by Ingemar Stahl, professor of economics in the University of Lund. His approach to preventive medicine is to ask informed people how big a premium they would be prepared to pay each year in order to guarantee the use by them of a kidney machine if the need arose: similar questions and answers summed together give an estimate, subjective admittedly, but still an estimate in financial terms of the value of a service function. Another of Professor Stahl's experiments is an attempt to estimate in economic terms the value of the deterrent for shoplifting against the benefits derived from a life of successful petty crime and against the risk of being caught: in other words, should the risk factor be increased by better detection methods? In a country dedicated to regarding the criminal as a fallen person to be redeemed, such an approach is unusual to say the least.

It would be out of place to embark here on a detailed description of the Swedish social services – only a few points of relevance to the main discussion will be highlighted.

Compulsory education starts at the age of seven in Sweden and continues to the age of sixteen, being comprehensive to the age of fourteen after which some regrouping occurs. It is hoped most children will also have at least one year in a nursery school before the compulsory period. 85 per cent of the children go on to a secondary school offering further either two years of vocational training with theoretical subjects included, or three to four year courses leading to university entry. Anyone over the age of twenty-five who has worked for five years is also entitled to study at a university without passing a qualifying test. The current number of new students entering a university each year is 20,000, although it has been as high as 35,000.

All school education is free and so are school lunches, regardless of means: educational allowances of £12.50 per month are payable for students between the ages of sixteen and twenty. Before that age, there are no child allowances on income tax, but the parent receives a grant of £150 for each child. University tuition is free but the students need to buy their own books and to maintain themselves – nearly all of them have loans amounting to £1,200 per annum, of which £1,030 must be repaid once the recipient is earning.

English is introduced at the age of nine and continues to be a prime subject. There are many good points in the Swedish system for the making of a competitive economy. The general impression is of a happy, relaxed relationship between parents and children, and between teachers and pupils. The only unsatisfactory thing some observe, and even this has its good features, is the element of propaganda involved in education which starts with proclaiming Sweden is best, the Swedish system is best and the present social system is the best. Propaganda maybe, but is it necessarily all bad?

Table 3.3 Expenditure on welfare services in Sweden (in m S. kr)

	1960	1970	1971
Health services			15,000
Unemployment			2,000
Pensions			13,000
Family and child welfare			6,000
Other items			1,000
Total	7,600	31,000	37,000

Table 3.3 shows that the expenditure on welfare services has been increasing at a rapid rate: 75 per cent of the expenditure is provided by the central government and local authorities out of income tax, and the balance is paid by employers through the National Pension Funds. There are indications that the rate of increase slowed markedly between 1972-4 because of the difficulty of raising taxation still further. Sweden spends more of the Gross Domestic Product on non-military spending by the government and the municipalities than any other country.

The largest item in the expenditure in the table is on the health services which, on average, amounted to £188 per head of population in 1971: there are indications that this will be substantially larger in 1974 because of changes introduced in that year, although new capital investment in this area is expected to become very much less. Medical services are largely free and independent of means tests – wage earners when ill are entitled to 90 per cent of their normal earnings up to a limit of £5,400 per annum. If a person is 'classified as a housewife or a man staying at home' (!), when ill, he or she receives a tax free payment of £0.8 per day.

The method of covering unemployment benefit was also changed in 1974 and is likely to increase the bill for the welfare services substantially in the future. Prior to that date, unemployment insurance was voluntary, but a large proportion of the working population elected to be so insured. From 1974, all wage earners between the ages of 15 and 67 years, and also many self-employed, have the right to compensation for loss of earnings due to unemployment. The base rate is £3.50 per day, increasing to £10 per day for most blue collar union workers: the period of eligibility has also been extended to 300 days or 450 days for workers over fifty-five years of age. It used to be said that the state in Sweden guaranteed the bread and butter and that the worker had to go out to earn his own jam. At the new level of benefits, the state is almost guaranteeing the jam as well, and it will be interesting to see how the Swedes react. As a nation, the Swedes have been much concerned with many aspects of security and this has been one of the factors helping to generate the remarkable strike free record of modern Sweden. For their sake, it is to be hoped the benefits of tradition will not be dissipated.

The welfare services in Sweden have passed through three phases. In the first, in the 1930s, welfare was concerned with the bare necessities of existence, provided only when requested. By the 1960s, welfare could be obtained as a right and if necessary social workers could seek out the needy and see they got the benefits to which they were automatically entitled. As the country became more prosperous, by the 1970s the emphasis was turning to preventive measures both in medicine and child welfare, with the state starting to play a dominant role in the latter field. All this on top of the magnificent municipal facilities of libraries and sports arenas is calculated to encourage the Swede to believe that his social system and his standard of living are the best in the world.

Note

The substance of the early part of this chapter was published in *The Times*, 8 January 1975, under the heading 'Lessons on Investment provided by Sweden'.

PART 2: INDUSTRIAL RELATIONS IN SWEDEN

4 TRADE UNIONISM IN SWEDEN

The growth of union activity

The high standard of material prosperity enjoyed by modern Sweden could not have been achieved without a labour force prepared to accommodate change and a management prepared to collaborate with labour in the avoidance of conflict. The roots of the present attitudes are embedded in the past – a past which was not always harmonious, but one from which the protagonists had the good sense to learn.

Trade unions came relatively late to Sweden for reasons that are easy to recognise. The early forms of industrialisation long predating the industrial revolution of the rest of Europe, were based on the natural resources of iron ore and timber, and as a consequence were located in relatively remote and usually dispersed areas of the country. Partly because of the isolation but mostly because of the traditional way of living (for farming as well as for the early industry) in tightly knit communities known as 'bruks', these production units were patriarchal in character with the head man being both the owner and the production manager. While wages were poor and conditions often extremely bad, the owner knew the workers individually and usually accepted a paternal responsibility for their welfare in so much as the old, the sick and the widowed were not allowed to starve. In these remote feudal communities, new ideas on the organisation of labour seldom had the opportunity for self-germination and rarely penetrated from outside.

The craftsmen and journeymen working mainly in the few townships of central and southern Sweden, although having contacts with each other and to a lesser extent with ideas from Denmark, seemed relatively slow in taking up the idea of trade unionism and even slower in seeing the union as a bargaining instrument for obtaining better conditions. The first trade union in the country was that of the typographers, founded in Stockholm in 1846, but this was more in the nature of a medieval guild concerned with improving the standards of workmanship and with educating for citizenship.

Still in the 1840s, the Communist Manifesto was translated into Swedish but this kind of thinking gained little ground. A few organisations were set up, outwardly as self-educating bodies, but in reality consisting of radically oriented groups bent on obtaining political power. However these organisations found little favour with Swedes, and petered out in the 1860s to be replaced by a few craft unions of the same kind as the typographers. Thus although a spirit of worker solidarity was becoming evident, it was far from militant.

Conditions might perhaps have remained this way for a few decades longer had not industrial relations altered. The well wooded coasts around the Baltic Sea became the hunting ground for foreign capital thirsting for timber. No longer was the manager the owner. The paternal attitude disappeared in these saw mills. The manager was pressed by the absentee owners to get more profit and the economic depression of 1879 saw bitter conflicts around the town of Sundsvall between workers objecting to cuts in an already inadequate wage and the representatives of absentee owners. With no resources and no backing, the workers lost; the strike was a failure since the workers had to return to the saw mills under the conditions to which they were objecting. Seen through other eyes, the strike was a success in that it was the starting point of organised, militant trade unionism in Sweden.

The 1880s saw the start of many local trade unions and at the same time the importation of fresh political ideas, again from Denmark, which assumed the self-imposed task of being a link between Sweden and the radical thinkers of the rest of Europe. Often the same people were involved in the new unions and the new political groups with the result that some confusion of objectives undoubtedly occurred. The Swedes resolved this confusion characteristically by refusing to accept an excess of dogma but recognising in the light of the Sundsvall experience the need for strong organisations. The effort was therefore concentrated on building trade unions strong in membership and strong in financial terms, even though how this strength would be used was not entirely clear.

Strength in this connection is, of course, a very relative term. As elsewhere, the employers in the early days certainly did their utmost to discourage the formation of the local trade unions. The ruling political party was conservative in outlook, unsympathetic to new ideas of any kind, and tended to be allied with the employers. This had a double effect on the unions, firstly of resolving the uncertainty of choice of partner from the radical liberals or the socialists, and secondly of seeking to strengthen the local unions through some kind of federation of interests. The united opposition also caused workers to be more eager to join the unions. As a result of these pressures, the first federations appeared on an industry of craft trade basis in 1896 and the Social Democratic Labour Party was formed in 1899.

After a period in which survival was the first requirement, the unions came to appreciate that to be successful in any conflict with the employers, they needed strength and they needed to act when the economy was buoyant. To increase their strength, even wider federation or alignment of interests seemed desirable and in 1898 the Swedish Confederation of Trade Unions (LO) was founded. This is the same organisation that still exists today as the main negotiating body on behalf of organised labour, but it nearly collapsed in the first years of its existence. Because of the alignment with the socialists, one of the conditions imposed by the founders of the LO was that the constituent unions had to promise that their membership would seek collective affiliation with the Socialist party: this was unacceptable to many of the unions who did not join the LO until the conditional clause was removed from the constitution in 1900. At the same time, another offending clause, namely the right of the Socialist party to nominate two members to the executive board of the LO, was withdrawn.

This summary glosses over a decade of attrition between the unions and employers who in defence organised themselves in 1902 into a strong, centralised organisation, the Confederation of Swedish Employers, SAF, which also still exists today and is the principal body watching the interests of the employers. SAF was a mixture of otherwise separate independent employers' associations for particular trades (although the metal industries elected not to join SAF for many years). During this period, neither side had any clear objective or planned approach other than opposing the other side as a matter of principle so, possibly unwittingly, the stage was being set for a major confrontation.

Viewing the industrial relations climate of Sweden today, it is difficult to realise that Sweden has had its share of major strikes in earlier years. The first of these was political in nature being an attempt by the Socialist party to extend the franchise: the strike only lasted three days but it involved 150,000 workers in a countrywide stoppage. It was the first powerful demonstration of worker influence and as such undoubtedly accelerated the formation of the employers' confederation.

There followed a strike in 1905 which lasted eight months and involved 30,000 workers. In contrast with events at Sundsvall, the unions were well organised and were able to support the strikers well enough for the employers to concede the demands, which were for the unions to negotiate on behalf of their members a national minimum wage for the trades involved. Other strikes followed, all concerned with the same principle. By 1906, the two major organisations, SAF and LO, were prepared to meet and between them produced an agreement which was the first indication of a collaborative approach. The employers conceded to the unions the right to negotiate on behalf of their members over wages and working conditions. The trade unions conceded to the employers the right to employ and to dismiss workers freely and to be responsible for the organisation of the work. Both of these concessions are still in operation today as important parts of the labour structure. It is characteristic that these concessions were not concerned with petty details but were both concerned with principles that have withstood the changes of nearly three quarters of a century.

One more strike will be discussed here: although it was certainly not the last strike in Sweden it was the largest and most significant as far as future developments were concerned. In 1909, a general strike occurred which resulted in the loss of nearly eleven million man days of production: at its peak, 300,000 workers were involved in a strike lasting between one month and six months in different parts of the country. The causes of this conflict were complex and have ceased to be of relevance since the issue developed into an open power struggle between the employers and the unions, and this at a time of recession. The outcome was a humiliating defeat for the unions, many ceasing to exist. The unions could have been crushed out of existence for the time being. Instead, because of a blend of indecision on the part of some of the employers and an appreciation by others that the unions did have a part to play in labour relations, the Confederation of Employers offered negotiations to the Confederation of Trade Unions. Thus at an early stage some at least realised that the best way to negotiate was through centrally organised bodies representing the inevitably contrasting interests of workers and employers.

The political situation of the time calls for some comment. The socialists representation in the Riksdag was negligible and was likely to remain so until the franchise was extended. A conservative government was in power with a strong liberal opposition. The government did not intervene in the strike of 1909 nor in earlier conflicts because they expected intense opposition to such moves from the liberals. Subsequently this viewpoint based on convenience has hardened to one based on the conviction that it is better for the employers and trade unions to settle labour disputes without government intervention, an intervention incidentally which would be resented by both sides to the dispute. On the other hand, the unions have always tried to put pressure on the Riksdag for legislation dealing with the social aspects of industrial operations, such as in the matter of hours of work for women, and compensation for industrial accidents.

The universal vote was introduced in the 1920s but to the surprise of many trade unionists it did not lead to an immediate socialist majority in the Riksdag. It was not until 1932 when the trade unions decided on a united political front to attempt to win a socialist victory in the general election that the socialists were able to form a majority party in a coalition with the Farmers Party. The coalition was formed in order to tackle the unemployment which had been a major problem throughout most of the 1920s: it was also the start of a long period of stable government in place of a succession of short lived minority governments.

From this it will be apparent that the main left-wing elements in Sweden looked at the revolution taking place within their close and too powerful neighbour of Russia, and decided that the fruits of revolution did not appear to be either sufficiently bountiful or sweet enough to tempt them on the same path. A splinter group of the Socialist party, however, did turn communist without gaining any real support in the unions or in the country as a whole.

Throughout the period 1909 to 1934, the trade union organisation had been growing in stature and had come to realise that power carries with it responsibilities. It has been described in earlier pages how part of the programme to deal with cyclic unemployment involved building and construction projects. The Confederation of Trade Unions supported this programme and indeed had been active in demanding a planned approach to the problems of the economy. It was a considerable blow when, in 1934, the Employers' Confederation sought to reduce the wages in the building industry because the extreme depression throughout the economy was affecting the viability of the companies involved. It was an even greater blow when the workers in the building industry refused to accept this proposal and went on strike. At first, other unions were solidly behind the building workers but when the financial pressure came on the members of other unions hurt by the strike, an approach was made to the Confederation of Trade Unions. This body, too, had initially been in support of the strike decision. The tradition in recent years had been for a mild sort of solidarity, that is mutual support short of strike action, but the tradition was now in question: the high unemployment of the 1920s and early 1930s with the consequent hardship and misery arising from inadequate insurance benefits were still very real spectres.

Eventually, and not without heart searching, the Confederation of

Trade Unions decided that the interests of society as represented by the economy must supersede the interests of a particular section; the building workers were then persuaded to accept the situation and to return to work. This marked a turning point in the ideology of the trade unions, being a clear realisation of the responsibilities of power. This act of statesmanship by the Confederation of Trade Unions is akin to a similar earlier act of statesmanship made by the Employers' Confederation in 1909 when generous conditions were offered to the defeated trade unions. Jointly they reveal at least to some extent why Swedish labour relations in the 1960s and the 1970s are the envy of much of the world.

Having demanded of society a policy of full employment implying the adoption of counter measures to eliminate or, at worst, to mitigate the effects of recurrent depressions, the Confederation of Trade Unions set out to analyse the contribution they would themselves have to make. One factor they identified was the need to collaborate with unlikely agencies. Another factor was that in the long run it was in everyone's interest to avoid the use of the strike weapon except as the very last resort when all other devices had failed. The success of this policy can be seen from the results. Since the Second World War, Volvo for instance have only lost one day's production due to strikes. More generally, since 1945 (when over ten million man days were lost) Swedish industry has been relatively free from the disruption of production by industrial dispute, the only years of any significance being 1951 (0.5m man days), 1953 (0.6m man days), 1966 (0.3m man days) and 1970 (discussed in a later chapter). Yet Swedish workers enjoy one of the highest living standards in Europe, if not in the world. There are very clear lessons in all of this for other countries. In the strike ridden economies of Italy and the UK (where one firm alone lost more than 0.3m man days of production in 1974), the standard of living is among the lowest in Europe.

Union federations

Although reference in this chapter so far has been exclusively to the Confederation of Trade Unions (LO) it is not the only grouping of unions in Sweden. The LO represents the blue collar workers of industry and of the service operations together with the manual workers of agriculture and as such is certainly the largest organisation, its 1.8 million members representing 45 per cent of the total working population. Moreover, it can claim to have the high figure of 90 per cent of its potential membership within its ranks. Currently LO is a confederation of only twenty-five different unions. A much smaller blue collar union is the Central Organisation of Swedish Workers – SAC. Forestry and construction workers are among its 20,000 members: although small this organisation has been a thorn in the flesh of the LO since 1910.

Unlike the situation in many other countries, salaried and professional staff in Sweden are usually members of a trade union which is active in pursuing the interests of its members. The largest federation of these is the Central Organisation for Salaried Staff – TCO. It was born in 1944 out of the amalgamation of two earlier bodies and has a membership of 800,000 drawn from twenty-seven different unions. Earlier differences in the methods of operation of LO and TCO have largely disappeared and they each recognise a commonality of interests particularly since wage differentials are often small. At first, the employers opposed the formation of staff unions on the grounds that such people were in positions of responsibility and trust and therefore it was not suitable in principle for them to be members of a union. However as the number of white collar jobs has increased over the years, and wage or salary differentials and 'privileges' have been less noticeable, it is now believed that this argument is no longer relevant.

SACO, the Swedish Confederation of Professional Associations, dates from 1947. It has 130,000 members organised according to professions or training, 7 per cent of its membership consisting of doctors, dentists and lawyers, many of whom are self-employed. Initially, the possession of a degree was a prerequisite for membership of SACO, but this regulation has been somewhat relaxed to permit other forms of professional training to be recognised. In 1973, a new organisation, PTK, the Private Employers' Salaried Association, was formed to negotiate on behalf of the 350,000 members of TCO and SACO employed in private industry.

The last organisation that will be mentioned is SR – the National Federation of Government Officers. It is quite small with only 19,000 members drawn from officers in the armed forces, high ranking civil servants and higher officials in that part of the railway that is state owned, and postal services. Since 1966, all of these have had the right to strike but there are misgivings in some quarters on how this right might be exercised.

The outcome of this fairly complex structure of union federation is that when a company like the large shipbuilding firm of Kockums agrees to establish a consultative body such as a Works Council, seven representatives are drawn from the company, seven from the shop unions, three from the salaried staff unions and one from the foreman's union.

As a race, and possibly also steered in this direction as a result of the educational system, the Swedes are great lovers of conformity, either achieved or manifested through the joining of groups of one kind or another; union membership is no exception to this generalisation, most strata of society being catered for through one or other of the unions. One major difference does exist between the attitudes of the blue and white collar unions. The blue collar unions are openly and frankly political in outlook, usually, but not always, having close association with the Socialist party. In contrast, the white collar unions are most anxious to avoid any suggestion of commitment to a political party. Otherwise they are agreed on the benefits to be derived from a powerful union.

Federation relationships

While membership of a union federation such as the LO has the advantages arising from combined strength and the possibility of creating specialised resources, it also brings certain obligations, notably in the framing of the statutes governing the union constitution.

A cardinal principle in the constitution of all unions affiliated to the LO is that membership of the union must be available to all who work in the area of activity of the unions. Equally important is the insistence on the right of the executive board of the unions to veto proposals made by the membership; in effect, this means that the executive board has the sole right to negotiate the collective or national agreements that determine the minimum wages of their members. The executive board of the union has the right to make these agreements with the employers without reference to the membership but in practice a large amount of consultation usually occurs. If a union amended this particular right of veto, it would face expulsion from the Confederation.

No union can start a strike involving more than 3 per cent of its members, or a strike likely to involve members of other unions without getting the express permission of the executive of the Confederation. If this permission is forthcoming, the striking union must then consult with the other unions affected before the strike actually starts. The intent of these provisions is very clear; the Confederation is determined to keep control of a potential conflict and to prevent rapid escalation. Although it is prepared to act forcibly in pursuit of what it believes to be a legitimate claim, the Confederation has always conceded that the authorities have the duty to ensure the essential social life of the country is not interrupted. One way of preventing a major clash is to keep the size of the conflict to controllable dimensions.

The Confederation has the right, which it generally exercises, of being represented during the negotiations concerned with collective agreements. Furthermore, this representative of the Confederation has the right to make proposals directed towards influencing the course of the negotiations. In other countries, the equivalent central union organisation might sometimes wish they had the same rights, since clearly the Confederation of Trade Unions in Sweden is in a position to determine to a large degree the activity on the labour front.

If a strike or lockout does occur, the Confederation has the duty to support the union involved financially and morally, but since the level of support is decided by the Confederation Executive, this gives an additional means of exerting pressure if the circumstances demand.

There is therefore a very strong centralised element in Swedish trade unionism written into the constitution of individual unions. In recent years, the centralised aspect has tended to increase rather than to diminish because some modern problems are tending to become more complex; changing technology can sometimes bring new problems to the fore very rapidly. The structural relationship of the LO is shown very clearly in Figure 4.1.

The two main planks in the blue collar union platform also happen to require a powerful central organisation for their successful implementation. Since the 1930s the unions have been dedicated to a policy of full employment achieved through economic planning and full cooperation with a government which is also fully committed to these concepts. Almost as important in union eyes has been the policy of solidarity, the raising of the wages of the lower paid to levels closer to those enjoyed by the more prosperous members of society. Although in the policy declaration there is a statement that the wage levelling must pay due regard to the skills involved, in fact considerable restraint has been placed on the pay rises of the more highly skilled. (Not unnaturally the professional unions not in the LO do not contribute to this philosophy.) Neither of these two policies can be furthered if the union organisation is fragmented. Success has been recorded in both directions, the only partial failure of note being in the solidarity involved in equal pay for equal work for men and for women. The idea was accepted centrally in principle as early as the 1950s and in a formal agreement with the employers in 1961, but it is at local level that the action takes place. For various reasons, the pay earned by women tends

Figure 4.1 Swedish Trade Union Confederation – structure and organisation

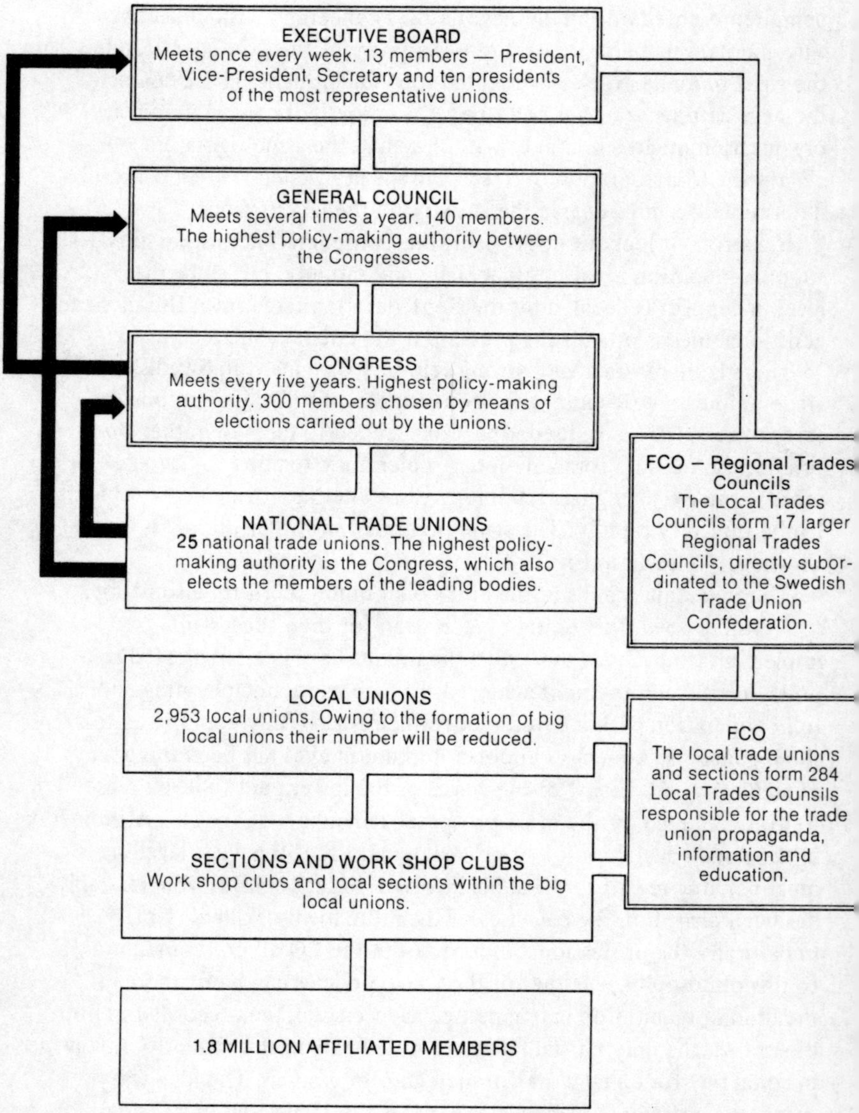

to be less than that of men, although women bus and train drivers and women welders are frequently seen.

The unions are well aware of the advantages of a centralised operation and are fully prepared to utilise them. The unions are also well aware of the inherent danger of a centralised position leading to a feeling of estrangement and even of divorce between the members and the executive. It will be seen later that much effort is devoted to communication and to keeping the members involved in union activities at local level.

Blue collar aims

As early as 1941, the Confederation of Blue Collar Unions defined three main aims which have remained unaltered for more than thirty years – a tribute to the far sighted union leaders of those days since the present generation seems to find the aims equally acceptable. With minor variations only, these are also the defined aims of the individual unions.

The first aim is to look after the interests of the members by seeking improved wages and working conditions. The second aim – to increase the efficiency of Swedish industry – is at first sight not so obvious as a union objective. Some have maintained that this means increasing the efficiency within the capitalist system: others have argued that it implies a take over of industry by the unions in order to improve efficiency. The existence of conflicting views has not prevented any union committing itself in practice to increased efficiency, because in this way the members get a share of a bigger cake.

The unions are aware that some companies may just not have the resources to increase the size of the cake due to economic or technical problems: under these conditions the unions can help by collaborating in the introduction of technical changes or indeed go as far as to include rationalisation of production into more efficient units as part of their activities. Rationalisation is a difficult issue because in the past it so often meant unemployment. The policy of full employment operated by the government through the Labour Market Board has done much to remove old fears on rationalisation. Further help in this direction has come from the educational courses run by the unions in which the virtues of economic planning, including rationalisation, deliberately feature very largely in order to foster the wider adoption of these ideas.

The most general of the three aims is to 'advance democracy in the political, social and economic fields'. Again the interpretation is wide open to debate. Some wish to see the trade union active in pursuing only its own affairs – minimising the political aspect. Others wish to see the unions pursuing political courses, and more specifically socialist enterprises, with missionary zeal. All are agreed in recognising there is no future for trade unions under a totalitarian regime.

The research department of the Confederation of Blue Collar Unions has produced a series of thoughtful reports which have formed the basis for discussion in successive quinquennial meetings of congress. The same themes have appeared repeatedly, these being almost entirely concerned with the means of achieving the first and second aims identified in this section. Reports on various sectors of the economy have led to more detailed investigation into the desirability of rationalisation and the effect on the individual worker. Requests have followed for the activities of the Labour Market Board to be strengthened in the particular area of job mobility and retraining facilities, job matching through the use of a computer and the provision of better information on job availability. Thus change is accepted as a means of maintaining industrial efficiency; the only question is how can the change best be organised with appropriate worker involvement. State ownership rarely features as an agent for change.

The need for further education for older workers in order to reduce the education gap between the generations and the requirements of the handicapped worker have both been highlighted over the years. It also appears that the research in these areas also has been the forerunner for action, which is a very satisfactory position.

The aims of the main unions are thus in no doubt: a steady pressure is evident for progress towards achieving them. The fact that the aims are reasonable and that steady progress is made with virtually no recourse to strikes may disguise to the casual onlooker the very real determination of the unions to further the best interest of their members.

One point of difference between the LO and some other national union organisations is that the former is itself a participant in capitalistic trade. It owns more than half the shares and takes an active interest in a building firm employing 15,000 workers, in a travel agency and in an insurance company. It is also the biggest shareholder in Aftonbladet, the second biggest newspaper in the country, read by one Swede in four.

Industry unions

Workers doing the same kind of job and having had the same kind of training have a natural affinity for one another and this is enhanced if they are employed in the same town or village. It was from such beginnings that the blue collar unions sprang, initially as craft type local unions. Federation upwards followed but always within the same craft. The disastrous general strike of 1909 revealed the weakness of this kind of organisation. A major weakness was that the pursuit of the best interests of one local union might be to the detriment of another local union. Some of the unions were weak, some were strong, even within the same craft, so there was no common form of organisation or strength. Lastly, there were just too many unions to enable the workers to speak with an effective voice.

As early as 1912, the congress of the Confederation of Trade Unions had before it a comprehensive study of the problem and proposals for its solution. The main proposal, which was accepted in principle, was that the number of unions within LO should be reduced to twenty-two national industrial unions, and these should be organised on an industry basis, that is, only one union in a plant. The reason for this was that the one union would be in a stronger position to negotiate; a supporting consideration was that in many work places or work areas, there would be sufficient members to sustain an effective organisation with a full time paid official on hand.

The argument has passed to and fro, one of the debating points being the difficulties of deciding borderline cases for different industries; likewise some of the highly skilled tradesmen were afraid of losing both status and reward if they were in an industry union together with unskilled labourers. Over the years, these difficulties have not been completely solved but decided progress has been made through the sheer logic of what was only a supporting consideration, that is, the organising strength of a single union is so conspicuously successful in practice. When the industry base is easy to define, as for instance in metal working or forestry, there is only one union. When the decision is not easy, LO has decided, perhaps reluctantly, to allow two or more smaller unions to exist even though the executive of LO in 1941 was given the right and even the duty to arbitrate in such situations – it has preferred to act as mediator rather than arbitrator. Thus instead of only one union for all transport workers, there are three, one for shipping, one for railways and one for all other transport. Sometimes, too, it has been found easier to have a separate union for municipal workers but, until recently, there have been no less than twelve separate unions for government blue collar workers! The number of national unions in the LO has varied over the years from a maximum of forty-six in the 1940s, to the current figure of twenty-five, which deviates but little from the twenty-two re-set in 1966 as a guide line. This is comparable with the sixteen industrial unions in Germany but is very different from the figure of 156 mainly craft unions in the UK.

Having only one blue collar union in a plant or works does not imply all employees are paid at the same rate, as a later chapter will show. Pay differentials exist but within a single negotiating system. In, say, a shipyard or a car firm there is a possibility of establishing the differential on a logical basis that will stand up to examination. Within such a firm, the single union believes it is in a very strong position to negotiate for all its members. The results indicate that the economy as a whole also benefits from industry as opposed to craft unions. The road to this situation has not been easy in Sweden but the Swedes have been prepared to look at it from several angles and then to apply the necessary effort to achieve a position which they believe is in the best interests of the trade union members as well as society as a whole.

Some have argued that the LO has not been entirely without self-interest in fostering the industry type of union; certainly the move has operated to their advantage. They believe the best way to secure stable industrial relations is through central negotiations between two powerful bodies meeting as peers, one representing the employers and one representing the workers. In this way a coherent, planned, general policy can be developed which at times has involved wage restraint and almost all the time has involved the principle of solidarity – the narrowing of pay differentials. Better conditions of safety, compensation and holidays, for example, have also been regarded as important issues. Naturally these policies have not found favour with everyone, but a central agency has a better chance of obtaining a successful conclusion than have separate bodies torn perhaps by internal and inter-union dissension. At works level, the union chief is almost certainly a paid official of the union, trained by the LO in the way the union thinks, so he will both support the union and be concerned to sell the union's ideas to the members. The wildcat shop steward would have little chance to sharpen his claws under these conditions and he does not exist in Sweden.

The position of the local trade union official is further strengthened through the procedure when a new worker joins a firm. An introduction to the firm is first given by the management when the rules and policy of the company are spelt out in some detail. Then in most instances the union official explains the benefits to be derived from union membership. Shortly afterwards it is the union official who invites the new entrant to become a member of the union, collects the first subscription, and so on. The emphasis throughout is that the union official is the man who matters in union affairs, although the new entrant is encouraged to take an active part in supporting the policy of the union.

To continue to be successful, this manoeuvre must be seen to produce results. In Sweden it certainly has. The standard of living of the workers has risen from rather a poor level in the 1930s to one of the highest in the world by the 1970s, by whatever measure is used, and this surely is what trade unionism is all about.

Membership of a union is open to all workers, the single exception being that a person involved in anti-union acts such as strike breaking, does not automatically obtain membership without investigation. To prevent the investigation becoming a witch hunt, procedure has been laid down for the right to appeal against an adverse decision, first to the executive of the LO, then to the congress of the LO, and finally if need be to a board of arbitration under an independent chairman sitting with equal numbers nominated by the LO and the appellant. He must be a brave man who invokes this procedure!

If a union member transfers from one job to another involving a different union, the membership is automatically transferred to the new union without additional cost and without loss of benefits – thus removing another potential barrier to job mobility.

Apart from the extraordinary position whereby a member of the master hairdressers' union can only employ members of the hairdressers' union, and the reverse – that members of the hairdressers' union can in turn only work for a member of the master hairdressers' union – there is no closed shop in Sweden. Some of the unions have raised this point somewhat half-heartedly from time to time only to be opposed by the employers. With a high membership already, the unions would appear to have little to gain. Of their non-members, many are immigrants employed on the more menial tasks, often ignorant of the language and only interested in getting back to their native land as quickly as possible.

The overall position is not quite so monolithic as the description so far might imply. Within the twenty-five national unions of LO, there are some 3,000 local or branch unions each possessing a certain amount of autonomy. There is a continual flow of information both up and down the chain but the national union reserves unto itself the right to negotiate wage rates; this is done at national level and establishes minimum rates. The local branch union is responsible for seeing the agreements are implemented and for dealing with local variations mostly concerned with bonus schemes. Certain of the skilled workers, while not at all happy with the reduction in pay differentials, have elected to go along with the principle at national level but have attempted and sometimes succeeded in using the local negotiations as a means of reinstating some measure of differential through the bonus scheme – this is sometimes described as 'wage drift'. Theoretically the local branch is acting on behalf of the national union and has no authority to initiate discussion without the approval of the national union; in practice the position is not quite so rigid. A further complication is that in a few plants, it is written into the local agreement that no outsider can intervene in negotiations, in which case the local official can only advise his members, mainly by acting as a link between them and the national union.

The final point in this section on industry unions is that when more than one union is concerned in negotiations (owing to failure to agree on a single union), the unions concerned are agreed to act in cooperation in what is described as a 'cartel arrangement'. The cooperation extends much further than in negotiations over pay. Joint union magazines of common interests are not uncommon and in some cases research costs are shared.

Communications and union resources

Because strikes have been so few, union resources in Sweden are little short of massive. As long ago as 1966, the blue collar unions affiliated to the LO had assets amounting to £84m and the LO itself had further assets of about £5m. The Employers' Confederation is also possessed of massive resources. Apart from the economic angle that strikes in the long run are in no-one's interest except that of the saboteur, it is sometimes suggested that the very size of the resources possessed by the unions and the employers is a guarantee that a peaceful solution will be sought through the channels of discussion, mediation and agreement. It is believed that resources are so large that an all out confrontation arising out of a deadlock on negotiation would wreck the Swedish economy – so it is avoided. The source of union funds is the subscriptions paid by the members. These vary from union to union but on average were in 1967 about £16 per annum with a further £5 per annum subscription to the local union: by 1973 union dues had risen to between £40 and £50 per annum. In addition many unions run

Figure 4.2 National unions in Sweden. Distribution of expenditure in 1966 (reproduced from *Trade Unions in Sweden* by Bo Carlson, with the author's permission)

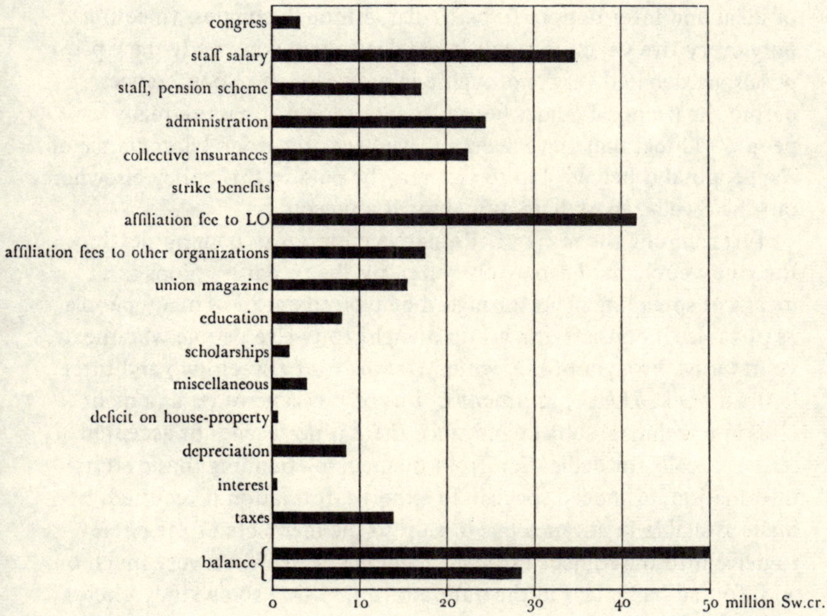

insurance schemes.

Figure 4.2 shows the distribution of expenditure for all the blue collar unions affiliated to the LO. The upper part of the diagram indicates the expenditure on administration much as would be expected: at £3.5m per annum on salaries there is no cheeseparing in this direction. £1.5m is spent on union magazines, £0.8m on education and £0.25m on scholarships, together with a considerable sum spent on conferences as part of the administration, indicate there is a real effort undertaken in this direction. The balance was increased in this year by about £2.8m out of a total income for the year of £29m.

The leadership of the Swedish trade unions is well aware of both the importance and the difficulty of communication between itself and the rank and file. The success of a union depends not only on its finances but also on the wholehearted involvement of the membership. As usual in such organisations, many conferences are held on a variety of subjects at all levels of the union in order to obtain a two-way flow of ideas and information. In particular, although congress (meeting only every five years) is the ultimate decision making body, new proposals are debated very thoroughly in a succession of conferences before the proposal comes before congress: thus if passed, many people will feel they have been involved and the general acceptance of the proposal is helped. Lip service may be paid to this policy elsewhere, but the Swedes work hard at making it a success.

From among the maze of alternative methods of communication, the study circle has been avidly seized by the Swedish unions as a means of spreading ideas through the involvement of as many people as possible. It consists of a group of eight to twelve people who meet voluntarily throughout the winter months for between two and three hours a week. The commitment is thus of the same order as a night class in a technical subject and since there is no teacher or accepted leader, it calls for dedication from the people attending. Basic course information, or indeed specialised expert information if required, is made available in advance but it is up to the members of the circle to delve into the subject through their collective efforts very much on an informal basis. It is in the nature of things that some study circles will be ineffective, but a remarkable number attain in this way a deep knowledge of the subject being studied and a skill in debate which can usefully be transferred to other union activities. Moreover, a successful study circle has the right to ask officials and other experts to appear before it to defend or to explain a difficult point. By thrashing out new ideas or new proposals through study circles it is claimed that the proposals have often been improved, while the attention of the experts has been attracted to an aspect which had been overlooked. It is claimed that no propaganda is involved in these exercises but it is difficult to see how it can be avoided if the subject happens to be a new act dealing with compensation for industrial injury, for instance, or even how the union dealt with a problem case.

The usual complaint is heard that the younger element under twenty-five years of age is not interested in giving up leisure to participate in either union conferences or study circles. But a surprisingly large number of Swedes, 140,000 each year from the ranks of LO alone, are prepared to devote their time in a spirit of perseverance to self-improvement in spite of the competing attraction of the TV, the ownership of which is widespread. It is just that there is a tradition of study in the winter that also becomes manifest in that other uniquely Scandinavian institution, the folk high school.

The government subsidises the folk high schools which are specifically designed to facilitate study by older students. The subjects can be of a quite wide range of general educational nature or, as is particularly the case in the two folk high schools partly owned by the unions, some instruction can be specifically oriented to trade union problems. All of the folk schools contain a fair proportion of courses in citizenship. The Workers' Education Authority play a large part in organising the course material in which particular attention is always paid to the avoidance of an academic, or too pure, approach. In spite of these qualifications, the folk high schools have played an important role in raising the educational standard of older people who may have left school at an earlier age than is the current practice. By making use of the grants that are available for study at the folk high school, and then subsequently by making use of the rule that anyone who has worked for five years and has attained the age of twenty-five years is entitled to attend university courses on repayable loans, it is possible for a late starter, or an early school leaver (because of economic pressures), to achieve a high standard of formal education.

The trade unions are very sensitive to this point because it is exceptional in Swedish trade union circles for officials to have come other than from the rank and file of the membership. A means of raising educational standards is therefore vital, not only for potential officials but also for the active union workers who may be in the older age groups. Part of this need is met through the folk high schools. Part is supplied by two residential colleges run by the LO, and in some cases, by colleges run by a union for its own members. Courses vary from a few days to several months, the shorter ones being concerned with special aspects of trade union organisation. The longer courses are obviously aimed at future organisers of the union movement. To quote Bo Carlson: 'it was no longer enough for an active trade unionist to know how to organise a strike, he also should be able to participate in the constructive shaping of society.'

Magazines produced by the unions have reached glossy status, usually being produced by professionals to include well written articles with suitable illustrations. The material is not restricted to union matters but is intended to embrace all of the family. It may not be a cradle to the grave influence but the aim is to make the workers realise just how important the union is to them, and how important they are to the union. The constant effort has produced results, but a later chapter will show there has been some movement away from complete identity with union ideas by some sections of the community.

The ultimate test by which a Swedish union organisation will be judged has at least two, potentially opposing dimensions. These are that it must be efficient and it must be democratic. If democracy means involving people in decisions, then much effort is devoted to making the unions democratic. The bloc vote simply does not exist in Sweden. The elaborate interlocking committee structure is deliberately designed to avoid the growth of a dictatorship within a union. Having said that, the fact remains that a decision to go on strike or not, and the decision on whether a wage offer is accepted or not, is made by a small union executive board of between five and nine members: this board has the sole right to make the decision and the decision can be in direct opposition to the declared wishes of the membership. But whether the executive board would then survive the next election (half the board is elected each year) is another matter. In fact, many such decisions have been made, the executive board generally acting as a restraining influence. One reason the situation developed in this way was that in union eyes it is 'inconceivable' that a particular group of workers should themselves decide to go on strike and then expect to be supported out of union funds.

To return to the recurring question of how much other countries can learn from Swedish experience, unions elsewhere would have a hard task to involve the majority of their members in the down to earth activities of union organisation, but it should be a rewarding effort if they were successful; this would, for example, mean that the executive and the officials might reflect the views of the shop floor membership more accurately than is presently believed to be the case. Detailed study by many people would lead to an appreciation of the unmistakable consequence that power brings with it responsibilities to be discharged with discretion. Constructive, planned union activity would then be able to earn higher increases in the standard of living of their members and of the society, of which they are a part. It could also be urged that the conversion to industry unions would bring benefits but this conversion would take time for old ideas to be replaced by better ones.

Holidays and insurance schemes

Economic conditions in Sweden were so poor that it was not until the 1920s that the working classes could afford to think in terms of holidays. About that time, the unions started a series of negotiations with the employers which resulted in most workers getting four days holiday, around the national midsummer day holiday, with pay but usually ar a rate rather less then the normal earnings. Further negotiations failed to obtain any increase in paid holidays and moreover, some of the small organisations were outside the agreements and paid no holidays at all. So reluctantly the unions turned to *political* action – not to strike action. In 1938 an act was passed granting every worker a holiday of two weeks to be paid in full by the employer.

The law has since been amended so that every worker now gets a minimum of four weeks paid holiday; local agreements on length of service and so on can increase the holidays above the minimum. Present day affluence has led to many people indulging in holidays overseas and the Swedes spend more than three times as much per head of population on overseas holidays as do the residents of the USA or the UK, and 25 per cent more than the Germans. The Swedes have experienced almost a rags-to-riches transformation in half a century.

A later chapter describes the national pension schemes which are completely outside the unions. Actually the initiative came from the Employers' Confederation in the 1950s for the alignment and regulation of many existing pension schemes but the blue collar unions refused to participate in discussions on the grounds that the smaller companies would again be outside any negotiations: a defensive note is observed in present day discussions on this point. The unions were also concerned that they would have no say in the investment of these pension funds. Instead state action has taken place, and tha national basic pension is presently paid by contributions partly from individuals and partly from the government, while the much larger national supplementary pension is financed entirely by the employers.

There was some alarm that the 'two conflicting sides position' that evolved in the pensions dispute marked the end of an era of peaceful existence, exemplified by progress in the social and economic fields. Fortunately, the alarm proved to be false. The typical approach can be seen in the way in which industrial injury insurance was established. The unions approached the employers with a request for a comprehensive scheme. The employers responded with proposals based on the commercial insurance companies, but the unions wanted the scheme to be based on the cooperative insurance house. The employers would have none of this, so a compromise was worked out whereby the scheme was based on a new insurance company established jointly by the unions and the employers. When such attitudes prevail, most disputes can be resolved without blood-letting.

A major difference in the function of the unions compared with, say the UK, occurs in unemployment insurance which has been operated by the unions in Sweden. From the earliest days, the unions believed they should try to help their members in a time of adversity be it due to sickness or to unemployment. When resources were slim, the ability to help was correspondingly small. Gradually, insurance schemes were established by the unions but there was disquiet that the insurance was being asked to finance an unknown risk: this disquiet was reinforced by the high unemployment of the 1920s. Approaches were made for government subsidies for the unemployment funds and while these were obtained, they were accompanied by regulations that the right to unemployment benefit was lost if the claimant refused to accept an offered job. This may sound reasonable but some of the unemployed were treated fairly harshly by the government servants under this rule and eventually the rule was amended so that the job had to be suitable for and within the capacity of the claimant, the administration passing to the Labour Market Board with whom the claimant must be registered as unemployed in order to qualify for benefot. The Labour Market Board also has the responsibility to oversee the functioning of the insurance funds, 66 per cent of which are contributed by the government with the balance coming from the unions, each national union being responsible for the fund in its own area of activity. Benefits are not payable for an indefinite period, so there is a considerable urge to find a suitable job if necessary through retraining and migration. During the recession extending into 1973 and 1974, the period of benefit has been extended to 300 days with a further extension of 150 days for the elderly or the handicapped. The government has also recently taken over the payment of continued benefits as has been discussed more fully in an earlier chapter.

Confederation of Professional Associations

Most of this chapter has been concerned with the Confederation of Blue Collar Unions which, because of its size, certainly dominates the Swedish industrial scene, but SACO, the very much smaller Confederation of Professional Associations is not without interest. Starting initially as separate and strictly professional bodies concerned with educational and ethical standards, for a long time their members viewed with some distaste the activities of the blue collar unions. They could afford to take this attitude as long as they were financially secure and of favoured status. During the Second World War and in the years preceding it, the position changed. University education became more expensive and at the same time rates of taxation were greatly increased, making it more difficult to repay the loans most professionals had during their university days. Reluctantly the professionals were driven to recognise that in a highly organised society such as Sweden, they too must become organised or continue to lose ground.

Hardship fell worst on the young professionals who could not find jobs in keeping with their qualifications or alternatively had to continue their training in lowly paid posts. So in 1943, an association with 5,000 members was formed to apply union type pressures to improve the financial position of newly qualified professional workers. This organisation demonstrated that greater strength came from unity with the result that SACO was formed in 1947. By the mid-1950s virtually all the professional groups belonged to SACO.

Membership of a professional association is not cheap: in 1974 it cost between £50 and £70 per year, depending on the association. The twenty-five associations then pay £7.50 to SACO for each of their members. The total membership, including some undergraduates at reduced fees, is now 130,000, so the budget is still relatively small.

The case for a separate confederation to represent the interests of such small numbers rests precisely on its size. If these people were absorbed in a blue collar industry union or a white collar salaried staff union, their specialised interests would be overwhelmed by the sheer weight of numbers. After struggling for a few years, by the mid-1950s SACO had earned the right to negotiate for its members in most spheres. About the same period, SACO succeeded in making an impact on public opinion by taking a non-political stand on certain issues: a few years later it received the seal of approval by being empowered to appoint delegates to official government enquiries or agencies such as the Labour Market Board.

The professional associations have adopted a distinctive position on three issues. It is believed the student loans should attract tax relief during the repayment period; the argument for this is that with the reduction in differentials, the earning power over the life span of a professional now compares less favourably (or even unfavourably) with that of a manual worker who starts earning several years before a professional. This debate continues. The other unions have also come round to accepting the second argument which is that gross income is the wrong measure to use in negotiations *vis-à-vis* the cost of living index; disposable income – that part of the income left after paying compulsory taxes – is a better measure. During the 1970 round of collective bargaining to cover the three years 1971 to 1973, SACO claimed that the professionals required an increase of 22 per cent in order to maintain real standards. The third distinctive position has arisen from the claim that the professionals too are entitled to a share of the increase in the standard of living that they have helped to create: the other unions responded somewhat tartly that the professionals should really be accepting a decline in standards since their present affluence was unwarranted in a socialist society. The government too was unsympathetic and public opinion was lukewarm.

Failing to win this, their first major conflict, by discussion, the professionals resorted to the strike weapon, calling 6,000 of their members out in the public sector. The authorities, who in this case were the employers, replied with a lockout, so that in all 45,000 people were involved in the only major industrial conflict since the war years – and this was with the professionals against the socialist administration! An average increase of about 13 per cent was obtained for professionals in the government sector and 23 per cent was obtained for those in local government, before the government introduced compulsory official duty, i.e. the job must be done. After one such trial of strength, it is interesting to speculate on what the future holds for SACO: time alone will show whether the authorities will be prepared to negotiate as freely with the professional unions as they do with the blue collar unions or whether political factors will intervene in spite of the apolitical stance of the professional unions.

In the nearly thirty years of its existence, SACO claims to have obtained marked improvements for the junior members. For example, a newly qualified physician now receives £5,700 per annum and a new entrant graduate civil servant is paid £4,000 per annum.

SACO has a strong research and policy making department. Naturally much of this effort is devoted to problems unique to a professional organisation but in addition the Swedish 'remiss system' absorbs a fair amount of effort also. This is part of the democratic process by which government and private members' bills are submitted to the state bureaucracies and other independent organisations such as SACO and LO for opinions and comments in advance of legislation. Each year SACO for instance passes comment on about 200 such motions.

The growth of industrial democracy discussed in other chapters is not expected to leave the professional untouched. As working groups become more widespread, the individual qualified professional is advised to participate with his own particular viewpoint in mind: training schemes and the dissemination of information are provided by SACO to assist the process.

There are signs that most of the factors mentioned in this brief survey are already operating elsewhere in the developed countries, so it would not be surprising to see the emergence of confederations to further the common interests of the doctors, the lawyers, the dentists, the teachers, the scientists and the clergy.

5 COLLABORATION BETWEEN UNIONS AND EMPLOYERS' ORGANISATIONS IN SWEDEN

Growth of collective agreements

The early associations of the employers took the form of trade organisations, but as worker power became manifest even in the weak version of the 1900s, the trade associations moved to a more defensive position against the activities of the trade unions. The general strike of 1902, called for political reasons, had demonstrated to the employers the weakness of their uncoordinated organisations. Moreover, many felt very strongly about the interruption of their production for political reasons which they believed were nothing to do with the work place. So the Confederation of Swedish Employers (SAF) was formed in 1902 purely as a defensive measure with much of Swedish industry being represented; the main absentee was the Metal Industries Employers' Association which was both the strongest association and already firmly organised on central lines.

In a few years however the metal industries had also joined SAF which today speaks for most of Swedish industry. Other bodies exist as will be discussed briefly later in the chapter, but just as LO, the Confederation of Blue Collar Unions, dominates the union scene, so SAF dominates the employers' picture. Generally speaking, it is now agreed this is a beneficial arrangement. Strength speaks unto strength. Both bodies are capable of looking beyond the short term and in spite of diametrically opposed views the collaboration between them has played no small part in giving Swedish industry the chance to reach its present favourable position. But it was not always thus. It was only after bitter conflicts involving both strikes and lockouts and even one shooting incident in which five metal workers were shot by the military, that the wisdom of collaboration was recognised. Some consider that it is only because the conflicts were so bitter that collaboration became acknowledged on all sides as being the only way forward.

Taking place in a tense atmosphere, the first discussions in 1906 and now known as the December compromise, centred on the form an agreement should take; eventually it was decided a collective agreement at national level would be most appropriate, implying the right of LO and SAF to negotiate at national level on behalf of their respective members. These collective agreements would have no legal enforcement procedures but would rely on the voluntary acceptance first by individual associations or unions and then be put into practice by individual firms and union membership. This is where the strength of SAF and LO can be of advantage. If need be, both can exert pressure to ensure that a collective agreement is kept. But the best way for an agreement to be kept is by means of voluntary acceptance through persuasion: both SAF and LO are closely in touch with their membership with this in mind.

In determining the content of a collective agreement the unions were anxious that it should include a national minimum wage. The employers were opposed to this but eventually conceded. Paradoxically it is now the employers who welcome the collective agreements for two main reasons. By fixing the wage rates for a definite period of either one or sometimes three years, a fair measure of stability is brought into labour relations. Secondly, the provision for negotiation at local level for increases above the basic minimum, has enabled limited wage differentials to develop – and it is the employers who favour differentials in opposition to the solidarity policy of the unions.

Officially, the collective agreement represented the full extent of collaboration until 1928, although unofficially, enlightened people from both sides were discussing further possibilities of defusing conflicts. In that year, the Conservative government took the initiative of convening a conference to discuss the problems of the labour market with particular reference to Sir Alfred Mond's work in the UK. Although the conference was able to agree on the value of collective agreements it could not agree on how conflicts could be avoided or resolved, or how joint production councils could flourish.

Pay negotiations

The early collective agreements were negotiated between employers' associations for a specific trade or industry and the particular blue collar unions involved, with representatives of SAF and LO in attendance. It was soon realised that with this system it was difficult to avoid inequalities or even injustice between different sectors of the economy: it became a favourite ploy to wait for other industries to complete their agreements. Gradually SAF and LO came to play an increasing part in the negotiations until in the early 1950s the present system was formalised under which the first stage in a wage round is a central collective agreement made directly between SAF and LO. The central agreements are currently of great importance not only because of the interaction between industries but also because of the supporting research that has been devoted to the preparation of the case.

SAF has a substantial research organisation working on past trends and future developments in the economy as well as on the impact on employers of current social change. The costs and effects of various strategies are explored by the research department as part of the employers' negotiators' brief. Wage and salary levels and trends are also analysed from raw data supplied by the member firms. These analyses and summaries are given to the unions and recognised by both sides as the factual basis of discussion. This avoids the cost of duplicated effort and, more important, establishes a mutual base in advance of negotiations.

Most collective agreements expire in the early months of the year so discussions start in the preceding November. The first stage is a general debate between the so-called 'large delegations' of between thirty and forty representatives from each of SAF and LO. A gathering of this size can only be concerned with general principles so each side presents a formal survey of the economy and economic trends relevant to wage negotiations. The formal demands for the new central agreement are next presented by each side and the proposals are discussed by the delegations. The SAF and LO now each appoint three delegates – the so called 'small delegations' – who take over and whose duty it is to negotiate an agreement with due reference to their parent bodies if need be. When an agreement is finally concluded, these six delegates are the signatories.

The outcome is a broad framework stating the principles for the industry agreements that follow. In theory, the central agreements are only recommendations from the central confederations but in practice they are adhered to very closely. The individual industry agreements are then negotiated in the same way, but these can only be regarded as drafts until they have been agreed by the executive boards of SAF and LO. No final approval is given until all the tentative agreements have been secured: whereupon all the agreements are then declared final and become mandatory. Both the Confederation of Employers and the Confederation of Blue Collar Unions thus keep a tight hold on wage negotiations and keep their constituent members very much in line.

Similar negotiations for collective agreements are carried out between SAF and the Central Organisation for Salaried Staff – TCO – with one difference. The agreement for an increase in salary is on two levels, a basic salary increase that everyone receives, and a gross amount for individual merit increase which can be disposed as the employer wishes.

The most recent agreement in principle on wages and salaries was contained in the so-called EFO report of 1968. After a detailed study of the interaction of wages, prices and the performance of the economy, SAF, LO and TCO concluded that future increases in profitability should be divided between capital and labour according to agreed principles. Moreover it was recognised that pay rises in the non-profit-making or sheltered sectors of the economy such as government service had also to be paid out of the extra profits earned in the competitive sector. This is an important change of emphasis in wage negotiations, recognising as it does that pay rises need to be earned if the real standard of living is to continue to rise; this principle is expected to be the determining factor in pay negotiations of the 1970s.

Rationalisation

Although the emphasis in collective agreements is on wage and salary levels, wider issues affecting conditions of employment are also frequently the subject of collective agreements. An important agreement on rationalisation was finalised in June 1972 superseding an agreement on work study made in 1948. The basic principle is that unless a firm undertakes a continuous rationalisation of its production methods, job security is at risk, as is the viability of the firm. Rationalisation should therefore be a joint effort with workers participating directly to make it a success. The overall goal of rationalisation is to improve productivity but this must be coupled with attempts to obtain greater job satisfaction and to create better working environments. While change and technical innovation are welcomed, a conscious effort should be made, particularly in mass production industries, to create jobs that the individual worker can perceive to be meaningful and rewarding.

It is agreed that in any worthwhile scheme for improving production efficiency, systematic methods of analysis and measurement through work study and similar techniques will have to play an important role. The only restrictions on such activities are that the people concerned shall be properly trained and that the union and workers shall be properly informed of the reasons for the investigation and, later, of the results. Access to the raw data can also be obtained by selected people on the understanding that confidential information will not be disclosed outside of the firm. It is recommended that sufficient training should be given in work study or other appropriate techniques to workers in the union ranks to enable them to contribute to the project at the consultative stage and also to be able to explain the position to other union members. To be effective in this capacity the trained worker should not be transferred out of his work place. The provision of suitable training in work study techniques has exercised both SAF and LO to the extent that the agreement on rationalisation contains a section establishing a small, joint working committee charged with the responsibility of being fully up to date in new developments in industrial engineering and in seeing that the training in Sweden is commensurate with the requirements.

The Swedish love of institutions appears even in this field. The agreement covers the formation of a new body, the Rationalisation Council, with three members from both SAF and LO, serving for three years under an independent chairman. Of its nine terms of reference, three are concerned with the dissemination of information on rationalisation, five are concerned with various aspects of work study and the last with enabling the Rationalisation Council to act as a board of arbitration in the event of dispute.

The technical department of the Employers' Confederation has considerable experience in rationalisation. If a company changes its system of calculating wage payments, every effort is made to quantify the results, particularly the effect on productivity. The technical department will help with the analysis in order to unify the basis for comparison purposes. In addition to undertaking research into control of organisations, it has the task of making known throughout the member associations the latest knowledge on production methods, scheduling, organisation and so on; it can assist an individual company to install a new system in any of these fields. It is thus in a good position to act as a catalyst accelerating change in methods.

Rationalisation can take many forms: closing a number of small production units in order to obtain the advantages of scale through the concentration of production in a single large plant; replacing the manual labour of say sixteen workers by a power machine operated by two men; or changing a production line to the group working system discussed later. Each of these will have its own separate problems. To help smooth the path, another body , the Development Council, with its own administration was set up in 1966: the Council itself consists of five representatives from SAF, three from LO and two from the white collar union TCO. Since 1970, this Development Council, and more especially its permanent working party (URAF) has been primarily interested in the growth of industrial democracy. Its mission is to advise on the likely effects of change, to keep track of the many experiments and to analyse the long term results. It is believed that five years is the minimum period required to assess the effects of a major change so it is still early days: so far the analytical work of the Development Council appears to be less conspicuous than that of the technical department of SAF, so the main function of the Council would seem to be that of a forum for an exchange of ideas.

Human relationships

Another important agreement not concerned with wages was the 1942 agreement on safety in working places, which was amended in 1967 to embrace wider considerations of occupational health. While LO and SAF are mutually agreed that improvements in safety are best achieved through cooperation, SAF have tended to take the lead in combating accidents and industrial disease through its medical unit which employs full-time doctors and professional hygienists. In addition to research into the potential hazards that might arise from new manufacturing processes, the medical unit advises on occupational health centres established in individual firms or sometimes on health centres serving several firms.

For the purpose of this chapter, only one other agreement will be mentioned – that on the provision of vocational training. Having agreed on the desirability of the scheme, SAF and LO have jointly established yet another body, the Labour Market Vocational Council, whose duty it is to devise suitable courses and generally to support the development of vocational training.

Still another body was funded in 1952 by SAF and still exists as an independent institution: it is the Council for Personnel Administration which not only carries out research itself into questions of personnel administration and industrial psychology but also finances university and some other professional research in similar areas. Part of the remit of this council is to coordinate the findings of the research and to see that the results are fed back into industry.

There is no doubt the Swedes treat very seriously the approach to human relationships in modern industrial life. Little is left to chance. Agreed and common approaches are set up as soon as a problem is identified or indeed sometimes to find out if there is a problem. The outcome has been outstandingly successful and it is not left there. Just as the unions have their own colleges, the Confederation of Employers has three pleasantly located residential colleges devoted to the development of managerial skills. A basic consideration of these courses (and indeed this point is pressed on the universities and other centres of technical training) is that the courses should lay a foundation upon which the participant can build and extend knowledge and personal skills with particular regard to the rapidly changing nature of twentieth century technology.

Organisation

The Swedish Employers' Confederation is unusual in that it has a dual relationship with each of the constituent member firms. It is a condition of membership that each firm is also a member of the employers' association appropriate to its sphere of activities – these might range from the Swedish pulp and paper mills employers' federation with fifty-two member firms employing a total of 47,000 workers to the Swedish bakery and confectionery employers' association with 14,000 member firms but only employing an average of twelve workers. To marry such disparate bed-fellows into a meaningful association is no easy task. The driving force initially was purely defensive and this is still reflected in the annual dues. Each firm pays to SAF an annual due proportional to the payroll: each firm also enters into an indemnity which can be used by SAF to compensate any member firm which may suffer loss due to either strikes or lockouts. This is a form of insurance against loss from industrial conflict and gives rise to the oft repeated statement that constituent firms are both members and part owners of SAF. Both the association and the firm are then members of SAF.

The insurance arrangement carries with it restrictions: it is also a condition of membership of SAF that a firm may not order or initiate a lockout without the prior approval of the executive board or the general council of SAF. Two other conditions complete the undertakings which must be given: a firm or association may not enter into a collective agreement with a union without approval of the details by the executive board of SAF; and the basic right of the employer to hire and fire, and to allocate and direct how the work shall be done, must be built into a fundamental agreement with the unions.

The constitution is thus designed to enable SAF to keep a very tight control on its thirty-nine affiliated associations and 26,000 member firms. The constitution has also been framed so that the power to take decisions is vested in the executive board (which of course is made up of representatives from the membership), without reference to the membership. The overall effect is to maintain the authority of a powerful body that can negotiate and otherwise collaborate with the LO, representing the 0.8 million blue collar workers employed by the members of SAF, and TCO representing 0.6 million white collar workers.

Although SAF is the largest of the employers' confederations, it is not the only one negotiating with the unions. In the private sector there are separate employers' organisations for agriculture, for ship-owners and for the cooperatives. The public sector and the state owned industries each have their own separate negotiating machinery and employers' organisation which are roughly matched by the union organisations.

Federation of Swedish Industries

Yet another organisation exists to provide a central focus to industrial problems: it is the Federation of Swedish Industries – known as SI – composed of twenty-six trade associations comprising 3,000 companies many of which are also members of SAF. The difference is that SI, founded as early as 1910, is not concerned with management/labour relations. It is more concerned to identify and then support economic and social policies that will promote the development of the real wealth or resources of the country. In this it is much concerned with securing sources of capital to maintain investment and is in effect a bridge between government and industry, in that it represents industry to government on questions affecting the growth and efficiency of industry and advises constituent firms and associations on these issues.

The Federation is divided into seven departments. Perhaps the most important is the economic policy department whose research is consistently of very high quality. To cite but one example: a report published in 1972 analysed in depth the international competitiveness of Swedish manufacturing industry. One of its conclusions was that because of the narrowing of profit margins in Sweden since about 1965, while this had not so far retarded investment for short term projects aimed at increasing productivity in existing plants, difficulty would be experienced in financing investment for long term improvements in productivity so that the high growth would not be maintained without a change in direction.

The development and planning department of SI is concerned with long term problems associated with community development, regional policy and the structure of industry as well as the more familiar area of computer technology. Associated with this is the environment and natural resources department. More prosaic perhaps but equally useful are the departments involved in taxation, legal matters, marketing and trade policy.

The Employers' Federation also has an interest in other bodies. The Taxation and Company Legal Department Ltd, and the Pollution Control Company are wholly owned by industry and exist to give advice and to undertake sponsored work. The Pollution Control Laboratory is financed 50:50 by the government and industry. The Industrial Institute for Economic and Social Research is an independent research institute founded by SAF and SI.

The government too is not idle: the Ministry of Industry has a research department investigating the changing structure of Swedish industry and it produces independent long term forecasts of future developments. The aim is to check and then to influence the position. The government also run the National Bureau of Statistics, and the National Institute of Economic Research which produces detailed analysis of the economic situation every four months. The government SOU publications continue to present an enormous amount of factual information on many subjects so that the effects of change can often be readily identified.

The national habit of analysis makes accurate data readily available in the quantified measures of statistics. The first collection of statistical evidence began in 1756 with the setting up of the Kungl. Tabelkommissionen: the process has continued so long that elaborate data banks exist, the most ambitious perhaps being that of land use based on a kilometre grid. According to Michael Drake, Scandinavia possesses a vast and in many ways unique body of quantitative data due to the happy accident that an administrative revolution preceded the industrial one. Amidst the wealth of activity on this front, two important features can be seen. The one is the large amount of research that is taking place under the aegis of many different organisations. The second is that the lack of friction between apparently overlapping bodies leads to a healthy cooperation aimed at improving industrial productivity and conditions.

6 LEGISLATION, THE EMPLOYERS AND THE UNIONS

Labour negotiations

Anti-union legislation has been very rare in Sweden, the exception being an act passed in 1898 making it illegal to force anyone to participate in a strike or to stop anyone accepting the offer of a job. At that time the unions were too weak to take the action they would have liked and the one Social Democrat in the Riksdag failed to make any impact, but the passing of that act is still a very sore point with the unions. The bill seems to have been initiated by top civil servants, ultra conservative in outlook, who persuaded a member of parliament to sponsor the bill: it is a measure of the feeling in trade union circles that this man is still described as 'a somewhat stupid member' even though in practice is appears the law was not applied over-zealously. Unsuccessful attempts were made up to the 1930s to pass other anti-union legislation, this time at the instigation of the employers, but since then it is probably true to say the legislation has either been of a social nature directed more against the employers or usually has been concerned with the need to seek peaceful solutions to conflict. But it must be added that legal action has been minimal.

Table 6.1 Date of passing of first of the social laws relating to industry in Sweden (many of these laws have been amended subsequently)

1881	Child labour abolished in factories
1889	First control of industrial hazards
1900	Regulations on employment of women workers
1901	Compensation for industrial injury
1913	Basic pension introduced
1919	8-hour-day and 48-hour week as maxima
1960	Earnings related pension scheme

Table 6.1 shows that Sweden even under the conservative (or bourgeois, as the unions like to call it) regime has been relatively early in passing

progressive laws aimed at controlling the social obligations of industry. Naturally these early laws have been considerably modified as the social conscience of Europe has developed, but Sweden cannot be accused of lagging behind.

The first two decades of the twentieth century saw a long series of damaging and very bitter conflicts between the employers and the unions. The government of the day did not interfere, partly because they were unresolved on the best course to take, and partly because they, and more especially the civil service bureaucrats who advised them, felt they were rather above the earthy activities of industry and its dissensions. However, it became increasingly clear that unless action was taken, the rest of the community would be at risk. The more discerning leaders among both the unions and the employers were also not unaware of their responsibilities to society and at the same time recognised that the level of conflict was damaging to their own interests. The development of the system of collective agreements was one aspect of the need to reduce conflict but it contained no mechanism to deal with the situation if the parties failed to agree, until the Riksdag passed the Collective Agreement Act in 1928 which converted the collective agreements into legally binding contracts.

Under this legislation, the signatories to a collective agreement are required to keep the peace in regard to all the clauses of the agreement for as long as it is in force. A Labour Court was also set up to deal with disputes on interpretation of a collective agreement – there is thus a means of obtaining peaceful solutions to the so-called 'conflicts of rights'.

However it was one thing to pass legislation and another to achieve the objective if the goodwill of the parties involved was lacking. The door was still open to disputes during the negotiations preceding the signing of an agreement – the so-called 'conflicts of interests' which certainly still caused many strikes for another ten years. It was believed by both the employers and the unions that unless conditions improved, the government would again intervene with more drastic legislation directed towards conserving the public interest. Accordingly, a conference was convened in 1938 between the Employers' Confederation and the Confederation of Blue Collar Unions, to be held at Saltsjöbaden and from which the basic or Saltsjöbaden agreement emerged.

There was in fact a fair measure of common ground between the two parties. Both were agreed that vital public services should not be disrupted by disputes and that sympathetic strikes or other indirect effects should not be allowed to injure other interests not concerned in the dispute – the so-called third man's rights. Both were even more strongly in agreement that government intervention in labour relations was undesirable. Each side was agreed that excessively militant conflicts were damaging to its own interests: this does not imply any reluctance to hurt the other side but is simply a recognition that in the process they at the same time hurt themselves. On this rather negative basis, an agreement was launched that has had a profound effect on Swedish life.

It is now generally acknowledged in Sweden that there are two types of problem in labour relations. In the one, management and labour have a common interest in devising the best solution, as for instance in safety, in rationalisation or in joint consultation: in these problems there is generally a harmonious pooling of experience and energy. In the other class of problem, the interests may be diametrically opposed: without relenting in any way the pressure to obtain the best deal each for its own side, management and unions now approach negotiations with a hard realism and a dispassionate appraisal of the evidence. The aim is to negotiate and the strike weapon is an unfortunate last resort denoting failure. This then is the spirit of the Saltsjöbaden agreement and in this respect is entirely a moral obligation.

However the agreement does have some teeth. As a result of the agreement, a Labour Market Council was established consisting of three representatives from the employers and three representatives from the blue collar unions. This body has functions which are a mix of arbitration and negotiation. It can act as an arbitrator in deciding whether a conflict will be prejudicial to the public interest, or indeed in deciding whether an action is contrary to the spirit of the agreement. More usually the Council acts as a negotiating medium helping to find agreement in a contested area. It may also be brought into action to help resolve the sensitive problems arising from dismissals and lay-offs when fact finding may be an important element in the Council's activities. The Labour Market Council is not a legal body and so its judgements can have no legal force. In spite of this it does have extensive influence because the combined weight of the Employers' Confederation and the Confederation of Blue Collar Unions is behind its deliberations.

The actions of the state mediator and of the Labour Court are in a different category because these functions were established by law. Sweden is divided into eight mediation areas and in each area there is a state mediator appointed by the government. It is the duty of the mediator to have his, or her, finger on the industrial pulse of the district. Seven days before initiating a dispute, the party involved must notify both the mediator and the opposing party. If the mediator thinks the intervention of his office is desirable, or if either party so requests, both parties will be invited to present their case. Failure to appear can result in prosecution. Under the law, both parties must be prepared to negotiate, that is to advance positive proposals which might lead to a resolution of the dispute; the emphasis is on the search for a solution. If unsuccessful, the mediator can suggest referring the dispute, which has probably still not yet led to open conflict in the form of a cessation of production, to a board of arbitration – there is no compulsory arbitration in Sweden so the mediator can only suggest arbitration. The number of cases of voluntary arbitration is getting smaller, most disputes or conflicts of interest now being settled by negotiation at the mediator level.

Labour Court

Misgivings on both sides of industry were apparent when the law establishing the Labour Court was passed in 1928. Nevertheless there was a need for such a body because the only alternatives available to resolve a dispute over the interpretation of a clause in a collective agreement were either through force or through actions in the civil courts – and if taken to the highest level it could take up to seven years to get a final ruling. This is obviously useless for a collective agreement which may be due to expire in less than twelve months. The Labour Court is now accepted as discharging a useful function; because of its specialist knowledge it can usually reach a decision quickly and the fact that there is no appeal against its decisions also helps to speed the process of litigation. Neither the mediators nor the Labour Court could have performed satisfactorily without the change of heart embodied in the Saltsjöbaden agreement.

The Labour Court comprises seven members all officially nominated by the Crown. The chairman and one member must have legal experience: another member must be impartial as far as employers and workers are concerned, and must have legal knowledge of the collective agreements and of labour market problems. In practice these three members are usually judges. Of the others, two are nominated by the Employers' Confederation and two by the Confederation of Blue Collar Unions. (If the dispute involves salaried staff or public bodies, the representation can be changed.) All seven members of the Court must take the judicial oath and so are sitting as judges, some with specialist knowledge, but none, it is hoped, with partisan leanings.

The prime concern of the Labour Court is to keep industrial peace. Once a collective agreement has become mandatory, all the signatories must abide by it and cannot seek alternative proposals or interpretations: failure to do so would be considered a breach of the industrial peace and would be referred to the Court. If either party fails to keep the agreement, say by not paying the agreed rates or by not discharging certain duties, or by striking, they can be brought before the Labour Court. While going to arbitration at the suggestion of either a mediator or the Labour Market Council is voluntary, failure to abide by the terms of the arbitration when made can also lead to an appearance before the court. In each case, the penalty can be compensation to be paid to the injured party. (If the case happened to be a failure to pay the agreed rate, only the union members would get the compensation but both union and non-union workers alike would receive the correct rate in future.) Individual workers can be forced to pay compensation up to a ceiling figure in the event of unofficial strikes and in fact a few cases occur in most years. While the compensation a worker has to pay is limited, there is no statutory limit to the compensation a firm may be called upon to pay.

There can be no doubt of the power of the Labour Court: equally there can be no doubt that it has established a reputation for impartiality. The approach has been strictly judicial. The Court has been concerned to hand down verdicts which are then regarded as precedents. Once a precedent has been established it is not changed without good legal cause. These precedents act as a very good filter, leaving well under 100 cases a year for the Court to examine. In fact, some workers feel grieved that the Court does rely so much on precedents because they feel this restricts the chances of a favourable verdict for them.

Results of collaboration

The high standard of living enjoyed in Sweden today owes its existence in no small part to the way in which the labour market has operated in recent years. The last three chapters have traced the development from a deplorable state of conflict in the early years of the twentieth century to the present situation when militant disruption of production is very rare. It is acknowledged by both management and labour that strong industry unions are an asset to the economy: they give strength to the workers in negotiation and management appreciate the stability derived from a firm agreement. Both employers and unions are well aware that failure to reach agreement can hurt both sides and the remainder of the community as well so they are resolved to do their utmost to avoid a breakdown in discussions. The law helps by making it costly to break an agreement by taking part in a strike or a lockout; the law also helps by insisting on negotiation, and is all the more powerful because it is in keeping with the spirit of modern industrial Sweden. Finally unions and employers make sure the spirit of collaboration is kept alive throughout their membership by a strategy that is a combination of firm discipline and consultative communication.

While never sacrificing the long term interests of their members, the unions have since the mid-1930s taken a responsible attitude to this power; this could be because throughout this period a Socialist government has been in office, helped there by union support, and committed to policies in line with union thought. Except perhaps during the Second World War when shortages predominated, the workers have seen a steady growth in standards and the adoption of union ideas that has made a responsible union attitude relatively easy to maintain, but none the less full credit must be given to the achievement. The employers too deserve credit for being able to adopt a flexible attitude to the new problems born of prosperity in the 1960s and the 1970s. Sweden appears to be well poised to deal with the difficulties of the future. Other economies have approached the same problems in different ways. Germany perhaps is nearest to the Swedish model. Japan so far has been able to deal with the situation through a heavy handed paternalism but there are signs of new needs. The USA to some extent, Italy and the UK particularly, are economies that have much to learn from the Swedish example. In their own interest, it is hoped these nations will also develop the good sense to tackle present problems in the common interest. Without this attitude, investment or state ownership or political dogma will do little to arrest the decline in relative living standards which must occur in a nation split with internal strife.

Job security

Two of the acts passed by the Riksdag in recent years with wider social significance are those concerned with worker directors (considered at length in another chapter), and with security of employment. The principal provisions of the latter are concerned with the laying down of rules for generous compensation to be paid by the employer for loss of employment for blue and white collar workers alike. This payment does not take the form of a golden handshake. It takes a rather fairer form of a continuation of full earnings for differing lengths of time, depending on the age of the worker. If during the payment period the dismissed worker succeeds in obtaining a post, the new earnings will be deducted from the compensation payments. Moreover, the worker must attempt to obtain a new job by attending the employment office of the Labour Market Board (private employment agencies are illegal in Sweden), and cannot turn down the offer of a job without good reason.

The act, replacing an earlier one of 1971, came into operation on 1 July 1974. Provided the dismissed worker has been in the employment of the firm for a total of six months in the previous year, or a total of twelve months in the last two years, and has reached the age of twenty-five years, full earnings are payable for a period of two months. An extra month of earnings is added for each five years of age so that at the age of forty-five, the compensation is payable for six months. The sliding scale may not be too popular with younger people but it is a recognition that the older generations tend to have greater social responsibilities. An addition to the scale of compensation acknowledges that older workers may have difficulty in securing new employment, so for each month of employment after reaching the age of forty-five, the period of payment is extended by a month up to a maximum of sixty months. Thus in an extreme case of a worker recruited at say forty-four years of age and declared redundant at fifty, the employer may find himself still continuing to pay the full earnings of the worker for a further five and a half years: while the intention of the act was undoubtedly sympathetic towards the older worker, the effect may be to make it very difficult for all but the best qualified of the older workers to secure new employment, particularly in a time of recession.

The provisions of the act do not apply to seasonal work or to temporary work when a clear indication is given at the time of the recruitment that the work is not permanent. Neither does the act apply to a worker dismissed on reaching a pensionable age. Similar exclusions are made for workers on relief work or receiving 'musician's aid', for top management, for members of the employer's family and for domestic employment.

During the period of notice, the employer is not allowed to exercise his normal right of transferring a worker to a different place of employment within the organisation if this might be seriously prejudicial to the obtaining of a new job. The worker under notice must also be given reasonable time off with pay to seek a new job – with the compensation levels as they are, the management would no doubt be eager to help the redundant worker find a new job.

The act specifies that a minimum notice of one month (two weeks for temporary employment) must be given on either side of intention to terminate employment. If the dismissal is for personal reasons the notice may be reduced to two weeks. Should less notice be given, the offender – be it employer or worker – may be taken to court for damages to cover the consequent loss.

Dismissal notices must be in writing if so requested, specifying the cause for the dismissal and at the same time indicating the worker's rights of appeal. The notices should preferably be given personally to the worker but failing that, should be sent by registered post to the home address or the normal post office for the worker. If enjoying part of the statutory four weeks' holiday at the time the notice is sent, the effective date will be that of the due date for a return to work. In normal circumstances, the union will be informed at the same time as the worker.

If the worker is not satisfied with the cause given for the dismissal, he may within two weeks request a discussion with the management. If he is still not satisfied, within two weeks of the end of the discussion he may submit an appeal to the Labour Court if he belongs to a union, or to the local court with the Labour Court acting as a higher court of appeal if the worker does not belong to a union. In the case of wrongful dismissal, the court may award damages or order the reinstatement of the worker.

The most usual cause for dismissal is redundancy through lack of work or due to plant modernisation, in which case the Labour Market Board is also kept informed (or even given longer advice of impending temporary lay offs). The worker may also be given notice for incompetence, for failing to carry out the duties of the post or for other personal reasons but the notice must be given within one month of the observation of any of these shortcomings. The cause for the dismissal must be stated objectively and if necessary must appear reasonable within the judgement of the Labour Court. The Court is given considerable powers of interpretation, again emphasising its authority, which will no doubt be exercised through the establishment of precedents.

When redundancies occur through lack of work, dismissals broadly speaking are on a 'last in, first out' basis. If circumstances permit re-employment, when trade picks up for instance, it will be on a priority basis with those of longest service having priority, subject to the employer's assessment of ability to do the job. The worker only gets this priority for re-employment if he submits a claim for it, and forfeits the priority if he accepts another job or turns down the offer of a reasonable job. The employer must normally give at least two weeks' notice of re-employment but in special circumstances can apply to the court for relaxation of this rule. Handicapped workers in specially prepared work places will be the last to suffer redundancy.

The provisions of this act are comprehensive in offering security of employment to the worker and give a reasonable cushion against potential unemployment during the changeover period: by having benefits tied to a limited time span, the worker is again encouraged to seek employment. Modernisation should also be easier for the worker to accept because of this and the other provisions mentioned in earlier chapters. On the management side, the dismissal procedures seem not unreasonable, although there is a marked curtailment of the previous right of the employer to hire and fire. Just what the effect of the act will be on modernisation is difficult to assess. In a recession, when re-employment may be difficult, there might be a falling off in modernisation activities – yet this is the very time industry should be re-equipping and when Investment Funds are readily released.

This act is an interesting example of the current legislation passed by a Riksdag in which the socialist and non-socialist parties are in balance with no clear majority. It probably represents the kind of price that has to be paid by industry when there is close collaboration between the employers, the unions and the government. At the lower end of the scale, the payments are small but because of the comprehensive nature of the cover, the scheme could prove to be expensive to the employers. Yet the comprehensive cover is socially desirable, the debate only being whether this is a social charge to be met by the government (and therefore the community) or whether it is a debt owed by industry to its former employees. Sweden has opted for the latter. If it assists the further progress of modernisation and collaboration, it could well turn out to be a small price.

PART 3: THE GROWTH OF INDUSTRIAL DEMOCRACY

7 NEW PROBLEMS, NEW SOLUTIONS

Signs of trouble

Earlier chapters have emphasised many good points of Swedish industry and Swedish industrial relations. The very successes described contained the seeds of trouble which germinated from 1968 to 1971 in the form of dissatisfaction and strikes, the number of working days lost per 1,000 employees rising in 1971 to the unprecedented high level for Sweden of 218, the actual figures being shown in Table 7.1. The table demonstrates two important points: firstly, that Sweden and Germany, both possessing a few industry based unions and a tradition of collaboration, are in a different class from the other nations shown; and secondly, that although Sweden had a problem in 1970 and 1971, steps were taken to regain the normally very good position.

Table 7.1 Days lost through disputes per 1,000 workers*

Year	1960	1965	1970	1971	1972	1973	1974
Sweden	5	1	40	218	3	3	16
Germany	1	2	4		3		
Japan	110	119	77		111		
UK	125	115	440	586	997	322	665
USA	352	383	840		357		

* The gaps in the table represent lack of data. [The ILO (International Labour Office) Yearbook quotes substantially higher figures for the UK for most years.]

Over the years there have always been a few wildcat strikes in Sweden, usually over working conditions or minor pay grievances when the workers have been more concerned to register a protest than to achieve industrial disruption: these issues have generally been resolved locally in a matter of hours so their occurrence would not appear in the official 'days lost' figures. The strikes in 1970 and 1971 were of a different nature, being a determined attempt to obtain an end result.

As we have seen the Swedish system is geared to avoid strikes but if in spite of all these barriers a strike does take place, then the individual worker is held to be personally responsible for a breach of the obligation to keep the industrial peace and he may be sued in the central Labour Court by the employer for damages. This is not just an academic ploy. Some four or five cases occur every year. The most publicised recent case was of 300 construction workers, working on a power station site in a remote area, who went on strike for three weeks: they were fined about £30 each. The unions accepted this kind of situation in early years in exchange for cooperation from the employers, but agitation from within the union ranks has turned the tide. The law still stands but the government has appointed a review committee. Hence if people strike in the face of these difficulties and against a tradition of no strikes, they must believe they have good reasons.

Graduate dissent

One sign of trouble appeared among graduates who could not get what they thought was the right kind of employment. This was a section of the community which had been taught to be articulate and did not necessarily accept the criteria of an earlier generation on the virtues of conformity and hard work. The Swedish educational system, operating mainly through a loan system, had seen the university annual throughput expand from 3,000 in the 1950s to 30,000 in the late 1960s. The solution adopted was to reduce the throughput to about 20,000 and to gear the number and content of the courses to the career patterns identified by the Labour Market Board as being consistent with future demands. The graduate dissent, more vocal than disruptive, looked like developing wider repercussions but was cut off at source.

This arbitrary method of dealing with student unrest has not been universally popular. In the universities there is a feeling that it savours of state bureaucracy, interfering with the liberty of academic thought because in general terms it is the arts subjects such as philosophy, economics, political theory and languages which have been affected. The more career oriented faculties of science, engineering and medicine continue largely as before. From the government's point of view, the action has been effective because in Sweden, as elsewhere, the career faculty students are usually too busy getting on with their careers to indulge overmuch in demonstrations. The action may have been ruthless but it was effective.

The actions of the establishment were not entirely negative. The Labour Market Board has opened employment offices in the university towns to help place graduates in fruitful occupations and, under some circumstances, will pay mobility grants to get the graduate to his first post.

Differentials

Sweden as a socialist state was committed to the aim of creating an egalitarian society and had a certain amount of success in that wage differentials were narrowing, especially at the expense of the more highly paid. With the blue collar workers for instance, in 1960 the range or spread from the average was from + 17 per cent to −13 per cent.* By 1972 the average hourly rate of pay had risen by 168 per cent (owing to a reduction in working hours to 33.4 per week – the average gross pay had increased by only 132 per cent) but the range had become +8 per cent to −7 per cent, i.e. about half of its previous value. Even at this figure the top had received marginally greater increases over the years than the bottom, in fact £30 per week increase compared with £28.4.

The Confederation of Blue Collar Unions expressed the view that this rate of progress towards equality was too slow, a view not shared by the more highly skilled of the blue collar workers, nor by higher paid salaried staff including those in government service, with the result that a series of strikes occurred in 1971. Legislation is now under review which might remove the right to strike from some groups of public employees (who incidentally only gained this right in 1966). In mid-1971, an agreement was made reducing the difference in fringe benefits between blue and white collar workers, with apparent agreement all round, and also apparently eliminating many of the grievances, although no doubt the pay rises obtained by the professional staff through the strikes also helped. At any rate by 1972, these strikes had ceased although their cause is a festering sore which may reappear. The trend for smaller differentials was reversed in 1973 but reappeared in 1974.

Table 7.2 which refers to the blue collar workers employed in what might broadly be described as productive industry – agriculture, forestry, mining and manufacturing – gives a detailed picture of the range of pay differentials.

The first observation is that the pay differentials narrowed more

---

* The method of calculating the range of wages is as follows. The average for all wages in a given year is first calculated. Next the average of all those earnings above this mean is worked out and is taken as the 'maximum' figure for the range. Similarly, the average for all earnings below the mean is taken for the 'minimum' of the range. This may not be an ideal method, but it does enable comparisons to be made for different years.

Table 7.2 Changes in productive industry 1960-72 (money units all in S. kr)

	Year	SWEDEN									
		Hours worked	Rates/ hour	Mean gross pay per week	Max of range %	Max gross pay	Min of range %	Min gross pay	Relative cost of living	Cost per man hr	Relative output
	1960	38.4	5.77	222	+ 17	259	− 12½	194	100	6.47	100
	1961				+ 17		− 12				
	1962				+ 16½		− 11½				
	1963				+ 16		− 11		107		
	1964				+ 15½		− 11				
	1965	37.1	8.37	310	+ 15	357	− 11	276	119	10.00	134
	1966				+ 14¾		− 10½				
	1967				+ 14½		− 10¼				
	1968				+ 14		− 10				
	1969				+ 12½		− 9¼				
	1970	34.8	12.61	439	+ 11½	489	− 8¾	401	146	15.60	169
	1971	33.4			+ 9½		− 8		155		
	1972		15.42	515	+ 8½	559	− 7	479	168	19.50	182
Change 1960-72		− 5.0		+ 293		+ 300		+ 285			
% change 1960-72		−13.0	167	132		116		147			82
Mean annual % change		− 1.1	13.9	11.0		9.7		12.2	5.7	16.3	6.8

$$\text{Wage cost 1972 relative to 1960} = \frac{\text{(Relative gross pay) X (Relative manning)}}{\text{(Relative output)}} = \frac{111 \times 0.977}{1.068} = 101.5\% \text{ or } 1.5\% \text{ change per annum.}$$

rapidly in the years from 1970 to 1972 (3 per cent change for the maximum) compared with the earlier period from 1960 to 1962, when the change was only ½ per cent for the maximum. Translated into money terms, at 10 S. kr to the £, this meant that over the years 1970 to 1972 the pay rise at the minimum was about £7.8 per week, whereas at the maximum the rise was only £7.0. No wonder the highly skilled were worried.

Over the twelve years shown in the table, the mean wage rate per hour in Sweden has risen from £0.58 to £1.54, a mean rise of 13.9 per cent per annum. But at the same time, the hours worked per week had fallen from 38.4 to 33.4, so that the mean rate of rise in gross pay was 11 per cent per annum – still a magnificent figure achieved without resort to the strike weapon. The cost of living index in Sweden had risen by about 5.7 per cent per annum so there is a clear margin between the rise in the wages and the rise in the cost of living which represents an increase in the standard of living of these workers.

The volume of output of this group of productive industries in Sweden had risen over the twelve years by a mean annual figure of 6.8 per cent – a very favourable growth particularly since the number of workers employed in these industries was falling at the rate of 2.3 per cent per annum. The nett result is that although the workers had been receiving substantial pay rises, the wages paid per unit of production in this area had actually only risen by the relatively low figure of 1.5 per cent per annum. This surely is what modernisation is all about. Before jumping to conclusions about the selling price, the productivity figure needs to be corrected for the extra cost of employing a worker which, because of the compulsory pension scheme and similar factors, rose by 14.1 per cent per annum so that the labour cost per unit of production rose by 14 per cent per annum.

The practice of small differentials also exists in the managerial field. The differential ratio of the gross pay of the top executive for a big company to that of the workers is the lowest in Sweden (9.4), followed by the UK (11.7), Holland (14.2), Italy (18.9) and France (28.8). After tax, the ranking order is not different because higher incomes are taxed most heavily in Sweden and the UK to leave the differential ratio of 6 compared with about 11 for Germany, the USA and Switzerland, or 22 in France. To a socialist, the small differential is an attractive political idea but taken too far it may not offer sufficient recompense for the responsibility of high office.

Bonus payments

A third factor causing trouble was the unpopularity, which became vocal in 1968 and 1969, of the piecework schemes which were widespread in Sweden – as many as 80 per cent of the working population expressed dissatisfaction with the piecework system. Once this factor had been thoroughly identified through discussions between the shop floor and management, changes in the method of payment were introduced fairly widely. By 1972, sufficient experience had been gained for the Employers' Confederation to carry out an analysis of the effects of changes in seventy-three cases. (The unions were invited to join in the analysis but refused to do so.) The report points out that the results summarised in the next table are not necessarily cause and effect but the trends are so marked and so uniform that 'it is not possible merely to shrug our shoulders and hide behind reflections on the complexity of working conditions'.

Table 7.3 Effect of change in payment system on productivity

No. of cases	Payment system		Difference in productivity 18 to 24 months after change
	Before	After	
36	Piecework	Fixed rate	−15% to −25%
21	Piecework	Premium	+ 5% to + 10%
16	Fixed rate	Premium	+ 25% to + 35%

The piecework system (i.e. more than 50 per cent of the remuneration being derived from payment by results and generally on an individual basis) was widely resented because of the conflicts it created between workers and with management. One section of the unions argued for a move towards fixed rates in line with white collar workers. Management replied they would really like incentive schemes for clerical tasks as well, but none the less made a change to a fixed day or hourly rates in half of the sample examined.

The sharp fall of an average of 20 per cent in productivity revealed as a result of the change must have disappointed the unions since it made future demands for day rates less tenable, but it left management studying its 'efficiency graphs with a worried frown'.

Premium payment is defined as less than 30 per cent (and more often about 15 per cent) of the remuneration being derived from payment by results, and is usually a group payment, the size of the group varying from 5 to 200 depending on the production circumstances.

The table consistently shows the premium system to have the highest productivity, the average gain being as high as 30 per cent in changing from a fixed hourly rate – and this is the essence of the UK National Coal Board proposals made in 1974 but rejected by the National Union of Mineworkers.

The case against fixed day rates is further strengthened by the fact that four of the examples reporting a fall in productivity when going to a day rate had changed again to a premium system and were in the sample showing a very marked growth in productivity.

Advocates of the fixed day rate claim that it leads to a more relaxed atmosphere, to less absenteeism and to higher quality in the product. None of these effects was found to be significantly present as a result of the analysis, a typical set of results being shown for quality changes in the table below. It could be, of course, that the very existence of the change in pay system stimulates interest in the job and so helps to maintain quality standards for the two years of the review – but two years is a long time for this effect to persist.

Table 7.4 Effect of change in payment systems on quality

Before	After	Quality changes in % of cases		
		Better	Unaltered	Worse
Piecework	Fixed rate	14	83	3
Piecework	Premium	14	86	0
Fixed rate	Premium	6	88	6

The figures quoted in Table 7.3 all contain a correction of 5 per cent for the growth in productivity which continues with incentive schemes whereas with the fixed rate schemes productivity stabilises at a constant level as shown by the curves on Figure 7.1. The original observations are quoted in Table 7.5 (which shows the immediate results of the change) in order to demonstrate that the range is much wider than the –15 to –25 per cent quoted in the summarised result. In fact the observed range is from +5 to greater than –25 per cent so that in any particular company, the outcome might not conform exactly to the original table, although the general conclusions seem valid.

Some further examination of the cases at the extremes of the distribution is merited. It was found that those showing the least falling off in production efficiency were precisely the ones with the lowest

Table 7.5 Observed change in production efficiency when piecework system was replaced by fixed day or hourly rate

% Change in productivity	Actual no. of cases	% of cases
+ 5 to 0	2	6
0 to − 5	4	11
− 5 to − 10	6	16
− 10 to − 15	8	22
− 15 to − 20	7	20
− 20 to − 25	5	14
> − 25	4	11

Figure 7.1 Effect of change in payment system on productivity

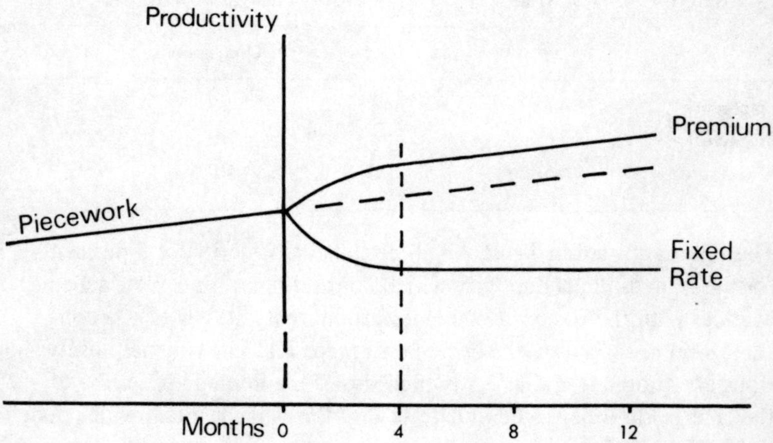

inherent efficiency and the least sophistication in the application of control and work study techniques like method study. It is therefore suggested that the falling off in performance was less because it was already poor. One of these cases was examined in still greater detail when it was found that the work study system had collapsed before the change due to overload. When on fixed day rates, the productivity of this particular case was only 60 per cent of that in a neighbouring department of the same company working on not dissimilar duties, but on piecework. A productivity drive was organised and as a result the day rate area raised its efficiency to about 80 per cent of its neighbour. In other words, further examination showed that this case, instead of being an exception, was in the middle of the range.

The change to group premium systems of payment was often accompanied either by a radical change in the organisation of the work as will be discussed in a later section, or in a new look at the way the incentive was calculated. In a saw mill, the former piecework system was based on the number of logs cut (with a complicated sliding scale depending on the log diameter) so it encouraged cutting regardless of wastage. It also contained allowances if stoppages were longer than thirty minutes, thus guaranteeing that stoppages were either very short or longer than thirty minutes. It also paid a bonus to all operators (on a percentage basis depending on the skill required) thus encouraging overmanning in order to ensure a high input of logs. By contrast, the new system was based on two factors only – the number of logs cut and the volume of good timber cut per man hour including stoppages. The effect of the latter was to keep manning down and quality up. There were actually four different scales embodied in the old piecework system so that the calculation of bonus payments was not easy. The premium system is much simpler and since it is more directly linked to output, it has been a success.

Not all of the changes to group premiums are as clear-cut as in the saw mill, but there is often an element of continual improvement involved. Figure 7.1 shows that about four months after a change the systems stabilised, but in quite different forms, the incentive based schemes continuing to show a growth in productivity whereas the fixed rate system stabilised at a constant figure. The Swedes draw two conclusions from these figures. The first is that most people require some form of financial incentive to energise them into looking for improvements in productivity. The second conclusion is that investment in new equipment in a fixed rate situation is likely to be unrewarding and therefore will not occur. The remarkable feature is that

Swedish industry faced up to its problems and with collaboration between management and unions was not afraid to try new methods. Characteristically, the Swedes have analysed the results of the experiment and are prepared to learn – for instance 50 per cent of the examples quoted as going to fixed wage systems are engaged in changing to premium systems.

The growth of industrial democracy

One of the successes of the Swedish economy has been the almost universal acceptance of modernisation as a way of life, and the recognition that effective modernisation achieved through investment in new equipment almost certainly involves a certain amount of redeployment of labour. For this to be acceptable, provision of new jobs is essential, and if retraining or relocation is necessary, then adequate financial support must be available. To this end, the Labour Market Board spends more of its budget on these items than it does on the payment on unemployment benefit.

Another factor helping mobility has been the so-called 'solidarity' policy of the unions – the narrowing of wage differentials. If a worker is redeployed, it is unlikely that the wages, particularly of the semi-skilled, will be seriously affected. The very success of the redeployment arrangements has created problems. It is so easy for a worker to change jobs that if he (or she) is in a boring repetitious job such as is claimed to be the case on conventional, machine-paced car assembly lines, then there is no great inducement for the worker to stay. By 1968, turnover had reached the high level of 33 per cent per annum for the Volvo company, and in certain jobs in the Saab lines was as high as 70 per cent. Not only was this inconvenient but it posed substantial training problems which were costing Volvo as much as £8m a year. Many of the incoming workers were foreigners so general training problems were compounded.

Economic success had also created another problem. Wage rates were so high that workers engaged in boring tasks could afford to take a day off when they felt like it and they felt like it so often that absenteeism in Volvo was running at 1 in 7. To keep the production lines in operation, 20 per cent excess manning (although this is a relative term) was necessary. Not only was this costly but since the absenteeism is unlikely to be spread uniformly over the days of the week, there were days when the excess (or some of it) was on the shop floor, underemployed and still more bored. The twin problems of turnover and absenteeism were thus aggravated.

The ways in which three Swedish companies tried to overcome these problems provide an interesting example of Swedish industrial democracy in operation. In the shipbuilding firm of Kockums at Malmö, collaboration started in 1965 and has taken the form of the extensive provision of social facilities both in and outside of the shipyard, together with an elaborate committee structure for joint consultation. In 1969, an existing assembly line in the Södertälje plant of Saab was converted to group working, and more recently, Volvo have constructed a new assembly plant at Kalmar designed on radically new lines to facilitate group working.

Kockums and the works council

The developments at Kockums are of importance because they were among the first of the Swedish firms to run into trouble with delivery dates due to dissatisfaction with piecework, absenteeism and high labour turnover, and this at a time when the yard was undergoing major reorganisation to break into a new market in large tankers.

The major social schemes of a sports stadium, high class health facilities, company visitors for wives, canteens, better working conditions, and so on, may seem paternalistic but much of the new labour was new to the district of Malmö and included foreign workers. There was therefore a need to create a company image in the best sense of the term with which the workers and their wives could identify. The Confederation of Blue Collar Unions had reported, in response to an invitation from management, that the company needed to treat the workers more as people, and believed that the welfare schemes, expensive at around £4m, were an essential part of the responsibilities of the company to its workers. The collaboration within the yard has been outstandingly successful. The basic framework is constructed around the Works Council. In April 1966, a collective agreement, amending an earlier agreement of 1946 governing the running of Works Councils throughout Sweden, was signed by the Employers' Confederation, the blue collar unions and the white collar unions. In this charter, it is agreed that the Council has 'the responsibility of working for increased production and work satisfaction'. The Council also has a 'duty' to provide an 'insight into economic and technical conditions and the results of the company's activities'. Provision for consultation, vocational training and safety are also built into the charter but wage negotiations are excluded. Both union and management claim that part of the success of the Works Council organisation at Kockums lies in all financial negotiations being taken out of the orbit of the Works Council and placed in the mill of the negotiating machinery.

The structure of the committees involved with the Works Council is fully defined at Kockums by the organisation tree shown in Figure 7.2 and in written specifications covering the makeup of each committee, its terms of reference and frequency of meetings. It is proposed to deal with only two bodies, the Works Council and the Department Council.

The Works Council has an extremely wide remit. The terms of reference state that it must be informed about, discuss and express its opinions on all the items shown in Table 7.6. The financing of the company is excluded from the remit which otherwise covers most of the company's activities. The Council has the right to take decisions in social areas within a given budget and the power to establish special project groups.

Table 7.6 Areas for discussion in Works Council of Kockums

Economics and marketing	Production	Personnel
1. General state of business	7. Planning	13. Personnel planning
2. Market developments	8. Organisation	14. Recruitment
3. Sales possibilities	9. Techniques	15. Selection
4. Projections	10. Development	16. Promotion
5. Budgets	11. Reorganisation	17. Introduction
6. Balance sheets	12. Production results	18. Education
		19. Transfers
		20. Working environment
		21. Labour turnover

The Council consists of eighteen members – who meet at least at three monthly intervals: seven company representatives, seven shop union representatives, three salaried staff area representatives, and one foreman's union representative. Chairmen of Department Councils who may not be in the above are also members. To ensure both the status and effectiveness, the Chairman of the Works Council is the Managing Director: the vice chairman is elected by the employee representatives who therefore can feel they have a very real voice in the organisation.

Figure 7.2 The consultative committee structure at Kockums, Malmö (reproduced by permission of the company)

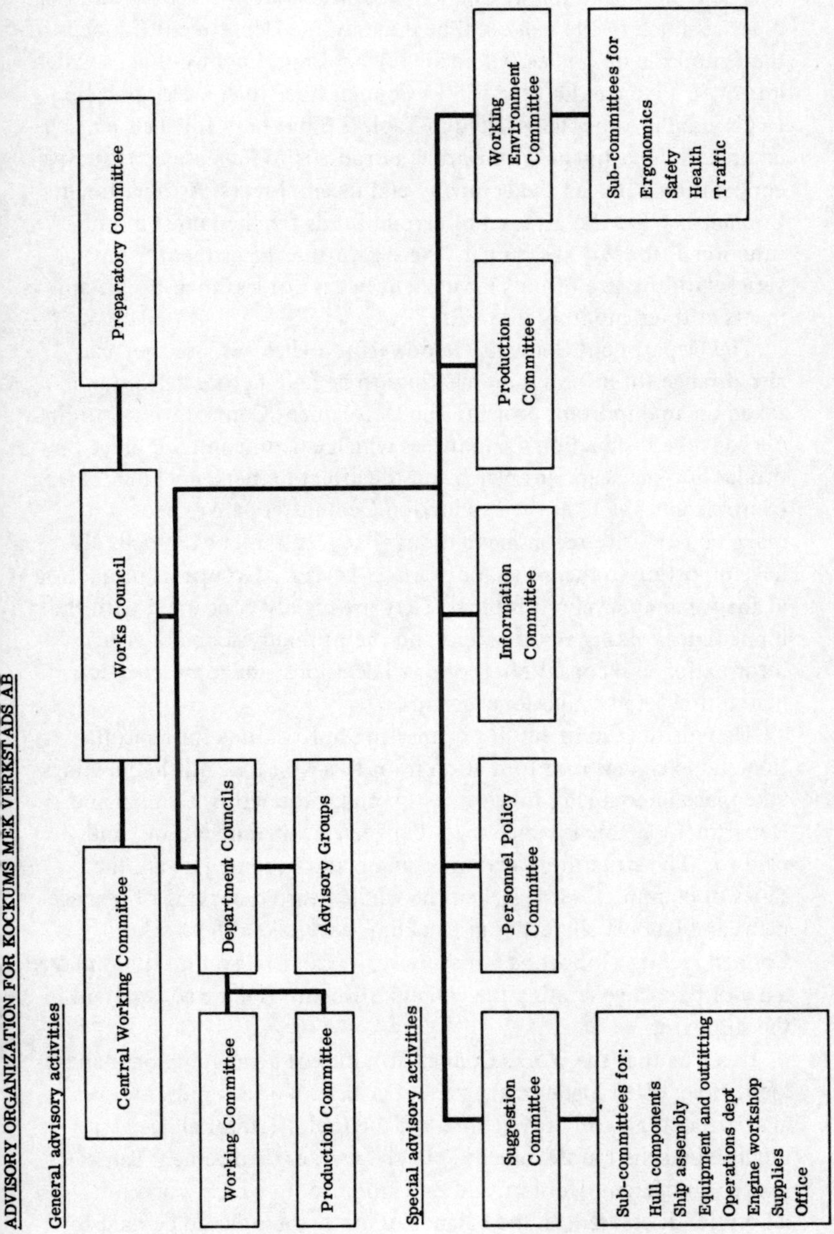

To bring individual workers into the picture, the activities of the Works Council are publicised through the shipyard newspaper.

The remit of the Works Council is so wide that one suspects that in practice much of the work will be done by the Department Councils or their subordinate bodies. There are several Department Councils which mirror to a large extent the Works Council since they are empowered to discuss the same items listed in Table 7.6 but only for their particular area or department. Their prime purpose is to increase constructive cooperation between the company and its employees. A Department Council also has the disposal of certain funds for the same kind of function as the Works Council. The size of the Department Council varies with the size of the Department but is not less than twelve and meets at three-monthly intervals.

The Department Councils are powerful bodies because they can also arrange for information meetings to be held before a decision is taken on an important project. The Department Council has subordinate to it the Production Committees which examine in their areas the production plans and problems and the effect on personnel numbers, overtime and the like: the Production Committees are expected to make constructive recommendations. The Department Councils also have reporting to them the appropriate Advisory Groups who function at the foreman level of problem. They are mainly concerned with the immediate working environment and their primary scope is with information and consultation prior to decisions: the representation here is down to occupational groups.

There is thus an in-depth organisation in Kockums for consultation and exchange of information prior to a decision. All the meetings take place in company time (except perhaps the Works Council and Department Councils which meet between 3 p.m. and 6 p.m.) and are paid for. The structure is elaborate and could become just another series of committees if it lacked the whole hearted backing of management and labour: all parties in Kockums have taken the work of the Council and its supporting structure very seriously, so that it has played a major part in generating the collaborative atmosphere so apparent in the shipyard.

It is true that the Works Council structure is demanding on management time, often higher management at that. Works representatives also spend a fair amount of time 'off the job'. Dictatorial decisions might be reached more quickly, but the worker involvement can often lead to a different decision, and one moreover in which worker collaboration is assured. In the balance of costs, the price to be paid for an effective Works Council does not seem high.

Worker directors

By an act passed in the Riksdag in December 1972, all companies employing more than 100 workers are obliged to appoint two worker directors to the Board if so requested by the local union organisations. Perhaps because of the success of the Works Council structure, worker directors have been less conspicuous in Sweden than in Germany. The difficulty lies in a dichotomy of interests. To be successful, the worker director must adopt a responsible attitude to his duties as a director. Yet he is usually a union official also, with responsibilities to the members of his union, and even in Sweden these two may not always coincide, as will be seen from chapter nine.

Working groups

For the successful introduction of group working in the Saab plant at Södertälje, the planning organisation shown in Figure 7.3 was set up first on an experimental basis but later as very much an operating system. While the numbers shown refer to Saab, the concept is in fairly general operation throughout Sweden wherever group premiums exist. A Reference Group of twenty members, jointly of management and workers, established the objectives. In Saab's case, these included job satisfaction through a widening of the workers' duties and responsibilities.

It is the function of the Development Groups for specific areas of the plant to convert the objectives into working realities: initially during the learning phase, there were only two groups but this has now been extended to sixty groups to cover the 1,500 workers on the lorry assembly and petrol engine sections of the plant. The Development Group must meet at least monthly and consists usually of seven people with the foreman as chairman, and the planner and work study worker very much in evidence. Each Development Group is associated with two Working Groups varying in size between four and fifteen but more usually consisting of ten workers. The members of the Working Group can decide how the work will be split and are responsible for their own rate of working subject to meeting the demands of the production schedule and indeed have a remarkable degree of autonomy. The curves bounding the groups are deliberately not drawn as identical circles to emphasise that these are dynamic groups of people whose interest and activities will change as the circumstances change.

It is now history how Saab converted the conventional production

Figure 7.3 Structure for organising Working Groups

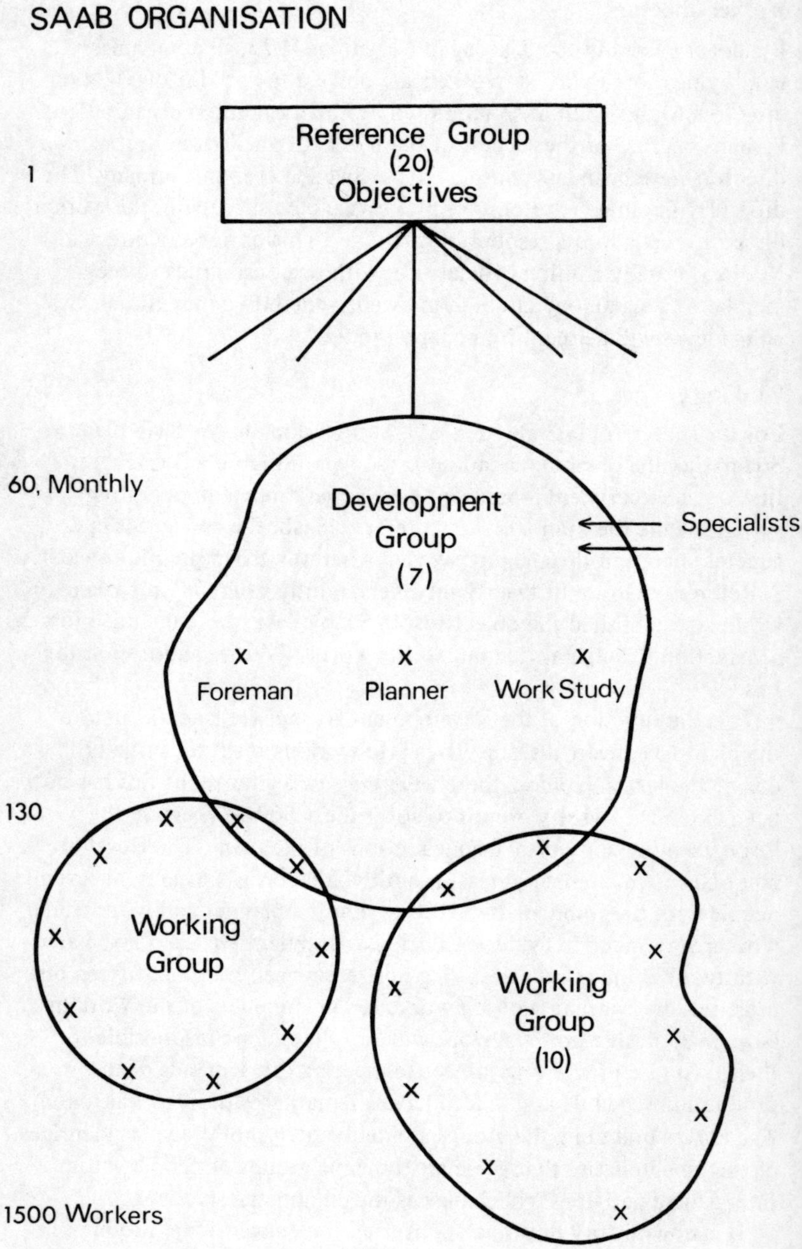

line into a series of loops separated by buffer stocks, the organisation within the loop being the responsibility of the Working Group. The system gave the structure for industrial democracy. How well it works depends both on the people operating it and on the philosophy represented in the objectives.

The concept, for which the structure is only the mechanism, is that workers on the shop floor should have a material voice in determining their working destiny. The Development Groups provide a planning control which prevents the anarchy which might prevail if every Working Group went its own way regardless of the others. The combination represents industrial democracy really at work.

Changes due to group working

In most cases, a deliberate attempt is made when group working is introduced to involve the operators in thinking about the organisation of the job and of the firm, and in so doing to identify with the objectives of the firm (e.g. to make better motor cars). Often the aim is to increase self responsibility, in the belief that this will lead to job satisfaction and a higher quality of work. It is typical of Swedish industry that change is accepted and that an all out effort is devoted to ensuring that the maximum benefit is squeezed out of the new situation. The changes in the saw mill described earlier or in the plumbing firm below are not epoch making – they are little more than sound common sense – but when the same kind of thing is repeated all over the country, the cumulative effect on the economy is considerable.

Under the old piecework system in a central heating and plumbing firm employing eighteen fitters, the foremen met all the fitters at the start of each day's work to issue jobs and equipment for these jobs. The fitters then made their own way, usually by public transport, to the job but often, like most plumbers, found the job required some joint or fitting they had not got, and so returned to the depot. The pattern is familiar. Customer and fitter frustration was mutual. When the task was completed, the fitter again returned to the depot for a new job. Group collaboration evolved a scheme in which the fitters were supplied with a van containing a range of tools, accessories and spares: radio contact was used to communicate with the depot. Although some investment is involved, the new system seems to have benefited everyone. Customer satisfaction increased and the fitters thought they were getting a better deal. The firm obtained a more effective use of skilled labour.

Changes in the car industry

Faced with production problems and rising costs because of high absenteeism and a high annual turnover of labour, the Swedish car firms of Volvo and Saab-Scania have endeavoured to rectify the root causes of the trouble. The approach in the two firms has been quite different although the end results are not dissimilar.

Saab took the first positive steps by experimenting in 1969 on a small scale in their Södertälje plant with two development groups each coordinating the work of two groups of workers. The group concerned with the assembly of petrol engines was very successful in its aim of creating job interest through participation in the organisation of the group and then moving on to different methods of working. Instead of intense specialisation, with each operator doing a certain small task continuously, the workers sought to amalgamate several operations into parallel jobs producing a visible end result such as a complete subassembly or function.

The second group concerned with small bore pipe installation was not so successful but the company none the less decided to extend the experiment gradually to cover 1,500 workers. In 1973 the company concluded that group working was no longer experimental but fully operational.

The change in practice involved changes in layout even within the constraints of an existing factory. In a conventional, machine-paced, straight line assembly the station time for the petrol engine, for instance, was 1.8 minutes. By introducing six loops into the production line with three fitters (women, incidentally, on this particular job) in each loop and each assembling a complete engine, the station time was increased to thirty minutes, or to ten minutes if the fitters elected to specialise. Moreover the job was no longer machine-paced so that the rate of working could be varied throughout the day provided the overall schedules were met.

The job span is certainly increased and the line is certainly less susceptible to disruption by absentees. It also has the merit that increases in production can be accommodated fairly readily in contrast to the conventional line where production increases may destroy the balance of the line and so necessitate a reallocation of tasks. On the other hand, there is a training problem in getting the operators fully trained for their wider functions – a seventh loop on the engine line is left for training purposes. This form of production is inherently less efficient than the highly specialised line so a balance needs to be struck between the loss in efficiency, the longer running-in period and

Figure 7.4 The effect of introducing group working

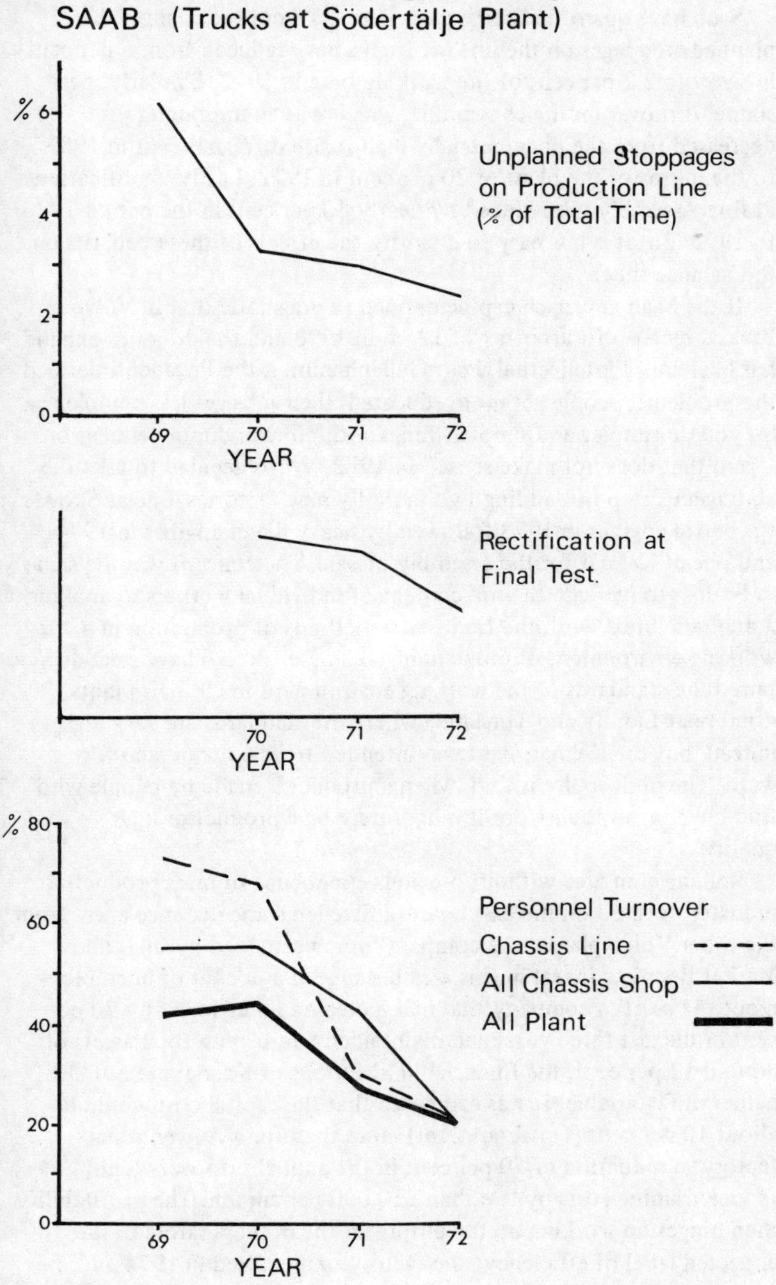

the gains derived from worker participation.

Saab have quantified some clear benefits from the changes. Unplanned stoppages on the line for trucks have reduced from 6 per cent in 1969 to 2.2 per cent of the working time in 1972. Similarly, personnel turnover on the chassis line, which was an unpopular job, decreased from the phenomenally high figure of 72 per cent in 1969 to the norm for the plant of 20 per cent in 1972. Lastly, rectification at final assembly has reduced by nearly 40 per cent in the period 1970 to 1972. But it is less easy to quantify the effects of these benefits on the balance sheet.

If the Saab approach can be defined as pragmatic that in Volvo, backed by a profit after tax of £25m in 1973 and the desire to expand, has been more intellectual. Pehr Gyllenhammer, the President, defined the problem: 'people get more educated, their jobs get less complex. So you do simpler and simpler things with more and more education – and that does not make sense.' In 1972, Volvo decided to take the courageous step of building two radically new factories, one at Skovde for petrol engines in 1973 followed by heavy diesel engines in 1974 and one at Kalmar for the assembly of cars. The concept was the same in both – to increase the job content of individual workers by making a dramatic break with the traditional methods of production in a working environment of outstanding character. Volvo have steadily raised the standards of the working environment in all their plants, notably at Lundly and Torslanda where the standards are very high indeed, but the Kalmar plant was intended to be a major step forward. The philosophy is that 'when a product is made by people who find meaning in their work it must surely be a product of high quality'.

Kalmar is an area without previous experience of mass production industry, located on the east coast of Sweden some distance away from the other Volvo plants: the company were persuaded by the Labour Market Board to invest in this area because of a pocket of unemployment. As befits a company that had increased its turnover by 70 per cent in the last three years and maintained a return on total assets of around 12 per cent, the financial implications of Kalmar are not altogether unfavourable. It was estimated that the capital cost would be about 10 per cent (i.e. about £1m) more than for a conventional factory: a reduction of 50 per cent in the annual turnover would reduce training costs by less than £10,000 per annum. The profitability then hinges on working up the output of the 600 operators to the expected lebel of efficiency: the factory only started in 1974 and the computer system, for instance, in early 1975 was not yet fully commissioned so the answers are not yet known. Kalmar is not regarded as a luxury but must pay off according to Volvo.

A new dimension has thus been added to the evaluation of capital investment. The cheapest scheme is not adopted. The inherently most efficient is regarded as suboptimal. Instead there has to be included an estimate of the less tangible influences such as absenteeism, turnover, job satisfaction and quality. In a company in the car industry that has only lost one day through strikes since the war, these factors must weigh heavily.

New concept in mass production

The prospect of computer controlled robots gliding through a series of hexagonally shaped production halls may sound like a science fiction vision of the future but it exists in Sweden at the Volvo Kalmar plant. Far from being a takeover by the machine, it is part of a scheme designed to increase man's contribution to his working lot. The operation of the assembly plant depends totally on the viability of the battery driven, robot carriers which move individually about the factory, unattended, guided by electrical impulses fed through cables beneath the floor. The main carriers are low level platforms about a foot high, just big enough to hold a Volvo car with space for the operator to stand on the platform to work, or if more convenient stand on the floor. The carriers are a complete break away from the idea of a conveyor line and represent a new (and previously untried) technology. It has been possible to throw away preconceived notions of factory organisation and to design the work place with practically no restrictions.

It was part of the philosophy that a deliberate attempt should be made to create the atmosphere of several small workshops within a factory. In the Skovde plant, this was done through an E-shaped building. At Kalmar, the assembly areas consist of three hexagonally shaped floor areas nesting together at the centre, and built on two floors in order to double the window areas. To enhance the group feeling, each hexagon and each floor has its own entrance. Coffee corners, amenities of a high order and the like occupy the outward faces of the hexagons, the work areas being immediately inwards of the personnel areas but separated from them by glass partitions.

Racked stores are held in the centres of the hexagons with only minimal stores held in the work spaces for immediate use. Siting the stores centrally has left the work areas airy and uncluttered by racks

Figure 7.5 Artist's impression of the Volvo plant at Kalmar (reproduced by permission of A. B. Volvo)

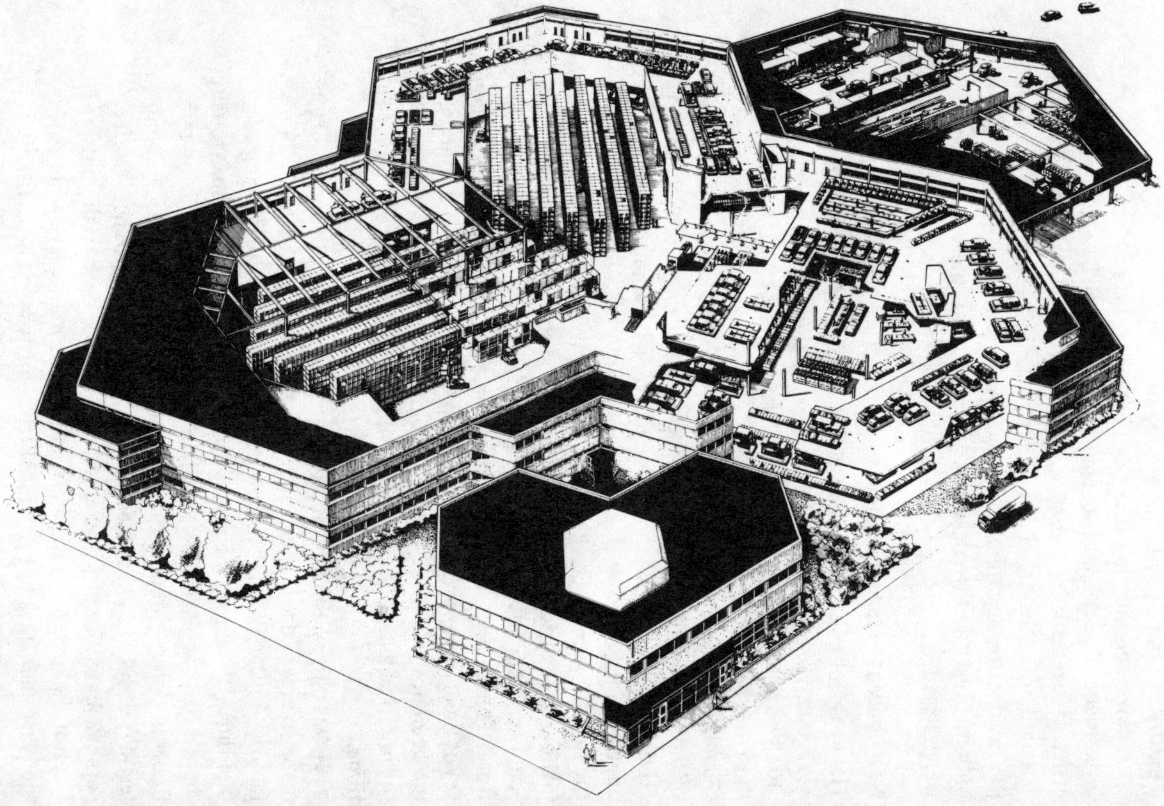

so that attractive, well-lit, well-ventilated facilities are created in which the workers have ample space to move around. Sound insulation to 65 decibel level in most places, or to 85 decibels where the process itself creates noise, completes the setting into which the robot carriers glide for attention by the workers.

The labour force consists of twenty-five groups of roughly fifteen workers. Each group has a specific function to perform and is responsible for the organisation within the group for the supply of spares and for its own in-process inspection. Conditions are radically different from a conventional assembly line and are as near perfect as current thinking would indicate for the fulfilment of human aspirations through work.

The layout is completed by an office and canteen block shown in the bottom centre of the illustration and by a single storey reception and despatch hexagonal area on the top right. This fascinating layout is clearly not open ended: it is designed to produce 30,000 cars a year with single shift working. Extra output can only come from extra shifts.

Computer control

So much imagination has gone into the creation of the Kalmar factory that it would have been disappointing if the company had failed to take the opportunity to develop the potential of the computer as a working tool. So it is welcome if not surprising to find that when a body shell is loaded onto a carrier, this information is recorded by the computer system which then keeps track of the carrier as it moves through the process areas. The computer controls the movement of the carrier by means of the underfloor electric pulse system to a vacant space which it has allocated in the next assembly function. While the carrier is in transit, the computer issues the appropriate instructions and stores requirements for the particular version of the car being assembled. Provision is made for human intervention through local controls for the carrier at each working station: pressure pads are also mounted along the edges of the carrier so that it can stop within 8 cm if it encounters an obstruction.

Part of the on-line computer system will be concerned with quality control data. After each function inspection (which is a more technical inspection over and above the in-process inspection carried out by the working group) the results are fed into the computer which analyses them, and if necessary issues new instructions to prevent the same error being repeated. Changes in quality standards and consequent action can also be advised to the groups as they arise. The computer system is thus acting as a factory coordinator in ensuring that up-to-date information is available on the shop floor as well as in the records section.

The results of the tests on the 'rolling roads' and any resulting rectification are also fed into the computer so that a complete dossier is built up for each car, and in addition to giving comprehensive information for the factory, the dossier is the purchaser's guarantee of quality. The computer system should be helpful not only in the immediate execution of the job but should help the operators to become very quality conscious.

Assembly at Kalmar

There are two types of carrier. The first is the basic low level platform which receives the body shell on the ground floor and takes a lift to the first floor where there are ten teams for the assembly of the upper part of the car – windows, head lining, doors, electrical system and the like. At the same time, assembly is proceeding on the ground floor of the engine, gear box, axles and exhaust system on a 'high level' carrier which differs from the first only in respect of jigs and fitments which can be adjusted so that the work is at the right height for the fitter. The high level carrier takes another lift to the first floor where the body system is united with the chassis. The carrier then returns to the ground floor for the brake system, steering and wheels to be fitted. The more or less complete car is then returned to the low level carrier for undersealing, final adjustment and test approval. At each working station, attention has been paid to the design of tools to ensure quiet and efficient working and full ergonomic consideration has also been given to the supply of support equipment.

This brief account outlining the salient features obviously fails to do justice to the changes made in the assembly process. The Kalmar factory represents a totally new concept in the organisation of mass production. Its success in financial terms is still not proven but its social implications are very interesting and at this early stage – production only started in 1974 – seem to have been successful.

What are the chances of the Kalmar experiment being tried in other countries? It requires a mass production company with a profitable and expanding order book. It requires a management prepared to devote the energy and resources to thinking outside traditional methods. It requires unions prepared to collaborate with management and to add their quota of knowledge and ideas. It requires a labour force prepared to appreciate the amenities and prepared to work to make it all worth while. How often is the combination of requirements likely to be available outside Sweden?

Note

Most of this chapter was published in *Management Today*, September 1975, p. 62, under the title 'Sweden's Modern Manning'.

8 WORKING GROUPS AND PREMIUM PAYMENT SCHEMES

Principles of group working

Chapter seven placed group working in Sweden and the concomitant premium payment system in historical perspective and also to some degree in economic perspective. The concept is so important a contribution to industrial practice that it merits further discussion on procedures and implementation.

By 1972, sufficient experience has been gained in Sweden on group working for the Employers' Confederation to publish guidelines to help and to encourage other firms in setting up working groups. The publication claims that the collaboration obtained through group working is visibly characterised by workers switching to different duties in the production system without instructions because this seems the natural thing to do in facilitating the work. Surely a most remarkable claim.

It is recommended that three formal targets be placed before a group when it is first formed, namely: to achieve a high and rapidly rising level of productivity; to stimulate interest in the job through a broadening of duties; and to maintain security of employment.

It is widely recognised in Sweden that job security depends on the firm remaining competitive, both through high productivity and by changing to meet new conditions. Some go so far as to say that change is actually a prerequisite for job security in modern industry.

To the widest possible extent, the work should be organised to make full use of the workers' actual knowledge and experience and they should be encouraged to widen their activities by rotating jobs within the group. This imples that as knowledge grows, the work would be reorganised – indeed the whole concept is closely associated with growth and self-adaptation.

Clearly expressed targets for production and a feedback on the degree of success achieved are not only an essential ingredient for the successful functioning of any business but are also good methods of encouraging workers. Yet as modern industry becomes more complex, it becomes more difficult to assign an exact target to an individual and moreover may invite demarcation troubles: group working solves this particular problem because it is almost always possible to get a clear and unambiguous target for the output from a complete plant or better still from a natural sub-unit of the plant. It is found that group spirit is enhanced when workers help one another to achieve the target and when they collaborate in a continuous effort to avoid unnecessary work by improving methods. Minor technical developments are expected to lead to frequent if minor changes in production methods which can be accommodated more easily in group working. But it is important for the success of the group that the payment system should not encourage the retention of old practices nor of excess work.

A further advantage of group working is that when part of a unit breaks down, or when absenteeism or a change in the makeup of orders calls for a different level of output or for different tasks, the local group organisation should be better capable of dealing with the necessary fast reshuffling of people and equipment than a remote administrative function.

Major technical changes are more difficult to accommodate but a working group should have useful practical experience to contribute through discussion with the managerial and specialist staff concerned with planning the changes. A broad based involvement at the study stage can help with implementation although designing by committee can be a difficult operation: a firm drill has to be established to ensure that executive action, outside of the committee, evaluates proposals advanced during discussion, and reports back on an agreed timetable. In other words, this collaboration is not a chatty exercise but needs to be constructed on a formal basis.

Lest it be felt that these remarks are too eulogistic, a reminder should be given that the introduction of changes in work organisation involves a lot of very mundane work if the outcome is to be a resounding success. The guidelines issue a further warning that group working and group premium payment schemes are merely good alternatives to other methods which should also be considered.

Objectives

At a very early stage before group working is introduced, a reasonably clear assessment should be made of the main objectives. Is the change mainly concerned with increasing production within an existing plant? Is it intended to consider the introduction of radically new practices? Is this a method of combating labour turnover? Are changes intended in the payment system? Is a change in product under consideration? These are the kind of general questions which need to be explored in an assessment described only as reasonably clear because it will almost surely be modified as the scheme evolves or indeed may be abandoned if the weight of evidence is against it.

The first practical step is the convening of a Reference Group (the relative position of which is shown in Figure 7.3), whose task it is to determine and to refine the objectives until they are agreed by the parties concerned. The Reference Group should be chaired by a senior manager and should include representatives from management and unions. Representation is simple in Sweden because normally the unions are industry based so that in general only two unions will be involved, one for blue collar and one for white collar workers. It will be noted that the Reference Group is collectively concerned with determining objectives, as opposed to being a body to which objectives are given by higher management or for that matter, by union leaders.

Categories of production

Before discussing a timetable, the Reference Group needs to take cognisance of the problems involved. It is believed in Sweden that productive organisations can be divided for this analysis into seven categories and that just as the organisational problems concerned with the introduction of group working will differ for these categories, so also will the outcome vary from outstanding success to near failure. It is therefore sensible to take a view of where in this spectrum one's activities lie.

Category A – the man-paced line

The essence of this category is that it is a mass production operation in which the flow of materials along the line is interrupted by a series of buffer stocks waiting attention at the next stage of the process. At one level, such as in a garment factory, the process stage might consist of one woman carrying out one task such as button holing. At another level, such as in car assembly, it might consist of a team of workers assembling a complete engine.

Organisationally it is very easy to introduce group working into the man-paced line – the buffer stocks are merely moved further apart to accommodate the team, but before doing so the gain must be assessed. Making the change in a garment factory does not create a team: each girl may now make a complete pair of trousers and in so doing has obviously broadened her activities, but she is still working as an individual. Moreover, specialisation has enabled the girls to become so proficient that the labour content of a pair of trousers is about one operator hour: one girl making a complete pair of trousers herself takes about four hours. Group working in this case is not economic. There will be other cases when the loss in inherent efficiency needs to be offset against the other advantages before a decision on group working can be made.

A further disadvantage is the longer training time required to reach proficiency in assembling a complete car engine compared with attaching the carburettor, for example. Also since the pace of working is determined by the operator, the output can be down due to lack of training or to lack of inclination. The output can be up due to enthusiasm and it is precisely this greater inclination to take an interest in the job and to get things done that is claimed to be one of the merits of group working.

The level of output is less susceptible to disruption by absenteeism in this form of group working – the work can carry on but at a lower pace whereas absenteeism or just absence from the line of a few key workers can paralyse a machine-paced line. In addition, experience suggests that absenteeism is itself reduced because of the greater job satisfaction that can be obtained from group working. The capacity of the plant can also be changed fairly readily by varying the size of the group, in contrast to the difficult rebalancing of function which can occur if large changes in output are required from a conventional assembly line.

Group working on this type of work can be more expensive to install because the buffer stocks need space and sometimes special handling equipment if heavy units are involved. In this latter case, a communication system is required to signal when work is to be moved, and this too can be costly. Volvo state the group working system costs 10 per cent more to install than a conventional system. In process stocks may also be higher than with a conventional line.

One method of creating a group working environment is to arrange for the workers to operate in a series of loops as illustrated in Figure 8.1 for the assembly of Saab petrol engines. This is a major change which is relatively easy to install in an existing factory at the expense of space. Saab estimate that to extend this principle to the complete plant would double the floor space, be very costly and so have restricted this form of group working in loops to relatively small components.

Merely putting workers together in a loop or in any other situation does not constitute group working. To be effective, the duties performed by every member of the group must, and must be seen to, lead to the joint result for the entire group. Extraneous jobs should therefore not be included in the group. Job enrichment can be enhanced by assuming responsibility for intergroup planning, quality and a certain

Figure 8.1 Group working layout in Saab works (reproduced from Reference [55] by permission of SAF)

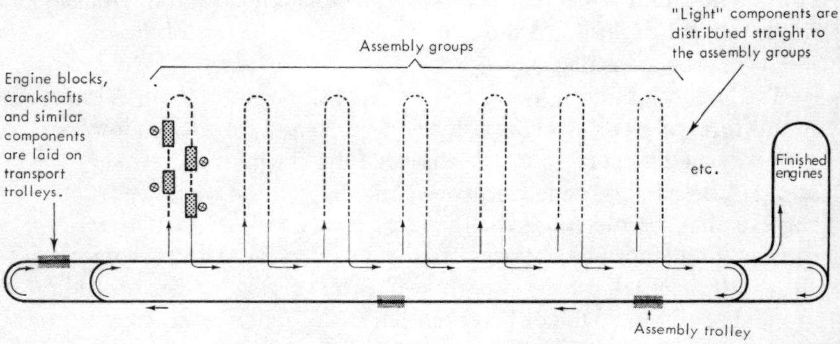

amount of maintenance and cleaning, in addition to the opportunity for a substantial amount of job rotation.

Increasing the job content can call for compromise. Too little work is regarded as boring while too much is difficult. Both extremes are unsatisfactory, but what is the right mix? There is no simple answer. To make a sweeping generalisation, it appears that the higher the skill involved, the more difficult it is for job rotation to be accepted as a satisfactory working arrangement. It is certainly easier to achieve job rotation if this is made a condition of appointment when the worker is recruited.

In a successful working group, there is considerable autonomy on how the work will be performed. This includes the degree of specialisation, if any, within the group, the rotation of jobs and the extent and frequency of rest periods. The autonomy does not extend, however, to the hours to be worked, or there would be chaos at the points of contact with other groups.

In the bigger companies it has been found desirable to extend the training in practical matters to include an understanding of how the company works and the importance of every individual work effort. A typical course of this nature will include some economics so that the relationship between personal effort and the company's total cost can be understood. It will include some method study so that the implications of work simplification can be appreciated. Product knowledge is also included so that the worker realises the extent of the company's activities, how these products function and the contribution he or she makes to the correct functioning. Finally, and ambitiously, some technology, heavily oriented to the worker's group, is given on such matters as the design and function of machines, maintenance, measurement techniques and quality control.

The function of the work study man is considerably altered in this form of group working. In individual working, he is largely concerned with the rating for bonus purposes of individual jobs: once the line is committed to operation, there is only a marginal amount of method study he can do on it (but of course a fair amount of work study can be fruitfully done in the supply services and so on). It is also not unknown for antipathy to exist between the work study man and the line operator. All of this can be different in group working, but the *can* must be emphasised. It will take time and patience for both parties to change but it has been done. The work study man can devote himself to the more rewarding tasks of method study with the collaboration of the operator and the working atmosphere does improve. One discordant note is heard, however: the work study men have the job of compiling minutes of the development group, and in conjunction with the foreman, ensuring that effective follow-up takes place – a sore point.

What of the foreman? On a day-to-day basis he still has the responsibility of ensuring output schedules and quality are met, but he can delegate part of this to the working group if that is performing satisfactorily. The foreman becomes less of a driver and more of a coordinating leader concerned with planning and development.

This category has been discussed at some length because it is the area of greatest difficulty and yet also the area of greatest potential reward. There is no universal answer on group working in this content. Circumstances may be unsuitable. When circumstances *are* suitable, group working will not become successful by itself. Effort and preparation are required to see that it becomes successful. As in so many other areas, the quality of the result depends on the quality of the effort that goes into the creation and maintenance of the working group.

Category B – the machine-paced line

The mass production assembly line with the product carried through the factory on conveyors, preferably on a straight line, with each operator discharging a small, specific but different function is the conventional example of this category. This line has the advantage that extreme specialisation leads to considerable manual dexterity after a short learning period and so is inherently efficient. Unfortunately it breeds the twin discontents of boredom and frustration born of a lack of job satisfaction.

It is not sufficient just to say operators numbers 1 to N will in future form a working group. There has to be some natural linkage and contact between the members of a successful group – in the machine-paced line, the operators are heavily dependent on each other but the contact is relatively small. It is easy to establish a group premium payment scheme but apart from that group working is difficult.

Some attempts have been made at job enrichment by widening the training so that the operators can rotate jobs. Attempts have also been made to widen the scope of the job by including responsibility for some maintenance (there is only one blue collar union in most plants) and for quality. Experiments are in hand on the influence of a systematic follow-up and discussion of the operating results including costs as means of developing a spirit of cooperation. Add to this extra training to increase interest in the company similar to that for Category A (but with which this operator can do comparatively little to influence the outcome) and that is about all that can be done towards group working in this situation. The preferred solution is to break into the production line so as to change the situation to Category A, but that is not always possible.

Category C – the automated process

The pinnacle of technical perfection can occur in automated process lines in paper making and chemical plants as well as in the generation and transmission of electricity. The common characteristic is that the main operating tasks are those of monitoring and checking a process which is heavily dependent on the satisfactory operation of equipment on which, in turn, there is usually a heavy maintenance commitment. The operating and maintaining functions are generally mutually exclusive in terms of time. With this definition, this category can be extended to include much of steel works plant and also extraction plant.

The aim in Sweden has been to integrate the operating and maintaining functions within a single team and with the same people moving from task to task. This would clearly be difficult if not impossible in a large organisation within the union structure of some countries, but even there it certainly occurs on farms where the worker is the combined operator and semi-skilled mechanic, and one suspects it still occurs with advantage in small works, more especially in remote districts.

A good example of the Swedish approach can be seen in a division of a company (Gullatt AB) engaged in excavating and part processing clay for the building industry. A detailed study, carried out before the site was opened, revealed there would be wild fluctuations in the work load of any particular skills. For instance, despatch would be concentrated in the evenings while discharging into final storage silos would peak on Thursdays and Fridays of each week. There would be a minimal commitment at the weekends but it could not be ignored. A seasonal element was present in that stripping and restoration of the clay pit were best done in the summer: the capacity and amount of work required in the processing unit was dependent on the water content of the clay. This kind of heavy equipment requires considerable maintenance which can be done on a planned basis, but to deal with breakdowns a certain amount of contingency capability needs to be available whenever the plant is operating. To man each function separately to meet peak conditions would be shockingly expensive and the project could not have survived.

Study indicated that the total work content amounted to thirty man-shifts per week, so six teams of five men were allocated to the site, two teams to work in the morning shift, two teams in the afternoon shift, one team in the night shift and one team to cover the weekends. To cover the work, all five men in each team would be trained for and capable of performing between four and six tasks each, while two men on each team would be trained for a further sixteen tasks. The only other manning proposed for the site was one manager, one process technician, one maintenance technician and one clerk (who also assisted in the despatch area) all on days.

There are three points of outstanding interest – the first is the variety of work each man is expected to do with absolutely no sign of demarcation between different production tasks and between production and maintenance. Once the scheme was underway, some revision was necessary because it was found expedient to do more maintenance on the night shift when production demands were less, but the principle had been accepted and is largely adhered to.

The second major point is that each team is responsible for its own supervision. A condition for the success of this bold innovation is that the workers learnt how to allocate work among themselves and, by means of theoretical and on the job training, learnt how to make the decisions necessary to keep the plant working efficiently. The idea was discussed with the teams at an early stage and fully accepted by them. The proponents of group working will express no surprise that these two points were accepted so readily, since these are two of the objectives which emerge as a natural outcome of increased job satisfaction.

The third point is that although the manager meets most of the workers daily, particularly at the shift changeover – for which a reasonable overlap of time is included in order that information can be exchanged – it is very much part of the scheme that a weekly meeting should also take place, with one representative (rotating) from each shift being present. These meetings deal with production and maintenance problems, changes in techniques or organisation, as well as the domestic affairs of holidays and so on. Work in this kind of industry is generally dirty and fairly arduous so it is not usual to find these workers meeting to discuss technical matters; on this site it is regarded as being of cardinal importance for the workers to have a continuous presentation of adequate and comprehensive technical and economic information. Currently this information is processed manually but it is expected that in the near future the company's central computer will be used, via a terminal, to give daily information to the operators on output, quality, costs, oil consumption, productivity rates and so on.

It is only fair to add that this venture was backed by the resources of a medium size company, but none the less the control is very ambitious and represents group working of a high order. It also demonstrates that good group working involves hard work at the planning stage.

Category D – the concentrated operation

The concentrated operation is the Swedish description for a bank of lathes or milling machines located together in a workshop but probably performing work for different items. This is fairly common practice because it offers the advantages of a high machine utilisation and effective use of specialist, and usually skilled, staff. On the debit side, in-process stocks are high and there can be planning difficulties.

The Swedes have decided this is not an area amenable to group working. Paradoxically this arrangement of machines, for quite different reasons, has been enjoying a vogue in the UK under the name of Group Technology.

Category E – the diversified line

In this category, part of the production unit is organised for single line working which then fans out into two or more parallel functions, possibly uniting again for further single line working. This kind of operation is typical of smaller plants and might include for example a bakery, when the same basic mix is formed into different shapes then baked in a common oven and finally decorated in different ways by different specialists before entering a common despatch bay.

An industrial example quoted in Sweden is of a group of twenty-five men operating fifteen different finishing processes in a factory producing art glassware at Orrefors. Before group working was introduced the factory was organised on a concentrated operation plan (of which these twenty-five men were a part) with banks of flat grinders, followed by banks of edge grinders and so on through the fifteen processes which dealt with all the products made by the factory. Queues in front of the machines were commonplace. An elaborate paper system was in operation to calculate individual bonus rates and to keep account of the flow of orders.

On changing to group working in 1970, the factory products were split into three types – individual pieces, service ware and special glass. The group under discussion was concerned with the individual pieces of decorated bottles and decanters, which can be further split into 'blown' ware and 'sheared' ware requiring a different mix of finishing processes. The finishing machines were moved to form two production lines, back to back, each served by its own conveyor. All the products united into a common inspection point at which the only records were kept, this time for the calculation of a group premium payment. To avoid an imbalance, the operators need to move to different machines in accordance with the pattern of the load. The aim, in a not very pleasant process, is to involve every employee in continuous efforts to make the work more efficient through simplification and better working methods. This, it is claimed, provides scope for personal initiative.

The sceptics may argue that this particular example is nothing more than the introduction of flow line techniques – but it would fail to work smoothly without the job mobility which is the essence of group working. The distinction between this category and say the man-paced line is a little artificial but the Swedes think that effective production targets for premium payments can sometimes be hard to establish in a diversified line.

Category F – the service group

Service groups are very widespread ranging from personal services with shop assistants and hotel staff, or medical services in hospitals to technical services in the plumbing example quoted in chapter seven or in garages. The common features are the contact with the customer, the varying nature of the work and the difficulty of obtaining an even work load. In a large garage, the degree of centralisation is critical because it is possible to lose any profits derived from increased specialisation at the work bench by inflating the costs of administration.

In one large chain of garages in Stockholm servicing Volkswagen cars under a system of intense specialisation, labour turnover was running at 50 per cent per annum; the management was also much concerned over the growing lack of a sense of responsibility for turning out a good job. Faced with the problem of deciding whether to try to recruit more highly skilled mechanics or to adapt the work to the skills available the company elected to employ teams of six mechanics of varying skills, with one foreman to a team and each team able to undertake any job. A typical garage would then have four such teams supported by a team responsible for spares and stores and another team responsible for appointments, costing, accounts and cash. An unusual feature is that customer contact is maintained by ensuring that the customer knows the name of the foreman in the team servicing his car, and moreover meets this foreman before and after the job is done. The team is now also responsible for its own inspection.

The main discussion in this area is to decide on the size of the group for the calculation of premium bonus and then to decide suitable targets. In the garage, it was decided to include everyone, manager as well, apart from a car hire clerk and a part-time canteen assistant. Labour turnover has fallen to 10 per cent per annum as a result of all the changes.

Category G – the construction group

The first advice the Swedes offer for the construction area is that good work planning and coordination of supplies are priorities on the path to efficiency. The methods might range from bar charts on a fairly simple erection job to PERT networks in major tasks. The shipbuilding firm of Kockums is a good example of how the building of tankers can be standardised to resemble factory production, but a close control is still kept on every detail in spite of the standardisation. The logistics of the supply and movement of heavy steel plate and welded assemblies throughout the yard must be smooth and under absolute control. This is achieved through a sophisticated computer system which first explodes the ship design into components down to the dimensions of the incoming plate. The computer then marshals the steel along the production line by feedback from numerically controlled flame cutting and welding machines. Production control is of paramount importance: considerable imagination was exercised at the design stage to ensure that the system works.

The next advice the Swedes offer is that group working and group premium schemes should emerge as a natural consequence of a situation in which all the effort is devoted to the completion of a clear task. The problems are two-fold, firstly to design a fair remuneration system and secondly to ensure that consultation and collaboration are meaningful, particularly if a new set of conditions arises with each new construction project. Kockums achieved the spirit of group working and liaison with a development group by means of a strong committee structure which had been developed around the works council before the formation of working groups had become fashionable. Kockums were vulnerable with a 250,000 ton tanker being completed every forty working days and a target for the next fifteen 350,000 ton tankers due for completion also every forty days. Labour disputes could have destroyed this planning system but the yard workers did not think of the tight schedule as a position of vulnerability in which section claims could be pressed. Instead they took an immense pride in being part of an outfit that could produce such near miracles. The management in turn made sure everyone in the yard knew the state of the order book.

A third factor in the conversion of a Kockums loss of £5.4m in 1969 to a profit before tax of £13m in 1973 was the high quality of workmanship. To help maintain this, temperature effects were minimised by building the port and starboard sections simultaneously and side by side, and continuous research is carried out for better cutting methods. Most of the operations took place in closed shops, major roof sections being removed in a single operation in summer to improve working conditions. The result is that when major sections of the ship are assembled in the dry dock ready for welding, the fit was so good (a tolerance of ± 1.8 mm is claimed) that rectification work was minimal.

Given the will and with effort, the construction group can thus be a very favourable area for group working.

The development group

Having surveyed the company's activities in general terms and decided that they fall within a favourable category, the reference group is able to frame objectives which are in the form of statements of principle, which it can pass on to a number of development groups: it is the responsibility of the development groups to convert the objectives into working realities. It is wise to commence with one or two development groups only and these preferably in favourable areas or where there is a genuine problem (such as very high absenteeism or poor morale) for which group working has a good chance of providing a useful solution. Usually each development group will look after the interests of two working groups – Figure 7.3 again shows the inter-relationship.

The essential criteria are that natural groups exist or can be created by adapting the production situation, and that it is possible for the development group to establish clear and simple targets in numerical terms for the output from the working group.

The development group normally consists of seven people, the foreman being chairman, with two representatives from each working group together with the planner (or scheduler) and the work study man for this area. There are no union representatives present as such; specialist designers, engineers or accountants can be called in as required. During the earlier stages of a group's existence, meetings may be frequent but once the working group is in action, meetings become less frequent until a major item develops but it is usually laid down that the development group must meet at least once a month. It will be concerned with production and personnel problems, training, quality, amenities, holidays and anything else that affects the performance of the group.

At all times, the emphasis in the development group is on formal (but not restrictive) procedure. An agenda must be produced in advance of each meeting, and on it must appear a follow-up for any action arising out of the previous meeting. It is recognised that executive action or detailed investigation cannot occur in a committee so the time of the meeting is limited. Investigations can be initiated and the investigator must report back to the development group by a named date. Minutes must be produced for each meeting. Much of the work of preparation and chasing methods and data falls on to the work study man, but he is relieved of the task of rate fixing and so can work on the more rewarding task of method study.

Once the working group is in action, it becomes not entirely autonomous but to a large extent self adapting to the constraints agreed in the development group, so the foreman has the opportunity to change his role to that of a 'father figure' guiding his 'family' and looking at the broader issues likely to develop in the future. The feedback is two-fold.

The working group has the opportunity to contribute to its own future through discussion in the development group. The results obtained will react on the group, probably through the pay packet, and certainly in the development group. The development group has therefore an important and continuing part to play in the evolution of the working group, partly through encouragement and partly by steering and controlling.

Group premium payments

To an outsider studying Swedish industry, it is often uncertain whether the desire for group working in any particular company preceded the desire for a better incentive scheme based on group premiums, or *vice versa*. What is certain is that the two are intimately connected and the success of one colours the success of the other.

It is no part of the function of the development group to participate in actual negotiations on wage rates: this must be left to the powerful negotiating machinery set up by the employers and the trade unions. However, if contained in the objective, the development group does have the task of studying the structure of the pay system and of making detailed recommendations on the structure on which subsequent negotiations can be based.

The development group has the guidance that a 'good' pay system has the following characteristics:

the workers must regard it as fair, and feel that differences in wages can be justified objectively by reference to the degree of difficulty of the task and to the individual's proficiency and performance: recognition of these points should encourage employees to self-development;

the incentive should only reward results which enhance the function being performed, i.e. it should be related to a direct measure of productivity and not to an indirect measure such as tons of coal burned: an ideal measure is cost per ton produced, or other suitable unit of economic performance;

the system should be simple enough for everyone to understand;

the wage system should promote collaboration on the job;

the wage system should facilitate rationalisation by accommodating minor improvements without having to change the system;

income variations from one pay date to another should not be so great as to threaten income security;

the wage system should keep the labour cost per unit manufactured at an acceptable level despite wage increases.

The development group has a formidable task in creating an ideal wage system since in addition it will need to suggest rules for payments when new staff come into the unit or when staff are transferred, or when major changes are introduced. The task is in theory made more complicated because some members of the development group will be discussing their own wages. Not everyone agrees this is a good policy but those companies who have tried it have found that no harm is done to the essential structure and some difficulties may be removed at a very early stage. But the procedure must be very formal indeed with supporting evidence being prepared carefully out of meeting. Any recommendations which emerge should be carefully tested against at least six months back data.

Experience has shown that in a good premium system the incentive element amounts to between 15 and 30 per cent of the gross pay. At this level, monthly fluctuations in wages are not too great. Downtime can be absorbed as part of the system and yet the incentive is large enough to form an effective spur to effort. Experience has also suggested that all workers in the group should receive the same amount of bonus, and that differences in skill of different employees should be embodied in the base rate only.

Differentials

In spite of official declarations by the Confederation of Trade Unions on 'solidarity' – the narrowing of pay differentials – the shop floor recognises that differences in skills and experience exist and should be rewarded. The only argument is how the difference should be established and its size. There is of course no single answer. One example can be quoted of rules which were agreed for a new factory at Bred.

The fixed component of the wages has the four basic levels illustrated in Figure 8.2. The new employee starts at level 1 but after being employed for six months and having completed the mandatory training programme, or otherwise demonstrated he has the knowledge, he is moved up to level 2, a rise of approximately 5 per cent. After being employed for a further eighteen months (or having 4½ years similar experience elsewhere) the worker is eligible for transfer to level 3, but

Figure 8.2 Proposed basic wage rates in one factory (reproduced from Reference [55] by permission of SAF)

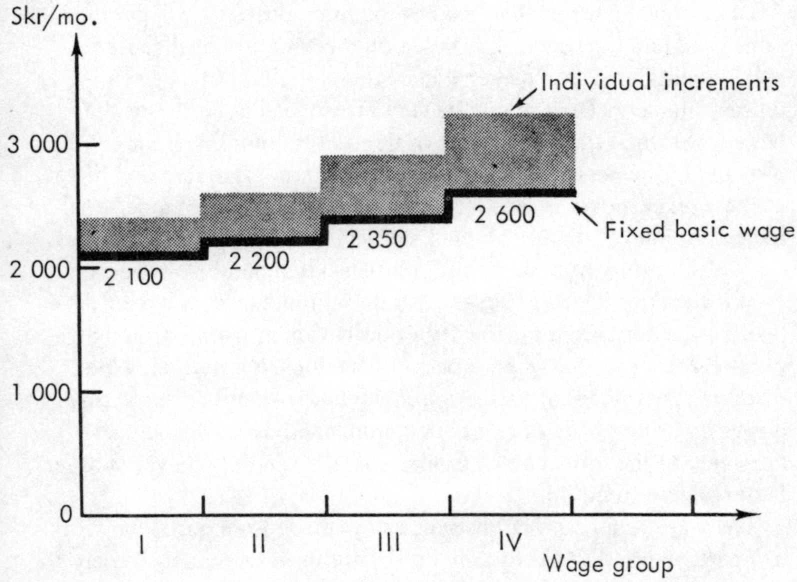

to gain the promotion he must have completed part 2 of the theory course and be able to undertake 50 per cent of the tasks in the group. The pay rise to level 3 is a further 7 per cent. To rise to level 4, the employee must complete a third course in theory and have acquired facility and knowledge in at least 70 per cent of the tasks of his working group; he must also have been employed for five years. The rise to level 4 is a further 11½ per cent on his basic wage. There is thus considerable incentive for the employee to improve his theoretical knowledge as well as to broaden his group experience.

The fixed component of the wage can also contain a personal increment. This was introduced to encourage the better worker and also to serve as some compensation for the fact that in time of trouble, it is often the better worker who is transferred to the trouble spot and this might involve him in loss of group bonus earnings. Evaluation for personal increments is on three levels. At the lowest level, the worker is satisfactorily competent – he gets no personal increment. If the worker is competent beyond normal requirements, he goes half way up the scale of personal increments shown in the shaded area in Figure 8.2. If his competence goes far beyond normal requirements, the worker can get the maximum personal increment which at level 4 amounts to a further 12½ per cent. In the same working group, it is therefore possible to have the highest paid skilled employee earning 52 per cent more on the fixed part of the wages than the new recruits. But they will get the same premium bonus which is based on the activities of the group.

It is considered that personal increments should not be given indiscriminately. They should be very rare indeed at level 1 of the basic wage when the employee is in the first six months of his employment. The personal increments become more frequent and bigger as the worker moves to level 4. It is expected that the total personal increment bill for the factory will amount to 5 per cent of the wages.

It is refreshing to find pay differentials based on objective criteria, even if the criteria of 'far beyond average competence' may be a little suspect because of difficulty of definition in words, although generally recognisable when it occurs. The converse method, which Sweden has avoided, of basing wage differentials on the negotiating power or strike power of competing unions, produces differences unrelated to the influence on production and can only be yet another factor adding to inflation.

The wage proposals just discussed were made for a particular works in a particular industry but they in fact conform reasonably closely to the average differences found in 1971 for the different degrees of skill among the blue collar workers (Figure 8.3 (a)). The average wages or salaries of the white collar workers of comparable skills determined by job evaluation, are also shown on the graph: these start at a marginally lower figure for jobs of the lowest skills but rise to about 200 per cent of the initial value at the fourth level of skill compared with 135 per cent for the blue collar workers. Moreover, the Figure 8.3 (b) shows that the white collar workers have a greater likelihood of rising to posts of higher skill.

There are always difficulties in assessing relative skills but it has been suggested by Borje Strender of the Employers' Confederation that the different levels among blue collar workers should be assigned on a scale of four reading

Assistant Operator
Operator
Process Technician
Process Engineer

The range of figures quoted above indicates that it is the more highly skilled craftsmen who are relatively least well paid, so much so that

Figure 8.3 Average effect of level of skill on wages in Sweden in 1971

(a)

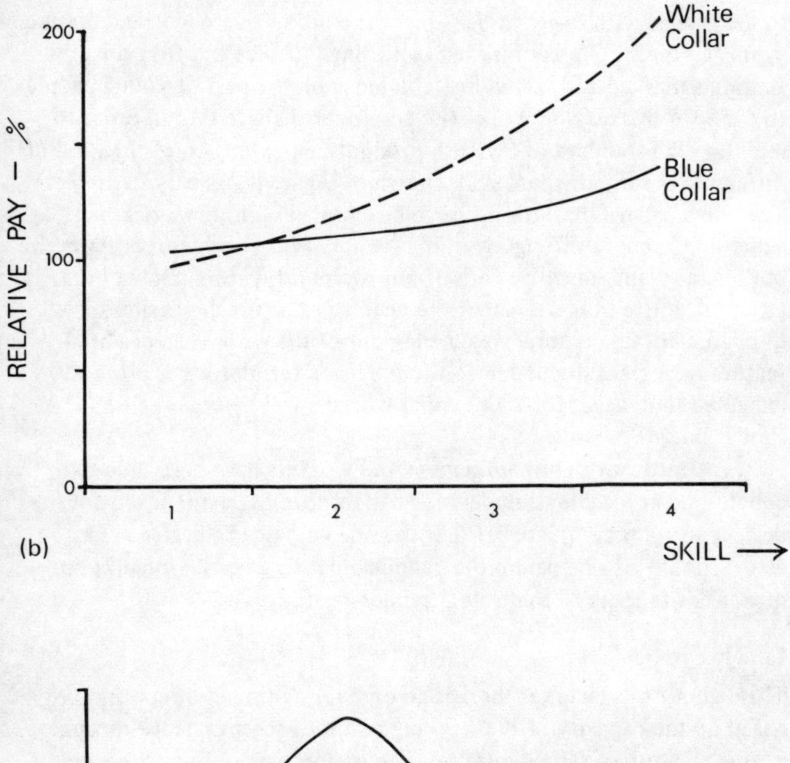

(b)

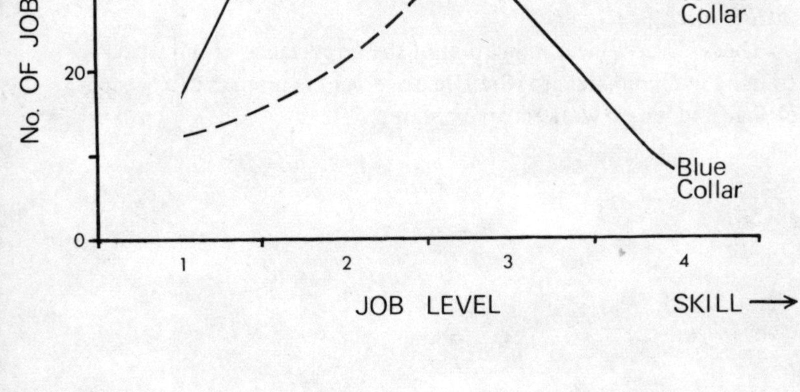

they have been nicknamed 'the forgotten men of Swedish industry'. This, of course, is the same kind of point that was made on pay differentials in an earlier chapter. Some of the unions have expressed themselves happy with this situation – the bulk of their members are in the groups with lower skills – but the employers are worried. Several years ago the employers forecast recruiting troubles and they are now finding a marked and increasing reluctance on the part of young people to train for this class of work. The employers believe that in order to maintain the standard of Swedish products, an extension of the kind of differentials for individual skills shown in Figure 8.2 is very desirable. They also believe that this needs to be coupled with job enrichment, achieved probably through working groups, with every worker given the opportunity and incentive for self-improvement, yet remaining in the group incentive bonus scheme: the need to cater for the desire for self-improvement in a natural way arising out of the work is an essential feature of current discussions on tomorrow's form of wages. It is also expected that wages for white collar workers will be organised on similar lines.

It is significant that management and workers have been able to collaborate at local level in devising suitable group payment schemes designed to satisfy 'the belief that the one who does a better work effort should also be paid more', an idea that 'is deeply rooted in our notions of fairness' – to quote Strender again.

Conclusion

Throughout this chapter, there is an underlying thread of continuity based on the capacity of the working group to accept change through a large measure of self-adaptation. The importance of this factor on the successful exploitation of capital investment schemes for modernisation cannot be too strongly emphasised and if group working achieved nothing else, this would be very adequate justification for its introduction.

There is also a clear indication of the importance of industrial training in circumstances where management is prepared to accept change and where workers are prepared to learn.

9 WORKER DIRECTORS

Worker directors on the company boards in Sweden are largely regarded as a political issue based on ideological concepts of industrial democracy. They have been less conspicuous than in Germany or Yugoslavia but this may be because it was not until 1966-8 that several unsuccessful attempts were made by the unions to obtain worker directors by negotiation with the employers' organisations. But as late as June 1971, Arne Geijer the then president of the Confederation of Trade Unions said he did not attach great importance to this reform. He defined the objectives very clearly in saying 'many people are wondering whether the time has not come for the trade union movement to take the plunge into the management pool – to take on managing functions and set itself on an equal footing with the capital owner in the direction of the affairs of the undertaking'.

Geijer continues 'we have always taken a cautious line in these matters, believing that to be able to assert ourselves both at work and in society, the trade union movement needs not only to be strong, but also to be free and independent'. The problem of the dichotomy of interests is highlighted in these words. To be effective, the worker director must take a responsible attitude to the problems of the company. At the same time, the worker director (who in the biggest companies is probably also a trade union leader) has responsibilities to the workers, and these two loyalties may not always coincide even in Sweden. It requires men of stature to resolve this problem and it says much for the people involved that the small experience to date is not unfavourable.

There were people in the trade unions who still wanted worker directors, in spite of Geijer's reservations, on the grounds that this would be a fairly easy method of increasing worker influence, and moreover a step which could easily be recognised as such. So having failed in negotiations with employers, the unions turned to the government, and in December 1972, an act was passed by the Riksdag to come into operation on 1 April 1973 and to continue in operation until 30 June 1976. The unions regard this three year period as a trial, not of worker directors, but of whether the legislation is strong enough.

The act is applicable to all joint stock companies (with minor exceptions covering banks, insurance companies and certain cooperative associations) employing a total of 100 or more workers, the white and blue collar workers being counted together. If the number of employees should fall below 100 after the appointment of a worker director to the board has been made, then the right of representation will continue. If the local trade unions so request, a company is obliged to appoint two worker directors (with named official deputies) to the board. The act states that, unless differently agreed by the unions, if more than four fifths of the employees under collective agreement belong to the same local union, then this union shall elect both of the worker directors: otherwise the two local unions having the highest number of such employees shall nominate one director each. In many quarters it is being assumed that in practice the representation will work out as one for the blue collar workers and one for the white collar workers. This is one of the indicators of the acceptance of common interests by the blue and white collar unions which has been very marked in Sweden since the minor strikes of 1971 and will be discussed again at the end of the chapter.

The worker director should be employed by the company and must not be a member of a board of another company: these two provisions are obviously included in the list to prevent a new generation of professional directors – this time representing the workers – appearing on the industrial scene. However, this act also sets up a council consisting of a chairman with legal experience, two representatives of the employers and two from the main unions concerned, which can, if it thinks fit, over-ride the conditions of this paragraph. By June 1973 the unions were already interpreting this to mean that since they alone choose the nominee, they have the right to 'select whom they regard as most suitable to represent their interests, whether employed by the company or not', according to André Thiria, the international secretary of the Confederation of Trade Unions. This declaration seems to run counter to the whole spirit of participative industrial democracy which has been apparent in Sweden.

Apart from one exemption, the worker directors have the full responsibility of other members of the board but are not allowed to take part in the board's considerations of action to be taken in the event of strikes or in the making or cancellation of collective agreements. The unions state the worker directors have the additional obligation to work for the interests of the employees and for more open information from the board to the employees.

The act came into force in April 1973, and requires three months notice to be given before a worker director can join the board, so by the end of 1974, experience of its operation is limited. However, a handful of the major industrial companies invited worker directors to join the board before the act was passed. Of these men, John Erik Olsson in Kockums, Gert Gunnarsson in Volvo and Carl Alf in the state owned shipbuilding yard at Uddevalla, all seem to be establishing a tenable position without surrendering their tough negotiating tradition on behalf of their members. All three were, of course, well known and respected in their companies through other activities such as the works councils and it remains to be seen how the smaller companies will fare under compulsion.

Recognising that worker directors may have difficulty in achieving parity with other members of the board, the Confederation of Trade Unions has established a training school to deal more especially with the legal responsibilities under the Swedish company acts. In addition the course will function as a clearing house for the exchange of experience as well as outlining common approaches to the goals of the trade union movement and economic policies. Part of this will be regarded by some people as indoctrination but clearly the worker directors will require some support initially, particularly in the wider fields of economic theory and practice and the problems of industrial growth including capital investment. It has been agreed with the employers that time off and financial compensation will be given to worker directors attending the course.

Gunnarsson and Alf have summarised their experience in order to help future worker directors. They agree that the most important task for a worker director is to inform the workers about the big decisions taken within the company: 'true it is the duty of the management to inform the employees, but the employee representatives must clearly state on the board that they reserve the right to inform the employees in case the management fails in this respect'. Another worker director, Erik Eriksson of the conglomerate Stora, admits that so far his role, to his disappointment, has been only in the information field.

Within a reasonable time, Gunnarsson and Alf believe the worker director will be recognised as an asset to the board. Other members will be expert in financial, legal or technical matters but the worker director will be an expert on practical matters, able to see both the difficulties and advantages in any practical situation within the company – and company knowledge is much stressed.

Asked if they have been in a situation of conflict of worker and board interests, Gunnarsson and Alf replied that they had expected this to happen but so far they had been able to resolve the issues satisfactorily. They quote two hypothetical situations which are of particular interest:

If a company has to close one or more departments because of lack of profitability, how should the worker director react? They suggest it would be advantageous for the worker director to be in on the discussion from the beginning, and perhaps thus be able to influence the decision. It would certainly be easier to accept the decision if they had been in on the discussions.

In environmental matters, the worker directors, after consultation in the works council or local union meetings, might convey a demand from the workers for measures to curb pollution. After costing and surveying the company resources, followed by further consultation it could be 'the employees will be faced with the choice whether to give up the next raise for the sake of an improved work environment, or the other way round'. Full information and discussion are believed to be the means to avoid a conflict of interests.

One of the next areas suggested for worker representation is that of accountancy in order to carry out an independent audit of the company's finance, and to pass this information onto the works council. An implication behind this, that the company accountants and the official auditors have in some way concealed the facts, is disturbing and at variance with the earlier spirit of collaboration that existed between the Employers' Confederation and the Confederation of Trade Unions even in such a potentially controversial issue as work study. As late as June 1972, the employers and unions were able to publish a statement to the effect that they were

> 'agreed that a continuous rationalisation of its methods of production is crucial in determining whether in the long run a particular firm will be able to maintain operations at a level that provided job openings and security of employment . . . rationalisation constitutes the foundation for advances in all branches of economic activity . . . helps to create the basis for successive improvements in the standard of living.'

It would be a pity if this process of collective collaboration, which is at the same time almost unique to Sweden and the envy of the western world, was lost through a battle of political dogma but there are signs of change. The works councils, which have proved their worth when taken seriously as in Kockums for instance, are being criticised as non-executive bodies concerned with discussion and consultation only. Similarly, voices are heard that the working groups of, say, Saab do not have any decision making authority in areas such as finance and profitability.

What is reasonably certain is that different sections of the community have regarded the working groups in differing ways. The management sees the working group as a means of solving two problems, absenteeism and turnover, and as a means of increasing productivity. The workers see the group as a means of obtaining self-expression through job satisfaction while some of the unions see the groups as a way of obtaining power. The latter also claim that effective working groups have only been formed where aggressive trade unions exist and that there are no working groups in areas of traditionally female employment – although in fact such a group has been considered for the sewing section of a garment making factory. (However, this particular proposal does not seem to have been implemented because the traditional method of specialisation on, say parts of trousers was inherently much more efficient than group working, in which each girl would tailor a complete pair of trousers.) Critics like André Thirià argue that worker directors are only one small step on the road to the ultimate goal of equality between work and capital: the decision making equality must be extended down throughout the companies' operations in search of this goal.

The dangers of the situation were recognised by Tage Erlander, a former prime minister, who said in 1972 that welfare policy in his time had been guided by a balance of power, but with workers claiming more influence on their own situation and working conditions, they would automatically come to demand influence over many other aspects of the enterprise. The worker directors were a first step away from the traditional balance of power towards a takeover of power.

A Swedish political commentator, Svante Nycander, is even more concerned. He views the newly found alignment of interests between the blue and white collar workers as the beginning of a movement that will have wide effects both in industry and in politics.

> 'When they unite and demand something from the politicians, as frequently happens nowadays, such an action carries considerable political weight, especially in a situation where the socialist and the non-socialist parties each have 175 seats in parliament. Some

people fear that political power will silently slip away from the politicians to these organisations.'

Nycander draws the conclusion that 'once a society has put ultimate power in the hands of ordinary people the old structure of power in industry is bound to fall sooner or later. In Sweden, organised blue and white collared workers are an absolute majority of the adult population and there is no definite limit to the claims that this majority can raise.'

It would be a tragedy if the continued growth of industrial collaboration in Sweden was disrupted for political reasons. In former decades ideology has taken second place to pragmatism, the test being 'does it work?' In Sweden the answer must surely be 'yes, industrial collaboration has worked'.

PART 4: FINANCE AND CONTROLS

10 CONTROL OF THE ECONOMY

First attempts at control

To the Swedes in recent years, control of the economy has meant steps taken in support of the objective of full employment. The control has been applied in two dimensions, spatially by applying pressures for future developments to be located in the regions, and temporally by attempting to absorb gainfully the surplus of labour arising from short term economic recessions. In practice, the latter has been the prime concern.

The National Pension Funds and the Investment Funds are both worthy enterprises within their own rights, but it is certain that from their inception, the government of the day has regarded these Funds very much as instruments by which the state could influence the timing of capital investment.

The concept of control has been a major item in the political philosophy: just how effective it has been will be explored in the following pages. The timing of events is shown pictorially in Figure 10.1 which can claim to be no more than an artist's impression. The movements of the economy for the years shown are represented in simplified form by the undulating curve in the middle of the chart, the troughs corresponding to periods of recession. Below this are shown the various actions taken, the tail of the arrow being at the initiation date and the head of the arrow at the date of the effective impact upon the economy. In the upper part of the figure, the box represents the period in 1960 and 1961 for which companies were allowed to set aside 100 per cent of their pretax profits in the Investment Funds; during this time, significantly, the discount rate shown at the top of the diagram remained unaltered at 5 per cent.

Sweden has experienced a sequence of minor recessions – in 1958, 1962, 1967 and 1972 – separated in some instances by boom conditions, notably in 1960. During the recession in 1958, it was the government's intention to combat unemployment by stimulating investment in construction projects. Ready release of the Investment Funds was given over the eighteen month period from May 1958 to September 1959, for projects which might take twelve to eighteen months to complete. Figure 10.1 shows this action was obviously too

Figure 10.1 Pictorial representation of the timing of measures taken to control the Swedish economy

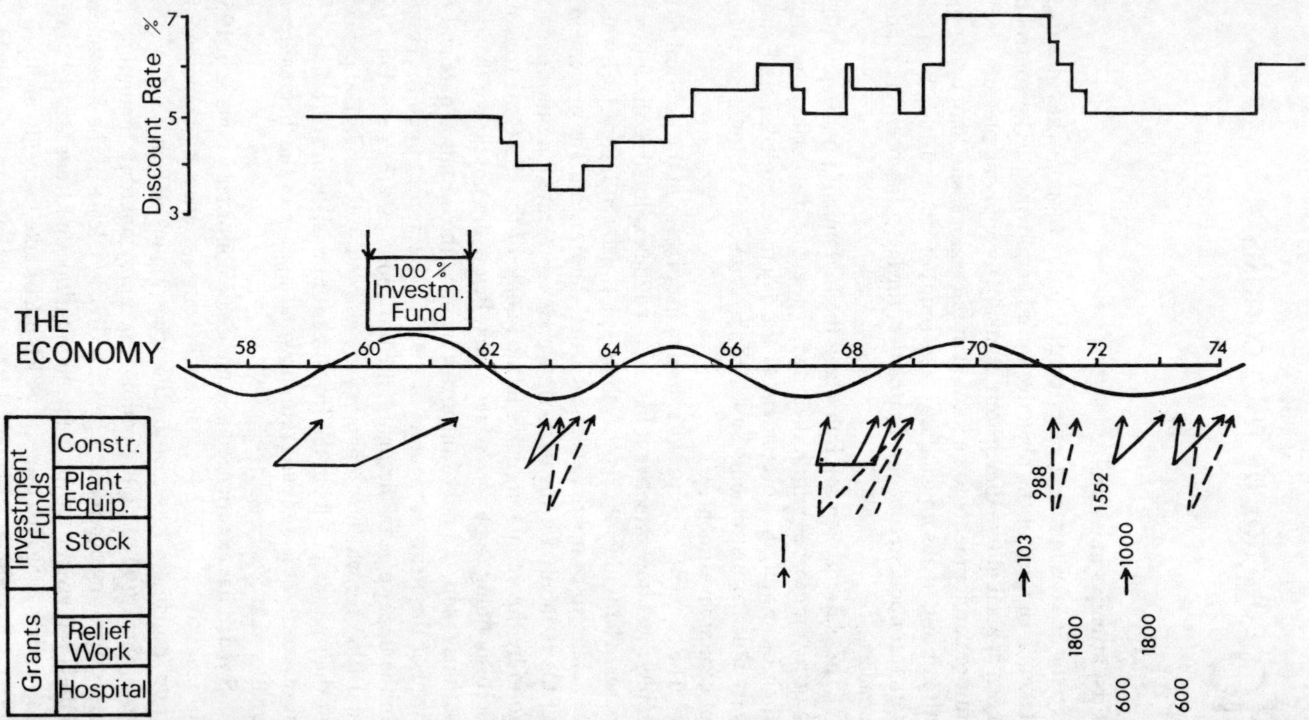

late and perhaps of the wrong kind in the sense that construction projects tend to be lengthy in execution. It is easy to be overcritical after the event; it does take time for the effects of a recession to work through the system and this could well account for the delay in reacting.

Learning from experience, when in early spring the 1962 recession appeared likely to arrive in the construction industry by the autumn, it was decided to restrict the release of funds to a ten month period beginning 1 July and moreover, construction had to start before 1 November. By late summer, a recession in the engineering industry seemed probable so funds were released for machinery and equipment from 30 November, but only for orders which could be placed before 30 April 1963.

The timing on this occasion seems to have been more effective, the chief criticism being that the developments took place in the main in central and southern Sweden which were relatively unaffected by the recession anyway. So legislation was introduced in 1963 for selective authorisation, i.e. the development areas (mainly of northern Sweden but also some other places), have preferential and almost automatic release of Investment Funds whatever the state of the economy. A variation on this theme has been that certain firms have received authorisation provided a proportion, and usually a small proportion, of the release has been spent in the development areas.

When the 1967 recession appeared, the Labour Market Board tried to refine the control mechanism still further but this time it seems to have been oversophisticated. Step by step planning was introduced so that successive stages of authorisation of Investment Funds took place in May, again in December, and yet again in April 1968, all to cover the placing of orders up to April 1968 for construction projects, and up to October 1968 for machinery and equipment. The idea was that by postponing definite decisions until more accurate information was available, a better control would be achieved. With hindsight, it seems clear that some of the decisions were left until too late since many of the projects were still not completed before the recession had disappeared. The control may also have been confounded because the Investment Funds were first authorised for the financing of inventory in October 1967.

Before discussing the events of the 1972 recession in greater detail, a brief look at the activities of the Board during the boom period of 1960 and 1961 is of interest. Authorisation for the release of investment fund monies was simply not given, except in very exceptional circumstances. Moreover, special legislation was passed to allow generous tax allowance for companies which placed 100 per cent of the investment fund (instead of the normal 46 per cent) in the blocked account in the Central Bank, the company in effect obtaining a far higher rate of return than was possible on the open market. So far as the government was concerned, this represented an attempt to absorb the maximum of business liquidity at the peak of the boom. The idea misfired. The companies obliged and £75m was transferred in six months to the Central Bank, mostly from company accounts in the commercial banks, which promptly ran into a liquidity crisis. The companies, too, found themselves short of cash.

A period of active use of monetary policy in an attempt to combat swings in the economy had been started in the mid-1950s. A credit squeeze was applied to commercial bank lending in the buoyant period of 1955-7 which preceeded the 1958 recession. In addition to the special measures described in the preceding paragraph, a credit squeeze was again in operation in 1960-61, again in 1963-6 and still more drastically in 1969-70. The discount rate was also varied being low at 3½ per cent in 1963 and high at 7 per cent through most of 1969 and all of 1970, with other corresponding but lesser movements in intervening years.

Forward planning

If only to be in a position to take advantage of the fairly rapid changes in policy on the release of Investment Funds, almost without exception Swedish firms have adopted forward planning as an essential component of their business expertise. Very firm plans exist for one year ahead. Detailed evaluation and technical design for projects covering a further four years ahead exist in most companies, although with a built-in elasticity to accommodate changes due to the trade cycle. Thus, when authorisation is given for the release of the Investment Funds, industry is well poised to take advantage of the position. This particular adherence to the principle of planning is born of convenience; there is also a deeply rooted conviction that forward planning is vital for continued prosperity. Changing working conditions and changing production methods are recognised, indeed welcomed on all sides as tactics in the fight for business survival and higher standards of living, and so must be constructed into an acceptable forward plan. And, incidentally, change is far from more acceptable if it has been planned and discussed than if it appears suddenly and unheralded.

Most of the technically oriented companies have clear objectives for a still further five or ten years ahead which have been evaluated and converted into the form of broad company plans. To mention but one company, Sydkraft (a privately owned company generating and distributing electricity to the bulk of southern and a fair proportion of central Sweden) has very detailed step by step developments planned to obtain the best mix of hydro, fossil and nuclear energy: at the same time, these developments are carefully phased to take advantage of the probable cycles in the release of Investment Funds and of the depreciation allowances for tax purposes. While similar forward plans undoubtedly exist in companies elsewhere, it is the widespread, almost universal, presence of in-depth planning which is so impressive in Sweden.

Planning is widely recognised as being at three levels, the Swedish definition being that short term immediate planning is concerned with annual budgets and control. Medium term planning is a continuation of the immediate planning, complicated by the presence of uncertainty but still concerned with the same concepts and constraints. With long term planning, generally for more than ten years ahead, the time span is great enough for most of the short term commitments to have been eliminated so that new ideas and targets need to be developed: if this does not happen, then in Swedish eyes, this is not long term planning but merely a further continuation of the medium term plan.

The position would be ill balanced if planning was restricted to industry and commerce. The Labour Market Board has a strong planning department which compiles a portfolio of relief work schemes in sufficient detail for rapid implementation when the economy requires remedial action. In reply to a question on whether there was a danger of running out of worthwhile schemes, Aksel Spendrup, Head of Planning at the Labour Market Board, replied that as the standard of living rose, so would new concepts appear desirable and he had no doubt there would always be relief work of a meaningful nature to be undertaken.

The 1971-3 recession

When the early danger signs of a recession appeared in the first quarter of 1971, the Swedish authorities resolved to utilise all the known procedures to avoid its worst effects. Even so unemployment rose from its normal level of about 1.5 per cent to 3.1 per cent in the first quarter of 1972 and again to 3.0 per cent in the first quarter of 1973; in the latter figure there were very few skilled people who by then

Figure 10.2 (a) Historical data for Sweden (b) Advance warnings of layoffs and closures

(a)

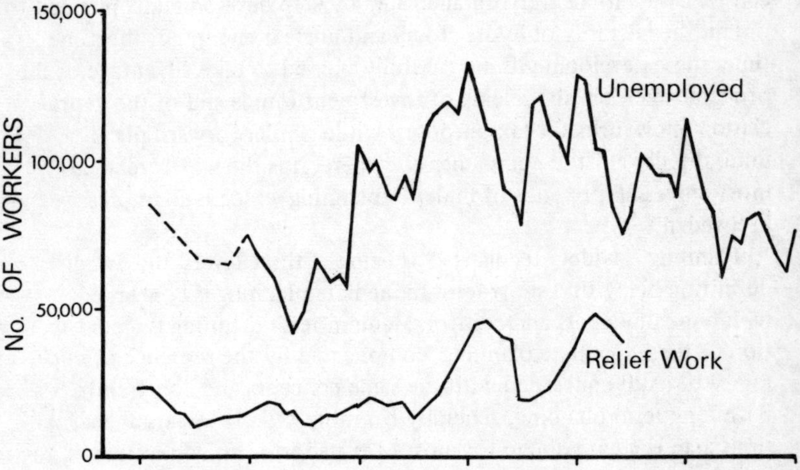

(b)

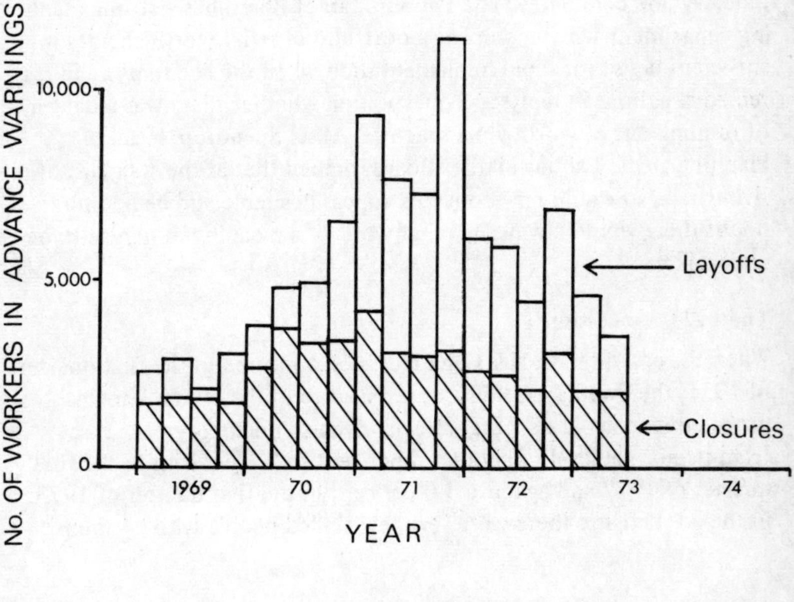

were in short supply but there were a number of salaried staff. Without the application of the controls, it is estimated, possibly rather conservatively, that unemployment could have been as high as 5 per cent or maybe 5.5 per cent.

The generation of accurate information is regarded as the first step towards effective action. By agreement between the employers and the unions, the Labour Market Board is informed by the firms six months in advance of any reduction in the size of the labour force due to cyclic influence (these reductions are known as layoffs). Any known closures due to modernisation elsewhere or due to other factors such as lack of demand, must also be notified six months in advance. The figures shown in Figure 10.2 (b) seem a useful indicator of trouble in spite of the fact that their level is only about one tenth of the total unemployed, shown in Figure 10.2 (a). It would appear from this chart that the layoffs lead the total by about one year. Be that as it may, nearly 12,000 were expected to be involved in closures or layoffs in the fourth quarter of 1971.

In addition, the Labour Market Board carries out sample surveys at monthly intervals from which, together with advice collected from many quarters, it makes forecasts of the labour demand by trade and by location for the next six months ahead. These forecasts are updated every four months. Longer term forecasts are also made based not only on statistical trends of population, but also to include school and university education which is to some extent 'steered' by the demand pattern established by the Labour Market Board.

During a recession the Board is much concerned to see that its normal machinery is working in top gear to provide employers with continuous information on available manpower. Job seekers (and others) are given – in an open report for all to see – the latest information on vacancies with task specification, pay and other conditions of employment, housing conditions and locality information. In passing, it should be said a steady effort is devoted to improving the quality of the information as well as its quantity so that job seekers can get a better grasp of the labour market. The information is put out weekly in newspaper form; each edition in 1973, for instance, contained between 5,000 and 8,000 vacancies, and some 46,000 copies were taken up in June when the recession had virtually disappeared.

The Investment Funds moved into action as a stabilising force in 1971, £95m being authorised for capital projects. A further £4m were utilised for investment but without authority and so became taxable.

In May 1972, it was decided to release Investment Funds to cover building projects up to the end of April 1973, and in March 1973 the general release was authorised to cover investment costs accruing to the end of March 1974 – which seems rather late for this particular recession. The result is that 830 applications were approved for the utilisation of investments totalling £200m, of which £150m was approved because of the business situation, the balance being in regions where authorisation was automatic.

Approval was given to industrial firms in November 1971 to use their investment funds to finance stock piling. One hundred and fifty applications totalling £10m were approved in 1971 and a further 500 applications for £100m were approved in 1972.

Not all of these measures were introduced simultaneously. There was clearly a month to month assessment of the situation and a corresponding extension of the resources involved either from the release of the Investment Funds or from government grants, relief work, etc.

Relief work was mounted on a large scale during this recession and at peak in April 1973 employed 47,800 people. The fluctuation in numbers on relief work are also shown in Figure 10.2 (a) and follow to a large extent the unemployment figures which they would have increased by roughly a third. Unlike the UK in the 1930s when relief work consisted of road making with picks and shovels so as to absorb the maximum number of men, Sweden has regarded relief work as an opportunity to create something of value to the community in a meaningful and efficient way. Whether the relief work consists of road making, flat construction or swimming pool complexes, the worker is armed with modern equipment and so relief work per man is not cheap (it costs about £80 a day to keep a man at work on the roads). Environmental improvements featured largely in this relief work, including a drive by the municipalities to improve sewage disposal. The government also helped by increasing the grant for this kind of work from its usual 30 per cent of the capital cost to 75 per cent – at a total cost of some £180m in both 1971 and 1972. A new feature was that nursing and other similar services absorbed an extra 5,800 people by 1973 all classified as being on relief work – one wonders whether these will become permanent posts.

So many activities were initiated to deal with this particular recession that their mere recital resembles a catalogue of disjointed items and so tends to obscure their importance. For instance building proposals were brought forward by the government for hospital and environmental projects costing some £60m in 1972 and about the same sum in 1973. It is normally essential to get planning permission from the Labour Market Board before any building can be commenced, and in the recent past, while council flats have usually received ready permission, the building of private houses has been heavily discouraged by means of a tight quota system. Because of the labour situation, unrestricted permission was given for building work commenced between September and December 1972 with the result that an extra 8,000 privately financed one- and two-family houses were started. Government grants were made available for improvements to the standard of both local government and private housing.

A further indication of the serious view taken of the recession by the government was that government orders to industry, mainly in the engineering industry, were brought forward both in 1971 and 1972 to the value of about £2.5m: local government was also encouraged to bring forward orders to industry. The effects of these orders were being felt well into 1973.

The regulator in perspective

Table 10.1 Order of magnitude of the 'economic regulator' in 1972 (in m S. kr)

Item		m S. kr
1	Investment Funds – approved projects	2,010
2	Investment Funds – for stock making	1,000
3	Regional development	400
4	Relief work	1,280
5	Extra help to place handicapped	150
6	Hospital building	600
7	Government orders brought forward	25
8	Total at the disposal of the LMB	5,465
9	Increase in National Pension Funds	10,000
10	Annual investment in the economy	46,000

Combining in Table 10.1 the measures available to the Labour Market Board, acting very much as the agent of government to combat the recession, yields about £550m; this, compared with the annual investment in the economy of about £4,600m is 12 per cent, which in itself is a powerful regulator. Add to this the £1,000m increase in 1972 of the National Pension Funds (which within the limits discussed in a later chapter, can also be invested in labour intensive projects in times of recession), and it will be seen there are powerful regulating influences at work in Sweden attempting to control the economy.

Another view of the economic regulator can be obtained from the mining and manufacturing industries for which the gross investment in 1972 was £820m. More than two thirds of the holding in the Investment Funds is credited to these industries. Two thirds of the allocation from the Investment Funds in 1972 amounts to £200m, so that by inference the Labour Market Board had at its direct disposal 25 per cent of the total investment as a regulator in this crucial sector of the economy.

One is tempted to do some crude arithmetic in spite of its dangers. If the combined effect of relief work and regional development at £168m reduced unemployment by about 1 per cent in the first quarter of 1973 (see Figure 10.2), by how much would the total of £550m reduce unemployment? The crude answer is about 4 per cent, so the unemployment might well have risen to around 7 per cent without the application of the regulator.

There are a number of points of significant difference between the 1971-3 recession and the recessions of earlier years. Not only did the Labour Market Board fail to control unemployment as well as it would have liked but instead of the previous two year span, this recession persisted throughout 1973 and it was not until March 1974 that clear signs emerged of the end of trouble. Unemployment then fell to 1.8 per cent and has remained low into 1975. Apart from a welcome fall in the unemployment figures, the downward trend in the discount rate from 7 per cent in March 1971 to a low figure of 5 per cent by November 1971 was reversed when the discount rate was raised to 6 per cent in April 1974, thus confirming officially, as it were, that the recession was over. At the same time, some restrictions were placed in the way of bank loans when the commercial banks were required to increase their cash reserve from 1 per cent to 5 per cent.

To deal with the recession during 1971 to 1973, several new factors were introduced on top of the previous measures. Grants of up to £600 per house were paid by the government for alterations to private houses started before 1975: this is a startling reversal of previous events when the emphasis had been on making private house ownership difficult. Authority was also given in March for the first time for the National Supplementary Pension Fund to be used to finance the purchase of ordinary stock up to £50m. In October, grants were revised for improvements to the environment so that the government paid 75 per cent of the costs to a local government scheme and 50 per cent of the costs for an industrial scheme provided 60 per cent of the costs was incurred before July 1972. The extra tax depreciation of 10 per cent in the year following the purchase of machinery as a result of a release of Investment Funds, was increased to 20 per cent in July 1971 and subsequently extended to the end of 1972. At the same time, new release of the Investment Funds, new relief work and new road making schemes were initiated. As a result of all these measures, it is interesting that whereas in the 1966-7 recession, the rate of investment was not maintained, the rate increased in 1971-3 recession and to this degree at any rate, the control mechanism was functioning.

One of the OECD reports sees in all of these new moves an indication that Sweden is beginning to lose its flexibility in dealing with a recession because of some degree of saturation in public spending on the infrastructure. The change in attitude to private dwellings would support this view, as would also the fact that in September 1971, the government through the Labour Market Board, elected to release the Investment Funds for use in the big cities – a reversal of the declared policy of encouraging provincial development at the expense of the cities. But it can also be argued that Sweden was hit harder than most countries by the world oil crisis of 1973 and wished to preserve an uncommitted situation in order to make a fighting return in the export market. Certainly grants of up to £25m were introduced in March 1974 for investments related to the saving of energy. Attempts were also being made to control inflation through price freezes for food (with compensation to the farmers through the budget) and timber: to have put too great a demand on the resources of the country would have been to increase the risk of inflation and the consequent loss of competitiveness in world markets.

To illustrate the problems involved when trying to apply outside constraints on the economy, it should be mentioned that some of the actions initiated during the recession will not be completed until well on in 1975 by which time they might be contributing to the next boom period.

The events of this chapter are considered at length in order to demonstrate that it is difficult to established equilibrium conditions in the economy through government (or bureaucratic) control. Even in a small economy like Sweden, where organised labour and the employers are prepared to cooperate with each other and with the state, the controls do not act as speedily or effectively as might be expected. The events of 1970 to 1973 in Sweden also show the need for a flexible approach to apply first one and then another form of control or incentive to meet an ongoing problem. In a larger and more diverse economy, unaccustomed to a planning philosophy, it seems doubtful if it would be possible to repeat the achievements of Sweden. The need for caution in regarding state intervention as a panacea should be very apparent.

11 THE INVESTMENT SCENE

Levels of capital investment

The investment ratio for Sweden – the amount of money invested in the economy each year as a percentage of the Gross Domestic Product – has been in excess of 20 per cent since 1955, in contrast with a figure for the UK which has varied between 14.5 per cent and a maximum of 18.6 per cent in 1968. Over the same period, the tendency in the USA has been for the investment ratio to drift marginally downwards from 17.7 per cent in 1955 to 17.0 per cent in 1972: incidentally, the USA is the only major country in which a downward trend has occurred.

Since 1964, the investment ratio throughout the industrial world has been fairly steady around the values shown in column (3) of Table 11.1 with Japan having the largest fluctuation from year to year but always well in the lead. On this ranking, Sweden is fourth, but if the gross investment per capita is examined (column 1), Sweden is in the lead with £539. In fact the differences in gross investment per capita for the first five countries are not very large – the exception is the UK with only £239, well under half that of the leaders. With these figures much of the emphasis in this section will be on comparisons between Sweden and the UK.

In some respects, the position is not very different for investment in machinery and equipment (column 4). In the west, the leaders are West Germany and France in this instance, with Sweden slipping into third place and the UK again well behind the others.

In Sweden, by far the largest investments – 20.1 per cent of the total of £4,600m in 1972 – were involved in mining and manufacturing, about half of this being in the metal industries and engineering. Agriculture, forestry and fishing absorbed 4.5 per cent of the gross investment with the power sector of the economy taking a further 11.7 per cent.

The capacity to invest is partly determined by the resources available, of which the GDP (column 2) is a good measure, and partly by the policy or the will to invest, which can be assessed by the percentage of the GDP set aside each year for investment (column 3). On this basis, the USA (at 17 per cent) is showing the least inclination but is partially redeemed because the GDP is the highest in the table: on the reasoning that investment, or more correctly its twin, modernisation, raises prosperity, the position of the USA with the highest GDP will be challenged soon by Germany and possibly by Sweden also.

Table 11.1 Investment per capita in 1972* (percentage figures for column (4) based on averages for years 1967-71)

	Gross Investment £/capita	GDP £/capita	% of GDP invested (Investment Ratio)	Investment in machinery & equipment £/capita
	(1)	(2)	(3)	(4)
Sweden	539	2,450	22.0	204
W. Germany	523	1,988	26.3	234
France	475	1,807	26.3	212
Japan	460	1,321	34.8	–
USA	445	2,617	17.0	183
UK	239	1,314	18.2	123

This gives little consolation to the UK which is doubly poor, firstly because the GDP is the lowest, and secondly because investment is also low at 18.2 per cent. The only good point for the UK is that more of the gross investment is spent on machinery and equipment (51 per cent) than the other countries in the table.

It is, of course, easier for a rich and prosperous country to allocate a bigger portion of the GDP for investment without feeling the pinch. It might be argued that Japan, with an investment ratio in excess of 30 per cent for every year since 1960, has modernised at the expense of the real standard of living of the mass of the populace. This argument cannot be sustained in the long run, as Table 11.2 shows that continuing restraint has paid off because there has been a doubling of the GDP over a period of seven years. After allowing for the investment of £195 per head in 1965, Japan had only £442 left for consumer goods, government spending and so on: by 1972, the same figures had risen to £861 – a doubling of the standard of living. During the same

* The figures in this chapter have been converted from Reference 2 at 10 S. kr to the £ sterling and from Reference 16, April 1975 (Switzerland) which give a corresponding figure of $2.10 to the £.

period, the investment ratio in the UK was between 14.5 per cent and 18.6 per cent and over the seven years the GDP only rose by a miniscule 15 per cent.

Table 11.2 Growth of Gross Domestic Product (per capita)

	GDP in 1965	GDP in 1972	Growth over 7 years
USA	£2,078	£2,617	26%
Sweden	£1,975	£2,450	24%
W. Germany	£1,517	£1,988	31%
France	£1,265	£1,807	43%
UK	£1,143	£1,314	15%
Japan	£ 637	£1,321	107%

The remainder of this table indicates that although the growth rate of the GDP is broadly in line with both the investment ratio and the investment in plant and machinery, the ranking order in 1972 is unchanged, except that Japan has overtaken the UK. Thus the GDP (and hence the standard of living which in the final analysis can only be paid for out of the GDP) is rising more slowly in the UK than in the other countries, and a contributory reason is the lower rate of investment.

The antithesis of the UK is seen in Sweden where the government encourages investment through tax allowances, both for investment and for depreciation, and where capital is made available by means of the retroverse loans system of the National Pension Funds discussed in this chapter. Workers are interested in raising the efficiency of the workplace, redeployment of labour is made relatively easy and workers and management collaborate. When these incentives are lacking, investment can only be expected to be at a low level.

To be effective, investment needs to be discriminating. The value of the high investment in Germany and Sweden, for instance, could be dissipated in projects of doubtful value. In practice, both countries are particularly exercised to ensure that investment helps to create an efficient, streamlined industry. Special regard is also paid in both countries to investment in human resources to avoid overmanning by means of redeployment into more productive jobs. Personal satisfaction through participation in a good job well done also features as a practical issue of the industrial philosophy of both countries, but that is another story told in earlier chapters.

Figure 11.1 Mean annual investment in plant and machinery (£/capita) 1968-72

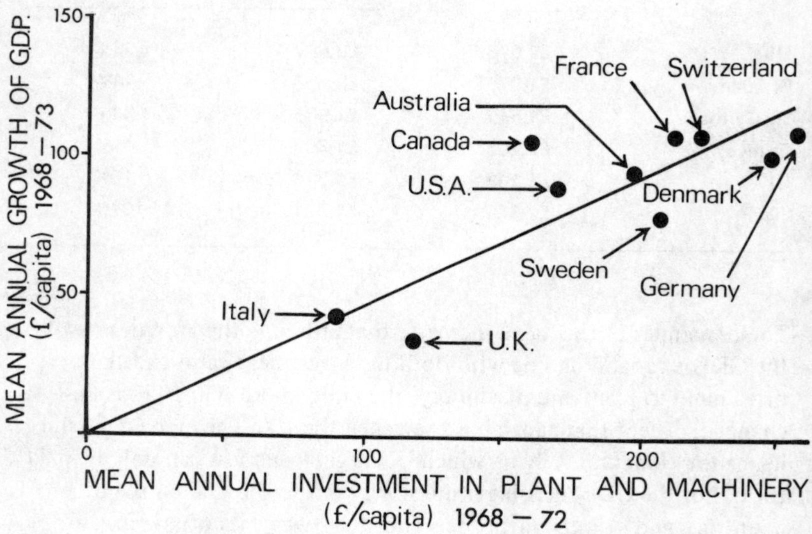

The effectiveness of investment in the different countries is further illustrated in Figure 11.1 which shows the conversion rate or the increase in GDP corresponding to investment in plant and machinery. The line, which might be described as the mean for a good relative performance, corresponds with an increase in the GDP of £47 per head per annum for an investment of £100 per head per annum. On this basis, Canada is showing the best return with remarkably little to choose between seven other industrial countries (including Sweden), both in the amount invested per head and in the effectiveness of the investment. The exception is the UK, with a poor return for investment and again the UK and Italy, with an investment per head which is markedly lower than the other countries (Japan is not included in this graph because separate figures are not published for investment in plant and equipment). A probable cause of Sweden showing a marginally poorer return in the GDP than some countries could well be the great emphasis placed in Sweden on improving the quality of the working environment. For instance in 1974, 20 per cent of all profits in excess of £10,000 had to be set aside to improve working conditions.

It would be unwise to attempt to read more than this into the figures because of the difficulty of making intercountry comparisons. Also the investment may not be the only reason for an increase in GDP as the graph might imply, and equally some investment might be used (possibly unwisely) for straight replacement of worn-out plant. The choice of axes, too, is not entirely satisfactory but can be defended on the grounds that the effects of investment will probably lag by about a year. Some of the investment in plant and equipment may also not directly contribute to the GDP – as for instance equipment in a hospital.

Public spending

Not all of the investment in any country will be in productive industry. In Japan, anxious to create a modernised economy as quickly as possible, the proportion so spent has been high. Other countries, of which Sweden is the most conspicuous, have, with the influence on the quality of life very much in mind, elected to invest more (greater than 40 per cent in Sweden in recent years) on improvements to the public and private service sectors of the economy. When the economy has required measures to combat unemployment, the opportunity has been taken to create a new standard of civic amenity – to pick one example, the enormous cruciform, totally enclosed and heated shopping precinct in the centre of Gothenburg is truly impressive. Yet it, too, has its critics because of the large amount of demolition that preceded the construction. But civic amenities of an exceptionally high order are to the benefit of the citizen. Spectacular traffic flyovers exist in the main conurbations and the main roads are well engineered and maintained (even though many miles of secondary roads are little better than dirt tracks).

The Swedish long term economic plan for 1972 to 1977 expects the growth in investment in the services side of the economy to be restricted to 1.7 per cent per annum in order that investment in the productive industries may grow at 4 per cent per annum. While this policy seems to be placing the emphasis in the right place, it also indicates some falling off in the growth of the gross investment which in the period 1951 to 1973 had increased at an average value of 4.7 per cent per annum – a value to be envied.

In the last few years, it sometimes seems as if the spending on capital projects by central and local government has been prodigious. The money spent each year per head of population on construction outwith houses in Sweden (£235) is exceeded only by Switzerland (£248) in the western world, with Canada (£228) the only other country to approach this figure. Yet at the same time, Sweden managed to invest £204 a year per head on machinery and equipment (Switzerland £197, Canada £193) compared with the £123 of the UK at the bottom of the league. So although it is essential that the rate of increase of government spending should bear a close relationship to the capacity of the country to pay (through the growth of the GDP), the failures of UK industry to invest cannot be blamed entirely on the absorption of the resources by government. Where then does the money go?

Private spending

When it comes to private consumption as a percentage of the GDP, the UK is well at the top of the list, just behind the USA, as column (1) in Table 11.3 shows. The first reaction is that this is because the GDP in the UK is so low that a high proportion of it needs to be spent on essentials; the rest of the table shows this reaction to be simply not true. Column (5), for instance, indicates that spending on food in the UK is much less than in the other countries and that in fact again with the USA, a high proportion of the GDP is spent on luxuries (column 2) such as tobacco and alcohol, betting and pools and travel – this last might be questioned as a luxury but as it happens, the percentage spent in travelling in the UK is the least in the table (presumably because distances are shorter). But once again, because the GDP of the UK is so low, in terms of the actual money spent on luxuries, the UK is at the bottom of the list with Germany (column 3).

Sweden is relatively lowly placed in the spending table although in money terms at £331 per head Sweden spends the most on food. It is remarkable that while Germany spends only the same amount on luxuries as on food, the residents of the USA and the UK succeed in spending twice as much on luxuries as on food. This suggests there are not unreasonable grounds for believing that, given the will, there is scope for a change in emphasis in the spending habits of the USA and the UK. Private savings, for instance, might become fashionable again if inflation can be controlled. A call to spend less on luxuries would probably not be well received but the proposal might be more acceptable if it is recognised it could be in the nature of a short term restraint leading to

Table 11.3 Private consumption in 1972 per capita

	% of GDP consumed privately	% of private consumption on luxuries	Luxury spending £	% of private consumption on food	Money spent on food £
	(1)	(2)	(3)	(4)	(5)
USA	63	47	775	18	297
UK	62	46	375	21	171
France	59	44	469	25	267
Sweden	54	39	516	25	331
W. Germany	54	30	322	30	322

still better conditions, as is happening in Japan.

The importance of personal saving to the economy can be surprisingly large – in Sweden, for instance, more than 7 per cent of the gross investment is financed out of private savings. As a socialist economy, the state has underwritten social security to a large extent. At one stage, the impression seems to have rooted in many minds that private savings were no longer necessary. Accordingly, consumption rose more rapidly than disposable income, so that by 1968 the percentage of disposable income saved had fallen from its previous level of 6 per cent in 1960 to a value of 2 per cent as illustrated in Figure 11.2. The growth of the recession from 1970 to 1973 and the well publicised steps taken to minimise unemployment seem to have greatly influenced the Swedes, for there were clear signs of a 'tightening of the belt'; consumption fell markedly with a consequent reduction in the import bill and private savings again became fashionable, rising gradually to the very high figure of 9.3 per cent of disposable income for 1974. Thus, if encouraged, private savings can make a significant contribution to the economy of the country.

Housing

House construction, and all that goes with it in the supply of services and components, consumed just over 20 per cent of the gross Swedish investment in 1972. At £125 per head, this is only exceeded by Switzerland (£156) and Germany (£151), while the UK can do no better than £45 per head.

Figure 11.2 Private savings in Sweden (reproduced by permission of Skandinaviska Enskilda Banken)

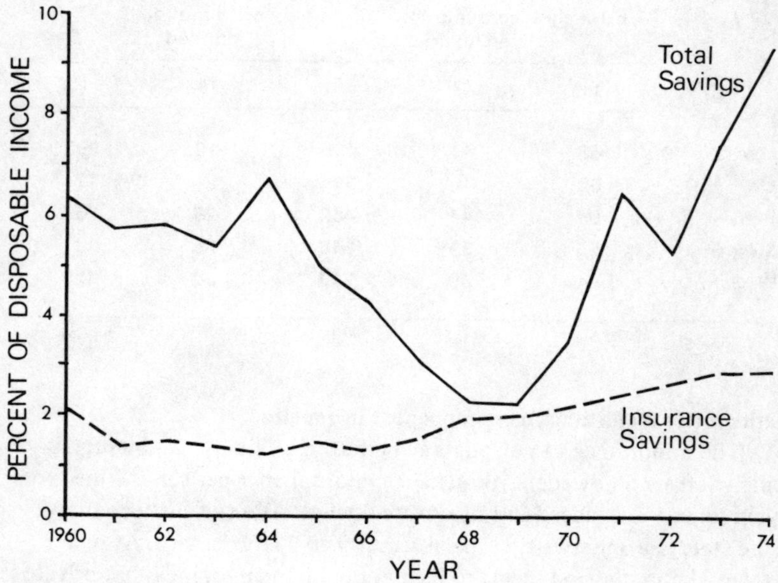

The housing story is an interesting comment on life in Sweden. In the sixteen years up to 1964, 0.8 million new dwellings were completed: this rate of progress did not satisfy the Riksdag who then embarked on a ten year programme to construct one million dwellings (that is, double the previous rate of building). This ambitious target, representing twice as many dwellings completed per 1,000 inhabitants as in the UK over the same years has just about been achieved but over the twenty-six years, 22 per cent of the dwellings were needed to replace houses which had been demolished or left to decay in the depopulated rural areas. The story then is very much of change, very often of families moving into flats in multiple dwelling premises but with a general raising of the standard of physical accommodation – in 1945, 44 per cent of the households were averaging more than two persons per room (excluding the kitchen and one other room) but by 1970, this figure had dropped to 16 per cent. In addition to the bare facts presented by the statistics, it should be mentioned that the standard of finish of fittings such as doors and plumbing installations is in general exceptionally good. But 19 per cent of the accommodation still consists of a single room, no doubt reflecting the tendency for young Swedes of both sexes to leave home at a relatively early age.

It is not surprising to hear that in socialist Sweden, rents were frozen in 1942. However, as interest rates and maintenance costs have risen, so have relaxations been allowed in the freeze, first for dwellings owned by the municipalities and by non-profit-making organisations, then for all property built since 1968, so that by 1974 only 35 to 40 per cent of rents of dwellings in multiple units have any form of control. By 1976, rent controls are expected to be abolished altogether (rent allowances exist for low income groups).

Many Swedes have always tried to preserve their country affinities through the ownership of a country hut to which they retreat in the summer, but over the years, as they became more prosperous, there has been evident an increasing desire for home ownership, preferably not in a multiple unit. The Riksdag contained this position through a system of building permits granted by the local authorities and start permits granted by the Labour Market Board so that less than a third of all new dwellings started were in 'small houses'. The policy was adopted in order that the average family could secure good accommodation at reasonable prices but by 1970, the first signs of saturation were appearing; small, privately financed houses were more generously permitted and by 1973 accounted for more than a half of the new dwellings started (which had dropped from its previous value of 100,000 per year to 80,000). At the same time, the government has extended mortgage facilities to private owners for houses built to certain standards. It may seem ironical that Sweden, the origin of so many sound socialist concepts, is creating a 'property owning democracy'! In fact, by the 1970s private ownership of private dwellings is in excess of 43 per cent.

The change in the pattern of housing has not passed unnoticed. Three state committees have been set up to investigate the causes more fully and to report on more equitable financing and tax relationships for single dwelling houses, which currently are at some slight advantage.

Foreign investment and foreign trade

The tendency is to think of Sweden as a self-contained and perhaps isolated community but by 1970, no less than 198 companies from overseas had elected to invest in Sweden, employing a total of 72,830 people and having total assets of £1,064m. (The definition of a foreign firm is that more than 25 per cent of the share capital is foreign owned.) In terms of the number of companies and employees, the USA is well ahead: the UK is second, while Germany, which is sometimes regarded as dominating the Swedish economy, is only a poor third.

Table 11.4 shows, however, that in terms of the ratio of sales value to assets, Holland presents the most profitable picture. The UK has the largest assets per employee but is well below the average in the sales/assets ratio. The mean sales value for all foreign companies has a high value of £18,000 per employee, a factor that is typical of the Swedish scene.

The total number of employees of foreign companies is increasing at about 7 per cent per annum but the sales value is increasing at 18 per cent per annum which seems a good omen for the future prosperity of these companies. In fact, the USA is the only country for which the sales value of the Swedish investment is rising at a lower annual rate than is the number of employees.

Table 11.4 Foreign investment in Sweden (1970)

	No. of companies	Mean no. of employees per company	Assets in £s per employee	Sales in £s per employee	Sales value/assets
	(1)	(2)	(3)	(4)	(5)
USA	67	404	16,200	17,800	1.10
UK	26	440	23,600	22,400	0.95
W. Germany	18	375	13,580	20,200	1.49
Holland	8	1050	11,680	19,400	1.66
Overall	198	368	14,500	18,100	1.25

The position has not been altogether one sided. While foreign firms have elected to invest in Sweden, Swedish firms have invested overseas, the capital involved being more or less the same in the nine years preceding 1969. From then on the overseas investments of Sweden have far exceeded the reverse process, including even the years 1970 and 1971 of the recession (which not unnaturally showed less overseas investment than the years immediately before and after). On a cumulative basis, which is the correct method of assessing the amount of investment, over the years 1960 to 1973, Sweden invested overseas a total of £1,240m compared with £730m foreign investment in Sweden. Of the overseas assets, the bulk (68.5 per cent) are in Europe, divided roughly two thirds in the Common Market countries (with only a very small amount in the UK) and the other third in the EFTA countries. About 15 per cent of the assets are in the developing countries and 11.5 per cent are in North America.

By 1970, the Swedish assets in manufacturing companies overseas (usually subsidiaries of a corresponding company in Sweden) amounted to £1,500m which is only 50 per cent more than the £1,060m of assets of foreign manufacturing companies in Sweden, yet the labour force was more than twice as great. Of these 183,000 people, the bulk – 135,000 – were employed in engineering of some kind, chemicals being the next biggest group with 25,000 employees. For the foreign companies in Sweden, the pattern is not very different, engineering employing 31,000 and chemicals 19,000 but with food manufacture employing 7,500. The pattern is clearly for the Swedish specialist companies of Volvo, Ericsson, ASEA for instance, to establish overseas subsidiaries for the part manufacture and assembly of their products with, to some extent, the same process happening in Sweden with foreign companies.

The residents of a densely populated area like the UK are frequently told that they work in a country that has to export in order to live, yet only 16 per cent of the Gross Domestic Product was exported in 1972 compared with the sparsely populated Sweden's 21 per cent. The UK exported only £210 of goods per head compared with £515 of exports per head for Sweden, the latter amounting in fact to about 40 per cent of the total industrial production, and this from a country 80 per cent self-sufficient in the production of food.

These figures need to be regarded in the context of the resources available. Sweden has abundant supplies of iron ore and timber so the preponderance of exports is based on these raw materials but generally with a high value added content – although there have been signs in recent years of the raw material content increasing slightly. Sweden has no fossil fuels so these have to be imported, together with certain food stuffs. There is also an import and export trade in machinery and instruments which is in approximate balance. In total, however, Swedish imports of goods consistently exceeded exports of goods right up to 1971 when the recession caused a marked diminution in demand. Since then, exports of goods have overtaken imports, so that by 1973 the values were exports £5,300m, imports £4,600m.

The earlier deficits in the balance of trade were made good by the income from Swedish shipping interests: in the latter half of the 1960s this balance was eroded by the increase in the number of Swedes holidaying abroad, a clear indication of the changing demands brought about by a rising standard of living. A further drain on the trade balance has been the decision of the Riksdag in 1968 to increase the aid to the developing countries in stages until it reaches 1 per cent of the Gross Domestic Product by 1975.

Table 11.5 Import-export trade for Sweden (1973) in £m per annum

	Imports	Exports
EEC	2560	2720
EFTA	843	1176
USA	305	330
Japan	102	69
Total	4630	5302

Table 11.5 indicates that more than half of Swedish foreign trade is with the Common Market (the EEC) of which Sweden is not a member. Of the individual countries of the world, the UK buys most of the Swedish exports at £780m per annum (imports to Sweden £575m), but Sweden imports most from Germany at £924m per annum (exports to Germany £545m).

The final point of relevance in this simple account of the balance of trade is that Sweden is unable completely to finance the modernisation of industry at the present scale, so a few of the big firms have recourse to borrowing money on the international market.

Source of funds for investment

The consumers of capital for the creation of physical assets can be classified under the main categories shown in the first four lines of Table 11.6. A certain amount of self-financing can be undertaken in each of these sectors from the gross savings, that is, the excess of income over expenditure. The table shows the distribution of self-financing in Sweden and the shortfalls. (The Investment Funds of an earlier chapter are included in the gross saving by the business sector.) In fact, the business sector is 65 per cent self-financing compared with

48 per cent of self-financing in the UK (by means of retained profits). Fortunately other aspects of the Swedish economy (in the next three lines of the table) show a gross saving with little or no commitment for investment so that overall the position is nearly in balance, leaving only 0.1 per cent of the Gross Domestic Product – a matter of £20m per annum – to be raised elsewhere.

Table 11.6 Mean annual investment and gross savings in Sweden for the years 1969 to 1972 expressed as a percentage of the Gross Domestic Product

	Investment	Gross savings	Shortfall in self-financing
The State	1.2	1.3	
Municipalities	4.8	4.0	0.8
Housing	4.9	1.5	3.4
Business	12.1	7.8	4.3
National Pension Funds		4.6	
Financial enterprises		2.2	
Households		1.5	
Totals	23.0	22.9	

One of the surprising features of the table is the relatively large size of private savings shown opposite the description of household savings. At 1.5 per cent of the GDP or £285m per annum, this is large enough to play a significant part in the Swedish economy. This figure may be a little suspect since it is a derived figure from the national accounts, being the residual between disposable income and consumption, but its order of magnitude is clear enough.

Disposable income, or the nett part of the income left after paying taxes and social security charges (which can be a credit for the low income groups), has been an area in which the influence of socialistic ideas is very evident. Social security 'transfers' paid by the state or municipalities or bureaucracies to households amounted to £3,000m in 1973, compared with the £5,000m paid by others in taxes and social security charges. There is thus a very considerable levelling in living standards brought about in this fashion apart from the comparatively narrow range of pay differentials discussed earlier. Moreover, the average income of a private entrepreneur is just under £3,000 per annum and as such is somewhat less than the wages of male industrial workers which will lie in the £3,000 to £3,400 band (1970 figures).

Taking an all round view of these figures, disposable income in 1973 rose by 11 per cent and is expected to increase by the same amount in 1974, much higher rises than in the previous twenty years, when the figure has been about 7.5 per cent per annum. No doubt this rise in disposable income would be very welcome but the Swedes reverted to their more characteristic love of discretion and security by increasing the level of savings as indicated earlier in this chapter.

Financial institutions

The Swedish banking system is a mix of privately owned commercial banks (with deposits of £6,300m out of total assets of £9,500m), a state owned central bank, a state owned savings bank (deposits of £4,000m) and a state owned post office bank (deposits of £2,500m). In 1974, three banks, owned equally by the state and private enterprise, were established to finance specific sectors of the economy; Företagskapital AB, for instance, was established to help with the financing of small to medium size firms. A much smaller state owned Investment Bank with an equity capital of £100m and with powers to borrow, has existed since 1967 to finance large and relatively risky industrial ventures, especially those involving the rationalisation of Swedish industry: by the end of 1973 this investment bank had advanced a total £160m. The investment spectrum is completed by the insurance companies which have capital resources totalling £4,100m but are subject to strict investment rules.

When the state owned Investment Bank was established in 1967, five important negative conditions were incorporated in the guidelines covering its operation. These restrictions will be mentioned and their implications discussed briefly.

Firstly, the Investment Bank should not compete with other financial institutions. This means that the bank cannot offer services to private investors or conduct other banking activities of a personal nature. The bank was expected mainly to serve two industrial extremes. On the one hand, major developments – in a new nuclear power station, for instance, or a new steelworks – because of their very size may have difficulty in raising the capital required. At the other extreme, the small new company might have difficulty in raising credit initially although, once started, such a company might be viable and indeed decidedly profitable. Table 11.7 shows how far these expectations have been realised: in 1974, there was a marked movement towards more transactions with small and medium size firms.

Table 11.7 Distribution of size of credits and guarantees made by Investment Bank and in force at December 1974

Size (in £m)	<0.1	0.1 to 1	1 to 2.5	2.5 to 5	>5
Number	100	143	35	59	21

In 1971, the terms of reference of the Investment Bank were extended to include export credits: by 1974, 31 per cent of the bank's total commitments of £360m were in this form.

Secondly, the Investment Bank should not grant subsidies. The corollary to this is that the bank should only help to finance ventures likely to be profitable and should then charge a rate of interest commensurate with the market conditions. In fact, because of the greater risk involved with some new projects, the bank has often charged between 1 and 1¾ per cent more than the market rate, but even so capital has been available at about 8 per cent, a lower rate than in many other countries in the same period: in the UK for instance, the interest charges have been in excess of 10 per cent. The bank itself borrows, largely from the National Pension Funds, as well as other market sources, so this helps to maintain interest rates at commercial levels.

Thirdly, during the initial build-up, the Investment Bank should not be expected to pay dividends to its sole shareholder – the state. This clause was inserted in recognition of the high risk involved in some schemes; it was deemed wiser for the bank to use such early profits as it earned to create a reserve against losses. Inevitably, the bank has been involved in a limited number of bankruptcies: in some of these, the loss has been written off. In other cases, the bank has taken over the firm for a limited period, in whole or in part, if the venture showed potential until such time as it could either be sold or stand on its own feet. In spite of these losses, the bank paid a dividend of £3.5m in the years 1972, 1973 and 1974: on an investment of £90m, this represents 3.9 per cent. The nett profit earned in 1974 was £4.1m which is 1.5 per cent on the gross assets of £275m. Such figures can only be regarded as very satisfactory in view of the function the bank discharges. The figures also illustrate the realism the Swedes bring to schemes devised in the first instance on theoretical grounds.

Fourthly, the Investment Bank should not operate as an instrument for government policy but should be an independent body. Some of the critics of the bank had feared it might be used, for instance, to foster unprofitable industries in an attempt to halt depopulation of the northern regions. A list of the companies and industries granted loans reveals no undue bias in this direction. The independence of the bank is ensured through its governing body of nine representing employers, unions, banking and government interests, uniting to make a success of an imaginative venture.

Finally, the maintenance of full employment should form no part of the considerations of the Investment Bank, *vis-à-vis* the creation of a streamlined, rationalised industry. Indirectly, the activities of the bank are expected to help employment because a competitive position will be achieved and one incidentally essential for the payment of high wages.

The articles of association for the Investment Bank were agreed on 22 June 1967, and the bank was in business on 1 July. By the end of 1968, it had a staff of six and had accepted 16 of the 113 applications made for loans. By the end of 1974, the staff had increased to thirty-one, still small for the money involved; 1974 saw a marked increase in the number of applications at a time when the rest of the world had not been outstandingly active in the investment area. The metal industry has accounted for most (37 per cent) of the loans, followed by timber, paper and pulp (21 per cent), chemical industry (11 per cent) and electric power (10 per cent). The Investment Bank is thus playing a significant role in the development of the modern industries of Sweden.

By tradition, many of the banks and credit houses are closely connected with particular sectors of the economy; sometimes they were even set up by these sectors, as is the case in agriculture. Many are interested in housing and building construction, and one is concerned with mortgages to assist in shipbuilding. The net effect of all these influences is that a relatively small amount of the new finance required by industry is coming from banks. After some fluctuations in earlier years, by 1972 the insurance companies and the National Pension Funds established their investments each with about 32 per cent of their resources supporting industrial investment, and it is from these sources that much of the new industrial finance is obtained. Since the National Pensions Funds are growing more quickly than any other financial resource, their influence on industrial development will become of increasing importance.

Some approximate calculations are justified to establish the order of magnitude of the effect of the Pension Funds. In 1972, some £1,600m was involved in the creation of new industrial physical resources. Assuming the same rate of self-financing as the rest of the business sector shown in Table 11.6, the following emerges:

	£m
Investment in industrial equipment	1,600
Assumed self-financing	1,040
To raise from external sources	560
Increase in industrial investment of Pension Funds	280
Balance to raise	£ 280m

In the past, the National Pension Funds have not been permitted to invest in share capital of industrial companies so the action has been indirect through the purchase of bonds or loans, usually of about five years duration, raised by other institutions. The guiding principle has been security of investment coupled with a reasonable rate of return – this has actually been about 6.7 per cent for the years 1971, 1972 and 1973, on total assets which in 1973 stood at £6,700m, a figure in excess of the deposits in all the commercial banks aggregated together.

The National Pension Funds

The organisation controlling the National Pension Funds occupies a position of unique importance in the Swedish economy by virtue of its influence in three distinct fields. Firstly, as has just been seen, it has considerable power in the investment area. Secondly, because of the completely transferable nature of the pension rights, the Funds have removed a fairly major obstacle to the mobility of labour in accordance with the varying requirements of modernisation. Thirdly, the Funds are playing a significant role in the continuing development of social justice.

There are two national pension schemes. The one, the Basic Pension Scheme started in 1914. The other, the Supplementary Pension Scheme came into operation in 1960. There are also minor complementary pension schemes to cover some employees in government or municipal service, or in the private sector: the complementary schemes will not be discussed further except to say they exist primarily to ensure that the salaried staff in earlier schemes will not be worse off than they would have been before the National Supplementary Scheme came into existence in 1960. Since the complementary schemes are largely contributory, they are regarded as beneficial in so far as they increase national saving.

The basic old age pension is available to all Swedish citizens resident in the country at the age of sixty-seven. It can be claimed on a reduced scale at age sixty-three or deferred to as late as seventy, when the benefits will be on an increased scale. Foreign nationals resident in Sweden can get benefits at the same rates, provided there is a reciprocal agreement between Sweden and the parent country.

The section of any community worst hit by inflation is normally the pensioners. With this in mind, Sweden has reduced the impact of inflation by tying the pension scheme to the 'base amount', a figure calculated from the consumer price index, the idea being to preserve a constant purchasing power. When the scheme was introduced in 1969 the base amount was £420, but this has risen to £900 for 1975.

All pensions are paid as multiples of the base amount. The single person basic pension is 90 per cent of the base amount. Married pensioners get 50 per cent more than this, and currently at the basic figure, receive about 28 per cent of the average earnings of an industrial worker.

About two thirds of the running costs of the Basic Scheme are borne by the government, the remaining third being derived from individual contributions which are levied at the rate of 5 per cent of that part of the income which is taxable up to a maximum contribution of £150 a year. The contributions are thus to some extent related to earnings, but the benefits of the basic scheme are independent of earnings.*

Disability and widows pensions as well as child allowances are payable under the Basic Scheme (and also under the Supplementary Scheme): moreover, rent allowances can be paid by the municipalities to cover the rental in cases of need. The Basic Scheme is thus reasonably comprehensive as far as it goes.

---

* In exchange for wage restraint, the workers contribution will be paid by the employers in 1975 as a result of legislation passed in the Riksdag.

Earnings related pension

It has been said of Sweden that the Basic Scheme provides the bread and butter, but you have to work for the jam of the Supplementary Pension which is earnings related and as such, caused bitter controversy before becoming a legal working arrangement in 1960. The formula used to arrive at the pension obtained from the National Supplementary Scheme is based on a points system. Only that part of the earned income lying between the base amount and 7.5 times the base amount is used for calculating the number of points earned in any year, one point being earned for each increment of base amount. Thus the maximum number of points that can be earned in a year is 6.5.

Points are recorded within the income tax system for every working year between the ages of sixteen and sixty-six but the pension is based on the average of the best fifteen years. The pension is then 60 per cent of the base amount multiplied by the average number of points earned. Thus at maximum, the National Supplementary Pension amounts to 6.5 × 60 per cent of the base amount = 3.9 × (base amount) compared with 0.9 × (base amount) obtained from the National Basic Pension.

Reducing the generalities to the particular, if the base amount in a given year is £900 (as it was in early 1975) this means that points are earned on incomes between £900 and £6,750 per annum – and the organisers of the Supplementary Fund say an increasing number of workers are exceeding this range. The maximum Supplementary Pension would then be £3,510 to which would be added the Basic Pension of £810, or £1,215 if married. That is a wage of £6,750 per annum earned a total pension of £4,275, or 70 per cent of the relevant earnings. The majority of people will not be at the maximum; taking a middle wage position of £3,200, the combined Basic and Supplementary Pension of the married person then amounts to £2,602, or 81 per cent of the wages – an even better 'buy'.

Qualifying for pension in Sweden

The rules state that to qualify for Supplementary Pension under the points system, a worker must have thirty years of point earning service. The points recording system has only been in operation since 1960 so that anyone born before 1924 could not possibly qualify: to reduce injustice for these people, the qualifying period has been relaxed to twenty years which would still exclude people born before 1914.

As the material prosperity of the country increased, it was believed to be only fair for the pensioners to share in this prosperity so the Riksdag passed a bill in 1969 to enable special supplementary benefits to be paid to pensioners who had only the Basic Pension or small amounts from the main Supplementary Scheme. These special payments increase the Basic Pension annually by 3 per cent until 1978, when the increase will be 30 per cent of the base figure for that year. A married pensioner could then receive 1.75 X (base amount) compared with the maximum earned pension under the combined Supplementary and Basic Schemes of 5.25 X (base amount).

An impression of the relative payments under the two schemes in 1970 can be seen in Table 11.8. In future years, the Supplementary Pension payments are expected to increase as more people qualify.

Table 11.8 Pension payments in 1970 (in m S. kr)

	Basic Pensions	Supplementary Pensions
Old age pensions	5,150	570
Disability pensions	1,070	347
Widows pensions and child allowances	600	243
Municipal rent allowance	840	
Total payments	7,660	1,160
Contributions received		6,100

Finances of the Pension Funds

The National Supplementary Pension Fund is derived entirely from payments made by the employers at rates determined by the Riksdag at five yearly intervals. In 1960, the rate was set at 3 per cent, to increase annually by 1 per cent until 1964 (when it was equal to 7 per cent), then to increase annually by ½ per cent until 1970 (equal to 10 per cent), and finally to increase annually by ¼ per cent until 1974 when it was 10¾ per cent. Originally a figure of 11 per cent had been specified for 1975, but late in 1974 this was amended to 10¾ per cent. This rate is payable on that part of the salary less than 7.5 times the base amount.

The size of the payments is thus very considerable and there has been appreciable debate as to who is actually paying for these charges. Initially the employers are paying, but it is suggested they pass this on in the form of increased charges for their products (where they can), in which case it is ultimately the domestic consumer who pays. Alternatively, the pension payment can be regarded as part of the wages, in which case it is the worker who is paying. Almost reluctantly, it appears, it is also conceded that since profit margins have decreased in recent years, the companies may actually be paying part of the contributions themselves.

Be that as it may, the size of the Fund has increased rapidly to £6,550m in 1973, and because of the very few qualifying for pensions so far, the interest earned on the capital has exceeded the combined administration charges and payments paid out in pensions. Not unnaturally, this has aroused the criticism on actuarial grounds that the contributions are too high, but in defence it is pointed out that by the year 2000 A.D. – by which time the Fund is expected to reach £76,000m – difficulty would otherwise be experienced in meeting the pensions due to the population bulge from the high birthrate of the 1940s.

During the protracted debate and repeated amendments made to the proposals over the years from 1947 that preceded the passing of the Act in 1959, several principles were developed to govern the organisation of the National Supplementary Fund. First of all, it was believed essential for the Fund to be of considerable size in order to compensate for the falling off in other forms of saving which was expected to occur – this accounts at any rate in part for the high rate of contributions. Secondly, the Fund must be administered in a totally independent way and the administration should invest the capital so as to obtain the maximum revenue consistent with monetary security. The Fund should not favour one group of borrowers at the expense of others, and lastly the creation of a new, large credit organisation with high administration charges should be avoided.

These several objectives have largely been achieved. The Supplementary Pension Fund is administered by a managing director aided by a staff of only six, the personal details being handled by the existing income tax and social security offices, any extra costs being recompensed by the Pension Fund. The first incumbent of the managing director's office was Lennart Dahlström, one of the characters of the Swedish scene, who retired at the end of 1973: his successor is Bo Jonas Sjönander, a former Under Secretary for the Ministry of Finance, who continues to administer the funds in very much the way a rather conservative and long established finance house would operate in other economies.

The Fund is divided into three main sub-funds (a fourth was launched in 1974) each representing a different sector of the Swedish economy and each with its own small governing body of nine members, nominated for a term of three years by the government, the employers and the unions. Each member has a named deputy. This then is a further area in which close collaboration takes place between all the interested parties in a constructive atmosphere so typical of Sweden and such an object lesson to the rest of the world.

Details of Pension Funds

The A fund consists of contributions made by the public sector, that is primarily by the government and local authorities: in 1973 it amounted to £1,900m. The money in this fund can only be invested in three ways, namely, by deposits in the National Central Bank of Sweden, in bonds and debentures quoted on the Stock Exchange or in loans to local authorities: 67 per cent of this fund is in the last category.

The B fund consists of contributions made by medium and large private companies employing twenty or more people. At £3,400m it is the largest of the four funds. In addition to the three investment possibilities of the A fund, this fund can also invest in the credit institutions provided this amount is within the framework of the 'retroverse loan' system. Under this system, contributors may borrow back 50 per cent of their own contributions provided the security is sound, the credit institutions acting as intermediaries with the normal responsibility of investigating the conditions of a loan before it is raised. (Before any loan can be raised it has also to be approved by the National Central Bank). Only 10 per cent of the fund is absorbed by retroverse loans with another 26 per cent invested in other industrial companies.

The C fund is made up of contributions from the small companies employing less than twenty people and the self-employed who must also belong to the Pension Fund. The assets of this fund are surprisingly large considering its constitution at £1,200m; the scope for investment is the same as the B fund so that it is again surprising to find the retroverse loans very small at 0.3 per cent, but the combined agricultural and other industrial company investments stand at 37 per cent.

The governing board of the C fund reflects its slightly different nature, the government nominating the chairman, the unions' four members, the small employers' two members and private contributors the final two members; of the two representatives of the private contributors, one is a farmer and former Vice President of the Federation of Swedish Farmers (a large marketing cooperative), and the other is a merchant and President of the Swedish Retail Federation. An indication of the serious view taken of the Supplementary Pension Funds can be obtained from a list of the members and their deputies of the three governing boards who undoubtedly consist of the leaders in their own fields of activity, embracing three members of the Riksdag (all nominated by employers' organisations, incidentally), three governors of provinces, together with presidents or secretary generals of the appropriate associations of unions or employers.

The fourth fund was established in January 1974 in order to invest in the ordinary share capital of selected companies, to the extent possibly of a total investment of £500m: for the years 1974 and 1975, £50m has been allocated to the fourth fund from the other three funds, in proportion to their size. The pressure came from the unions in 1972 who believed the funds should be in a position to benefit more completely from the growth of industry; this is not regarded as the back door to nationalisation, but is simply a desire to profit from the good points of private enterprise.

The system works through the managing director tabling firm proposals for investment eight times a year for discussion in principle by the various boards. Maximum yield is not the only criterion by which the investments will be judged. There is a desire to spread the influence of the funds throughout the economy and to this end a purchase, sometimes small, sometimes large, is made if possible of every new issue of bonds. Other things being equal, projects likely to increase exports or to lead to improved modernisation find favour, as do also labour intensive schemes provided the latter are not at the expense of modernisation. Survival of a firm is not in itself a sufficient criterion for the funds to invest: there must also exist good reasons to suppose the firm will be profitable and yield an adequate return.

In order to maintain a high yield, the liquidity of the funds is kept as low as possible. Yet the first requirement is that there must be sufficient cash available tp pay the pensions on the tenth day of the month. The main contributions are received from the employers on the twenty-fourth of the month, some months with bigger intakes than others since some payments are only made six times a year, so a constant watch is kept and some juggling is required with the liquidity of the funds.

Throughout the activities of the Supplementary Pension Fund, two recurring themes are apparent. The provision of a nationwide, guaranteed pension with an assured purchasing power and based on the occupational activities of the recipient is regarded as a prime social necessity. Having caused a certain amount of disincentive to private saving for this reason, and also having drained off a certain amount of investment capital through the large contributions from the employers, the government is deeply conscious of the need to maintain investment on as wide a scale as possible. It would appear success is being achieved on both counts: this bold and significant social experiment seems to be working.

Financial criteria

For investments of the type just considered in which a financial institution of some kind is concerned with investing its money through fixed interest bonds, debentures or even in the purchase of share capital of another organisation, the usual figure adopted as principal criterion is the yield or percentage return on capital. For the National Pension Fund, this has been around 6.7 per cent for several years with no stock appreciation. Over the same period, the mean yield for common stock purchased on the Swedish Stock Exchange has been about 4 per cent, and for engineering companies the average was as low as 2.32 per cent. By world standards these are low yields but have not prevented Swedish industry from investing heavily in modernisation (a cynic might comment that perhaps this is why the yields are low!). At least one Swedish economist has expressed the view that shareholders in the UK have been too greedy in the matter of dividends which take the money out of the firm.

There are signs, however, that some of the Swedish companies are not satisfied that the present (or immediate past) rate of return is sufficient to maintain the viability of the business. In the producing sectors of the economy, the rate of return on total capital employed is the corresponding measure: while the published accounts of the company will be based on the maximum depreciation of equipment permitted for tax purposes, more realistic periods for depreciation are usually employed for internal calculations.

On this basis, Sydkraft – the firm responsible for the generation, transmission and distribution of electrical energy in much of southern Sweden – show that in some recent years the return on total capital has been between 2 and 3 per cent. To rectify this position, tariff charges were increased in 1973 (apart from the automatic increase tied to the price of oil) so that the return on total capital increased to

6 per cent. In order to remain viable, the company consider they require a net yield in future of double this amount, and their forward projections all assume this will be forthcoming. In the short term, Sydkraft have a programme of work in hand directed towards increasing tariffs in line with real costs: this work involves the computer recording and analyses of loads, so that short term peaks can be related to transmission costs and long term demand related to equipment costs more especially in generation. As a matter of interest, part of the Sydkraft difficulty is due to the fact that although about 40 per cent of their generation is in hydro-electric stations, the scope for further expansion of capacity in this area is very limited.

In a general survey, a report published by the National Pension Fund mentions with concern the diminishing profit margins of industry and thus reinforces the opinions expressed by Gränges, the fourth largest company in Sweden engaged in a diverse series of operations in mining and heavy engineering. The return on total capital for Gränges has been about 5 per cent (3.5 per cent in 1972).

> '. . . compared with other Swedish firms Gränges must be regarded as fairly close to the average . . . if we take into consideration the kind of yield that would be needed, with interest rates at current levels, to attract additional venture capital, then . . . the level of yield . . . simply will not do in the long run. Accordingly, Gränges and other major Swedish companies, particularly in exports, feel that the yield on their capital must eventually be raised and are addressing themselves vigorously to this.'

This passage* has been quoted at length to emphasise that changes may well appear on the Swedish industrial scene in the near future.

The one conspicuous exception to the trend of low yields for producing companies is Volvo where the return on total capital in 1972 was as high as 12.9 per cent.

The common factor throughout Sweden in assessing investment is therefore the use of the percentage yield on capital, both for share capital and total capital, with considerable emphasis on the latter. A minor variation also employed when assessing whether physically to go ahead with a new project is the pay-off period – that is, the cost of the venture divided by the annual profit. A few companies also

---

* Page 42 of Reference 10. Gränges increased the return on working capital to 10.6 per cent in 1973.

employed the net present value concept and Volvo employed the internal rate of return as a method of discounting inflation when deciding between projects competing for the same, limited available capital. In all of this, of course, the position is not different from other countries.

Computer models

Various computer models have been proposed, notably in the UK and elsewhere, to assist in the determination of an optimum (or even a balanced) portfolio of capital investments: there appeared to be no evidence that such models were used in Sweden. Some of these models are based on the techniques of linear programming or dynamic programming: while the major companies at any rate were well aware of the scope and nature of these techniques, it is perhaps disappointing to find that in Sweden, the home of quantification for many generations, these techniques were not employed in the choice of capital ventures. On the other hand, Gränges Stal, the steelmaking subsidiary of the main company, used linear programming to decide the least profitable orders which would not be accepted for production in the limited capacity of their plate mill – a neat twist on a conventional technique.

However, some computer models do exist in the financial field. Volvo, for instance, use a computer to prepare the final company projections which are a composite of the hundreds of cost centres operated in Sweden and overseas: in this case, the detailed work is done in depth at the cost centres and the computer undertakes the task of assembling the data, and then explores, on demand from the planning division, the influence of different financial factors.

Sydkraft employ a computer based corporate planning model to assist in their long term projections. In a corporate model, many – ideally all – aspects of the company are quantified and brought together so that simultaneous consideration is given to the load, the equipment, the manpower and training that manpower will require, costs, profits, depreciation and methods of financing. The output from the model is designed to highlight deficiencies or excesses in each of the vital areas year by year. Kockums claim to have a comprehensive corporate planning model live in late 1974.

Interesting though the Volvo and Sydkraft models are, they can be matched with parallel developments in other economies, although admittedly not on a widespread base.

Liquidity and solidity

Liquidity is a quantity which is watched very closely throughout Sweden. The aim, obviously, is to have sufficient cash in hand to meet the outgoings but equally, never to have an excess of cash that could be better used in an investment. The concern of the National Pension Fund has already been mentioned, that the liquidity is sufficiently high to meet the immediate demands of the monthly pensions, but never so high that investment is sacrificed.

Gränges has learnt the hard way. In the 1920s, the company worked on a relatively large amount of borrowed capital and a small liquidity reserve: during the economic troubles of the 1930s, the company's very existence was in danger. At a later stage, the company's share of LKAB, the iron ore mines in the far north, was bought out by the government with the result that for a period, this company had an embarrassing surplus of cash. The company now endeavours to strike a golden mean with the liquidity not too low and not so high that development potential suffers. It is claimed that the optimum point is gauged on the basis of systematic calculations.

Gränges is also concerned to utilise its borrowing powers to the fullest extent on the principle that failure to do so means failure to achieve development potential. This policy, too, can bring its own problems. Throughout Sweden there is concern to see that the 'solidity' – the ratio of the equity or own capital to the total capital employed in the firm – does not get out of control. In many companies the solidity is of the order of 30 per cent: a lower figure than this would be most unwelcome. The fear is that if the total capital contains a large element borrowed at fixed and often high interest rates, in times of low profitability the company would have difficulty in paying the interest to the prejudice of other activities and even in the extreme, to the survival of the company. For these reasons then, both liquidity and solidity are major factors in the life of the financial division of the Swedish company: it is not pretended these factors are ignored in other economies but it is doubted if they feature so largely in normal times.

Decison theory

Management science theory has developed a technique known as decision tree analysis which is regarded as a suitable means of improving decisions in the investment area. In its simplest form it is largely descriptive yet it is useful in identifying the alternative courses of action available and their possible outcome. Suppose a company is

Figure 11.3 Example of decision tree

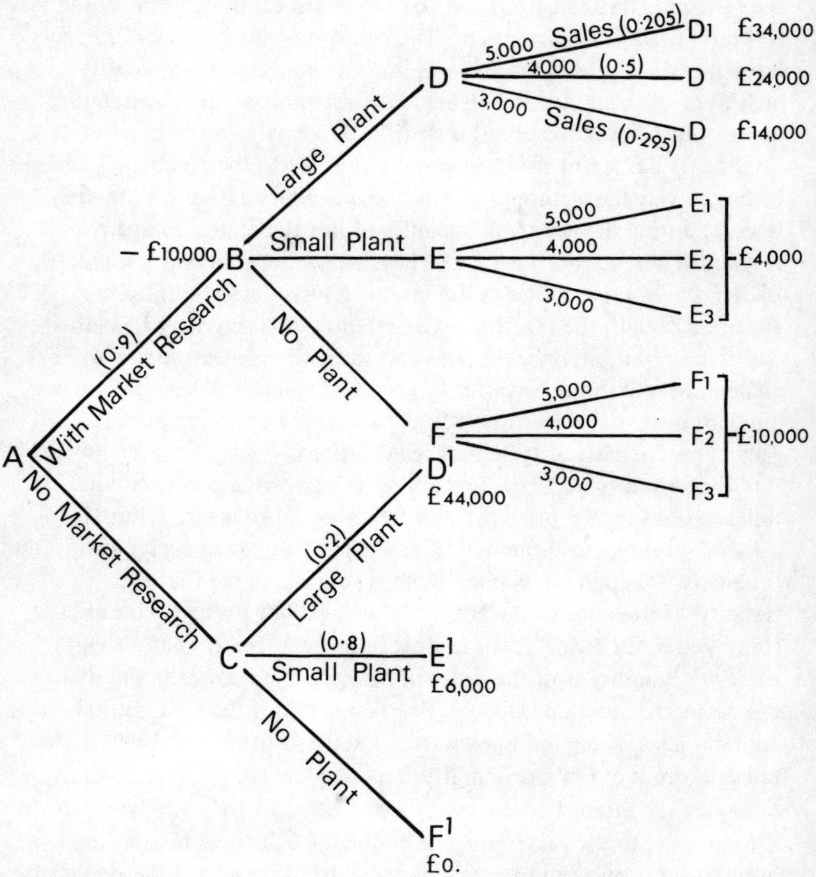

Expected Monetary Value in first year for no Market Research = (0·2) × £44,000 + (0·8) × £6,000 etc.

= £8,800 + £4,800 etc.

= £13,600 etc.

examining the potential profitability of building a factory to produce a new type of refrigerator. Eventually, one decision which ought to come up for consideration is whether or not to undertake a simple form of market research costing say £10,000 to ascertain the potential demand for their new product. The present position is represented in Figure 11.3 as at A. The decision in favour of market research is shown at B, while that for no market research is at C.

Suppose further that two alternative plants or processes are possible, the one at D being highly mechanised with a potential throughput of 5,000 models or units a year, each showing a clear profit of £10, above a breakeven minimum of 600 models a year. The alternative at E is a less sophisticated plant with a maximum capacity of 400 models per year, each unit showing a profit of £15. A third possibility shown at F, is to abandon the project after the market research.

The profitability is clearly influenced by the decision route that is taken. By the route A B F, the result is a loss of £10,000 because of the cost of the market research. By the route A B E at best the first year will show a loss of £4,000 but there will be an annual profit thereafter, provided sales materialise. The route A B D has a potential maximum profit in the first year of £34,000. It is also possible to go ahead with either of the plants without the market research, in which case the position is at F^1 E^1 and D^1 with maximum possible profits in the first year of 0, £6,000 and £44,000 respectively.

The major Swedish companies are well aware of this technique and use it at this level of sophistication in most developments involving capital expenditure. At this level, the technique is used first to clarify the issues in the mind of the investigator and then to expose or explain the alternatives to others involved in the decision making process. It is, of course, a comparatively rare situation for the investigation to be concerned with a brand new product: equally, market research may not form part of the decision tree, but the process can be appreciated from this description of a simple situation.

The next stage in the life of the illustration will depend on what people believe the likely outcome will be. Salesmen and managers in touch with the market will have opinions which, without the support of market research, will be subjective but none the less may be the best information available. Suppose that it is agreed collectively there is only a 20 per cent chance of achieving the maximum sales of position D^1 but an 80 per cent chance of achieving the sales of position E^1. These probabilities are then marked on the decision tree (in brackets) together with the subjective probability of 90 per cent that the market research would provide reliable information, but at three different sales levels of 5,000, 4,000 and 3,000 models a year. These figures are shown on the decision tree which is then expressing in graphical form the best known information at this stage. (The story has been simplified by omitting reference to the conditional probability that the market forecast will be achieved.)

The major companies in Sweden are well aware also of this stage of decision tree analysis and at least two practice this whenever it is thought the probabilities would yield helpful information – around which discussion could occur.

Even with this very simple example, the best decision is not immediately obvious at this stage. The next step according to decision theory is to evaluate a pay-off function obtained by summing the products of the probabilities and the profits of the system. Although the answer so obtained is called the expected monetary value, in practice this never appears in money as an outcome of the decision: the artificial nature of the function is held by some to be one of the weaknesses of decision theory and militates against its wider adoption. In fact, none of the Swedish companies appear to be going this far in the use of decision theory in the investment area. Another reason for the lack of enthusiasm possibly is that in a real life situation many other factors not included in Figure 11.3, such as the availability of manpower and money, and company policy, also influence events.

Conclusion

The Swedes have no magic formula for success in the investment area: they are no further advanced in the use of quantified management techniques than their opposite numbers in other countries. But they do work very hard at success. They have created a modern and efficient industry through hard but discriminating effort, coupled with a clear recognition of the importance of investment in modernisation. One of the keys to this success has been the appreciation of the relevance of the three requirements for successful modernisation discussed in chapter three: these are so fundamental that they will bear repeating here. First the idea or concept must be studied in depth to ensure its correctness. Then the money must be available, and finally, the climate must be suitable for the introduction of the concept. The Swedes work diligently to secure the right industrial climate through collaboration and experimentation with various forms of work organisation. Collaboration and a willingness to work is apparent on all sides. The success of modern Sweden is closely associated with the hard work undertaken to earn success. And once started, success breeds success.

Note

Part of this chapter will appear in the O. R. Quarterly under the title 'Can OR learn from Sweden?'.

12 THE WAY AHEAD

Background considerations

The way ahead for Sweden has its uncertainties. 1974 was a difficult year in which the planning resources of the country were strained in a successful attempt to maintain the twin policies of full employment and a balanced economy. Professional people view with increasing disquiet the falling off in their relative standard of life. Employers too are concerned that the pressures of an egalitarian doctrine can leave industry with insufficient skilled workers among the blue collar unions to continue to exploit the high standard of precision products upon which the prosperity of the Swedish economy largely depends.

Recognising the growth of a new challenge to existing values, the Swedes followed their traditional line of approach by appointing a working party, chaired in this case by a member of the cabinet, Mrs Alva Myrdal. The group was appointed as early as 1971 to examine the long term attitudes and changes necessary to preserve, among other factors, the balance between increasing demands for material prosperity and world ecology. A principal concern was to ascertain if a small country like Sweden could continue to control its own destiny in the face of powerful outside influences. Unlike the other consultative bodies discussed in this book, the six members of this working party were all academics distinguished for their researches into economic and social problems. The first report made in 1972 is not unnaturally coloured by the experience of the group in that there is a strong emphasis on the need to establish satisfactory data bases on which objective assessments can be made.

It is a just comment on the Swedish approach to objectivity in public life that the Prime Minister, Olof Palme, when setting up the working party thought fit to refer to the dangers of 'one-sided views of the future'. The working party supported this view particularly in regard to the inherent dangers arising if decisions on the global scale were left in the hands of an elite bureaucracy maintained by and therefore watching the interests of either multinational companies or military agencies. The need then is for accurate information, widely disseminated in an understandable form so that the processes of democracy can function.

It is a further interesting comment on the Swedish approach that although this very distinguished working party had substantial ideas on many issues, the first main recommendation was that the report should be circulated among interested parties for informed comment. The feedback would then be analysed by a new secretariat, attached to the cabinet office, which the report recommended should be established for future studies. Another recommendation was that a series of symposia should be organised around certain concepts developed in the report so that there should be a full and free exchange of views. The working party concentrated on the function and content of long term studies rather than on the organisation through which the studies would be financed and controlled: in other words, the function should decide the institutional framework and not the other way round. The committee recommended that after the discussions had been analysed, the new secretariat should have the task of devising the organisation. All four recommendations have been implemented and a budget allocation of £0.4m has been made for the financial year 1974-5.

The democratic influence on decisions arising out of long term planning studies is believed to be particularly important because the future of unborn generations may be under discussion. There is a danger of some predictions becoming self-fulfilling if only one set of conditions is presented for discussion: hence model building in which the outcome of alternative actions can be explored in sufficient detail to yield comparative results must feature largely in such studies of the future. The future is inevitably uncertain, so the studies should also attempt to estimate, even if only subjectively, the degree of uncertainty inherent in any set of solutions. Any major model of the future built within the confines of a single intellectual discipline is almost sure to be inadequate if only because it will fail to identify all the constraints: hence an interdisciplinary approach to model building is advocated. Sweden does not possess many people working under the banner of operational research, yet the long term studies of the future contain all the characteristics of good operational research if it is regarded not so much as a set of techniques but as a method of tackling problems.

An interesting suggestion for broadening the debate has been made. The classical method of approaching a problem in Sweden has been through a commission of enquiry appointed by the government. The work of such a body is usually thorough, being supported by an enormous battery of statistical analyses, and accordingly it is so costly that it is rare for more than one alternative to be explored. The suggestion is that for each 'heavyweight' investigation, there should be at least one less costly survey of the other choices carried out by independent workers. This should help to make the remiss system – the consultation with interested parties – more lively and probably more valuable.

While not unmindful of the work of Jay W. Forrester and the Club of Rome that led to the 'doomsday' predictions, nor of the more optimistic technocratic work of Kahn at the Hudson Institute, Sweden believes it is a special case for comprehensive modelling because it is a small country with restricted resources and perhaps even more because it has evolved a set of social values at variance with the material interests of those global models. Swedish interests are more allied to the modelling work of the European Cultural Foundation centred on Amsterdam but with international projects in various countries, of which Sweden has acted as a test bed for some educational ideas. Underlying this trend is the growing belief in Sweden that the Gross Domestic Product is not the only measure of the success of the economy. Although a high value of the GDP is an essential first step in the development of a socially conscious environment, it ignores other factors that affect the quality of life. The modelling work should therefore be extended to embrace factors such as those discussed in this chapter.

State intervention

The first and perhaps most obvious manifestation of the changing values is expected to appear in the area of public planning. So far public planning has tended to be fragmented, the larger municipalities undertaking their own, often major and frequently impressive, developments without sufficient research into either the long term needs of the community or the integration of the developments on a national scale. This is expected to change. Central planning is expected to play a far greater role in the future. Research into the effect of telecommunications may reverse the policy of concentrating the population into large conurbations, although this also involves major examinations of the transport system of the country in which alternatives are examined with a full appreciation of their significance. To some extent the government would welcome such a change so intervention from the centre in planning procedures may take place for political as well as fundamental reasons.

The main implication behond these changes is that more attention needs to be paid to the needs of the individual as a human being. The indicators of material prosperity should be augmented by measurements developed in perceptive psychology to test the reaction of the individual to the environment in which he lives: planned experiments on the environment then follow naturally.

Among the factors to be varied will undoubtedly be the amount of external stimulation. It is widely believed that in private life many people living in large conurbations are overstimulated from many directions by too much noise, too much information from the mass media and too many people in the form of anonymous crowds. In contrast, the working life of many suffers from the understimulation arising from monotonous, dead end jobs of a repetitive nature. The one does not necessarily compensate for the other. The experiments in working groups spring from a recognition of this problem and the desire to find a solution. But in fact the working groups are analysed from many points of view. Apart from stimulation, it is believed participation in an effective group gives rise to a self-esteem which has a distinct bearing on the physical as well as the mental health of the worker. A second factor has been mentioned earlier – the effect that the joy or satisfaction in working has on economic results with fewer defects, less absenteeism and less labour turnover. There is also an ideological element involved which can be important to the worker. Finally, the involvement of the worker can lead to suggestions which can alter the working environment.

Important as they are, the working groups are seen as only part of the attack on a wider problem, namely how to improve the quality of life in a modern state which has already made sure the basic physical needs of man have been satisfied. The welfare state in Sweden already makes considerable provision in the shape of hospitals and other medical care. But, some researchers are asking, is this enough and is it going in the right direction? There is obvious scope for development in the fields of preventive medicine and rehabilitation. Many would be less happy with 'the new potentials for bringing intentional influence to bear upon man's most fundamental constituents: the brain and the germ plasm'. True this phrase is used* in connection with mental diseases where the 'direct chemical-biological manipulation of the central nervous system' could be used advantageously, or knowledge of genetic infection might be used selectively. The Swedes acknowledge the ethical implications of this work, but a horrifying picture of state intervention in malevolent hands is difficult to avoid.

Experiments with animals have demonstrated the importance of the environment in the early years after birth on the ultimate development of the adult: in some cases, irreversible damage was done by malnutrition. The converse is the importance of providing the correct

* Page 100 of Reference 76.

conditions during the early life of the child. More information is needed in this area, but the state is already exercised to ensure that early conditions are clinically and nutritionally correct. Further action of the welfare state on these lines seems inevitable. This represents one of the dilemmas of the situation. Concern is expressed for the rights of the individual. Concern is also expressed to ensure the individual does the right things – both the things and the rightness being decided for him, objectively and scientifically, but none the less for him and not by him. The state has become *le grand patron* in every sense.

Safeguards for the individual

Awareness of the dangers of state intervention has led the Swedes to speculate about the democratic process. Traditional democracy in the western world has been based on the exercise of a free vote through a secret ballot. In the past, it has usually been fairly easy to identify the issues involved and the man in the street likes to think these were explained to him in such a way that he could appreciate their significance. Intellectual cynics may say the man in the street was also misinformed but in an age of rapidly changing technology and one in which more subtle values are being introduced, it is less easy to keep the average man informed. Moreover, man himself is not really adapted to accept rapid change: it usually takes a generation for radically different conditions to be fully accepted. So there is a danger that in the interests of speed and efficiency, the democratic process may be short-circuited.

The practice has developed in Sweden of consulting with many organisations before legislation is passed. This has merits in that faulty or inadequate laws can be corrected before reaching the statute book, and having been passed, the legislation has every chance of a favourable reception. But the system undoubtedly lends itself to lobbying by pressure groups. The adoption of comprehensive state planning creates a new and powerful pressure group in a uniquely strong position – that derived from specialist knowledge. Bureaucracies have usually been able to achieve similarly favourable stances, but the effect of pressure can be particularly acute in modern conditions.

Acknowledging the problems, discerning people have advanced pleas for fundamental research into the methods by which public opinion can be moulded and for two diametrically opposed motives. The one is so that the dangers can be recognised and highlighted. The other, strangely often held by the same people, is so that the influencing or moulding of public opinion can be made more effective. It is believed that the research should also embrace the capabilities and willingness of the voter to comprehend difficult or obscure problems. At present the way ahead is believed to be through the provision of more frank and intrinsically accurate information.

The rate of technical innovation is all too apparent. The mechanism of social innovation, by which is meant the speed or kind of reaction to changes (often brought about by technical innovation), is not properly understood: such evidence as there is suggests the rate of social innovation is lagging far behind technical innovation, and in fact is barely changing. Yet this is the root cause of the political dilemma – how can the process of replacing one thought pattern by another be accelerated? Education helps to a limited extent. Without a solution, state planning raises many threats for the individual of which he is probably blissfully unaware.

Of the mass media, television is regarded as offering the most potential for the dissemination of the accurate information required for the survival of democracy in the planning utopia of the future. It also offers, however, the possibility of biased and often glamourised presentation of issues. A positive change is expected in the coverage of political news by Swedish television so that a deliberate attempt is made to present major problems to the electorate, not just at election time, but on a reasonably continuing basis. It is important that alternative solutions should be presented with equal clarity and impartiality. This may make for dull TV but it is believed to be an essential step to prevent the domination of the state by a planning elite.

Great care is needed to ensure that broadcasting remains unbiased otherwise the medium (or the party controlling it) would be guilty of trying to brainwash the community. Experiments carried out in Sweden have shown that in the short term, television has less effect on the moulding of people's opinions and actions than would be expected. Rather dangerously it has been suggested that behavioural science should carry out more research to ascertain the mechanism by which people can discard the trivia that characterises so much of TV entertainment in order to retain information on the planning or political problems of the day. It is not certain how far the cumulative effect of information (as opposed to propaganda) influences long term judgement but it is believed television is more effective in this respect than in the short term. The Swedes may be right or wrong in the conclusions they draw, but they cannot be accused of not facing up to one of the pressing problems of the age – information provision.

It is also believed that greater attempts should be made to convert TV into less of a one way transmission of views by changing the nature of the presentation so that a steady procession of accurate information can enable the viewer to build his own quantitative background. Against this background, he can then ask the question 'how does this affect me?': he can even be helped in the answer by phone-in discussion, study groups and so on. Without this kind of process the Swedes fear for democracy. Their normal consultative processes in labour relations might also fall into disrepair if the planners were to take over.

The other dangerous aspect of mass information arises from the processing of data banks. In Sweden, because of the pervasive influence of the social services, in preventive medicine for instance, and because of the personal information on education, training, intelligence and even attitude tests compiled on behalf of the Labour Market Board, an unusually large amount of personal information is on file. When this is manipulated to obtain anonymous trend data, the use of data banks can be justified without difficulty. When the data banks are utilised to obtain information about an individual, the position is different. Being aware of the potential abuse for commercial reasons or simply as an invasion of personal privacy, the Riksdag passed a Data Act as early as May 1973.

Under the act, a data inspection board is established consisting of a chairman and eight other members with a supporting staff. The board has wide powers to visit automatic data processing premises, and if it so wishes, to supervise the actual processing to ensure that information does not fall into the wrong hands. Anyone can start a file or data bank of personal details but must apply to the board for permission stating the personal details to be recorded on the file and the purpose for which the file is to be used. The board may refuse permission or issue instructions on how the file can be used, the aim being to avoid invasion of individual privacy. Significantly, none of the provisions of the act apply to files established by the government.

Details of convictions under the criminal or temperance laws of the country, or detention under mentally retarded acts are not permitted to be recorded on the files. As a further protection of the individual, if so requested the keeper of the file must disclose free of charge the full entry to the individual: if the entry is in error or incomplete in such a way that may be prejudicial to the individual, the keeper of the file must correct the entry, make known the correction to whomsoever has received the previous information, and is liable to prosecution for compensation. Religious or political views may not be recorded except in the case of associations wishing to keep a record of their own members. Failure to comply with any of the above renders the keeper of the file liable to a fine or to imprisonment for one year – a great inducement to accuracy.

Furthermore, if an unauthorised person alters or obliterates a data file, that person on conviction by the board is liable to a fine or a period of imprisonment of up to two years. Although there is far less use of data banks for statistical analysis in other countries (because very often the quality of the information is just not good enough for the analysis to be of value), many people would regard this piece of legislation as timely and a worthwhile protection of individual rights. The use of credit rating through a data bank, for instance, does seem reasonable ground for misgiving: the Swedes have dealt neatly with this problem and in this area at least, the way ahead seems well prepared.

State planning

Conscious since the 1940s of the conflict between the demands of industry and a desire to preserve the amenities of the countryside, Sweden has followed a policy of protecting environments of outstanding interest for outdoor life. This policy from its very nature is negative, specifying what can not be done. In the mid-1960s a distinct change of emphasis led to a more positive approach, the first real manifestation of which was the formation of an expert group to coordinate the collection of data on the environment. About this time, the pressures started to build up. Structural changes in the private sector of industry to obtain economies of scale were leading to greater urbanisation. Reduced working hours, longer holidays, more affluence were all creating new demands on the environment because of leisure activities and because of the spread of second home ownership (even if many were little more than country huts). Expanding industry and a sudden awareness of the risks of pollution, all continued to generate renewed interest in preserving the countryside. It became the declared policy of the government to prevent further environmental degradation and to restore already damaged areas as far as possible. Land and regional authorities started to take a more constructive approach by zoning certain areas for use by industry, because depopulation also was a problem in some areas.

Gradually a series of local plans, not always compatible with each other, were drawn up. The need for a national plan of land and water use thus emerged and was produced in its first form in 1971. By this means, the government can control the use to which land shall be put. The first stage was the preparation of a map showing the land demands of the key industries for ten years ahead precisely and in outline for thirty years or more ahead. Each industry was asked to supply this information on a capital project basis, and the ministry of physical planning and local government reconciled the data in a form of density map, after consultation with the environmental protection board, trade unionists and others.

An outcome of the survey was a recommendation on the legislation that would be required to put a national plan into effect. An additional and typical recommendation was that research teams should be organised to obtain factual information on the current state of the environment and to study the sensitivity of various aspects of the environment and human beings to external changes.

The national plan for the physical use of land and water is in existence and is expected to be an important influence in the future. To date, its contact with long range planning for the economy has been limited but this is expected to change in the future, particularly as economic planning becomes more formal. The plan so far has only been concerned with expansion according to known technology and its deliberations have been coloured by existing values: wider considerations including some degree of uncertainty of the future and the irreversible nature of some decisions on the use of water resources, as for instance when a dam is constructed, are expected to feature in the next stages of the formulation of the national plan. The pressures are for the plan to be dynamic, flexible enough to change if there is a major change in technology or in the economic state of the country. But the national physical plan does exist on a quantified base and government control can be expected on an increasing scale. An environmental protection act has been in force since 1969 to control air and water pollution and noise nuisances. The national board for environment protection also sits as a specialised court with powers not dissimilar to those of the Labour Court and has wide powers to control the location of certain industrial processes.

At first sight, in opposition to the aims of the national plan, the regional policy of government is to attempt to stop or slow down depopulation of the rural areas by encouraging industry to develop there, and of course the rural areas are usually the areas of beauty, solitude and so on. Fortunately the reconciliation is not difficult because Sweden is such a large country for the population it carries, but none the less there is a problem. It was in fact at about the same time as the national plan was starting to appear as a concept, that an expert group for regional studies was established in 1965. One outcome has been the stimulation of research into regional problems, as many as one hundred researchers financed in various ways currently being involved. With a research effort of this magnitude, much of it in universities, a wide range of work can be undertaken ranging from the influence of economic factors to studies of the ethnographic characteristics of the different regions: the complementary problem of the growth of urbanisation and the pressures this brings to bear on people receives a good proportion of the effort. So far, cost benefit analysis does not seem to have featured at all largely in the investigations in spite of the fact that this is the very area in which it should be of value.

The implementation of regional policy takes place through the Labour Market Board using the persuasive force of grants and the priority release of investment funds. In future it is expected a closer liaison will occur between the administrators of the national physical plan and the research findings of the regional groups. Typical of the expectations are investigations into the possibility of a far reaching integration of education, work and leisure. The effects of new methods of distributing wealth such as a negative income tax or a cessation in the growth of consumption of goods are also possibilities under examination.

The production of a five year economic forecast, started in 1948, has become traditional in Sweden, the published analysis dealing with the different sectors of the economy in some detail. In the past this forecast has largely been compiled from the aggregation of individual forecasts made by the major companies. Gradually this has been changing so now there is an additional independent element in the forecast made by the Ministry of Industry. The assessment is actually made from an input-output econometric model covering twenty-eight sectors of the economy through eighty-five equations and about 200 variables. The output from the first run is fed back to the suppliers of data in industry and adjustments made for a re-run if necessary, so that a restricted form of dialogue does take place during the preparation of the forecast. It is generally believed the forecast has a useful function in disclosing the activities of one industry to the rest of the economy with which it will probably react. It is considered in some quarters that the time is now ripe to change this from a passive forecast accepting the events as they occur, into an active economic plan in which steps are taken to control the events.

A model with fixed relationships cannot sensibly be used for forecasting for longer than five years ahead. Yet a strong case can be made for longer term projections of up to say not less than fifteen years ahead. Changes would obviously be needed in the equations and methods of the model. It is argued by some economists that at the same time the model should be made capable of testing the effects of radical changes in government policy, such as in taxation, location or manpower restriction, to mention but three obvious areas. Additional outputs would correspondingly be required from the model which would be used to explore the effect of several alternative strategies.

The balance of evidence from all of these separate indications is that the government intends to take a more active part in planning or controlling the economy in the future. In the past, direct intervention by the government has been minimal although the indirect effects of government actions have been considerable and generally beneficial – the generation of investment funds through tax reliefs, the redeployment of workers through the activities of the Labour Market Board, and the helpful influence of the Labour Court are three examples of indirect effects. It is hoped direct intervention will be equally beneficial.

Before turning to a consideration of where these developments leave private industry, it should be said that Sweden expects these ideas to make an impact on the international scene. In addition to a long established pattern of neutrality, Sweden has, for years, been committed to helping the underdeveloped countries (1 per cent of the Gross Domestic Product is committed to this end in 1975), so Sweden expects to speak with some authority backed by analytical expertise which is rare outside of the big power blocs.

Productive industry

The productive sector of the economy is very much the goose that lays the golden eggs. No matter how laudable the intentions of government controls and no matter how praiseworthy the multiplicity of investigations, in the final analysis these all have to be paid for by the goods produced by industry, by forestry and by agriculture. If the capacity to produce is seriously impaired, then the capacity to sustain the growth of the welfare state will be similarly impaired.

If on the other hand, the changes lead, as they well might, to a greater involvement of the workers and management, unions and employers, in the will to succeed for the common good, then the productive sector should be able to continue to produce the goods still more efficiently. In fact, the need for still greater efficiency is inescapable. The same tendencies of investment, modernisation and redeployment, supported by effective market research seem inevitable for the survival of Sweden. Without them, the goose is at risk.

To maintain the position, the private sector is urged by government sources to develop long term planning with clearly defined goals in order that applied research can be steered into the most effective areas. Linked with them, the use of the twin techniques of technological forecasting and technological assessment are advocated – the one to anticipate new technical developments and the other to explore in depth the potential applications of a technology. In other words, the government is fully alive to the need to get the correct concept built into capital investment, but they are probably preaching to the converted since Swedish industrialists are already very good at this, particularly because the exporting sector is already largely specialised and efficient.

The effective socialist state is thus seen to demand an ever increasing level of productive efficiency from the productive, and largely private, sectors of the economy. The evidence of earlier chapters suggests there is little reason to doubt that Swedish industry will continue to respond.

BIBLIOGRAPHY

Chapter 1 and general information used throughout:

1 W. R. Meade and W. Hall, *Scandinavia*, Thomas & Hudson Ltd, 1972.
2 Anon., *Some Data About Sweden 1974-75*, Skandinaviska Enskilda Banken, Stockholm.
3 Anon., *Historisk Statistik for Sverige*, 1955.
4 Anon., *The Swedish Economy*, Swedish National Institute for Economic Research, published three times a year, Stockholm.
5 Anon., *Industri*, National Central Bureau of Statistics, annually, Stockholm.
6 Anon., *Sweden*, Swedish Institute, August 1973.
7 Anon., *Profitability League*, Veckans affarer, 2 August 1973, Stockholm.
8 Simon Caulkin, 'Sweden's Strikeless Wonder', *Management Today*, London, p. 699, January 1974.
9 Simon Caulkin, 'Volvo versus Ford', *Management Today*, p. 44, January 1973.
10 Gőran Smith, 'Gränges – Portrait of a Company', *Prisma*, Stockholm, 1972.
11 Anon., *The Statsfőretag Group of Sweden*, Solberg, Gothenburg, 1973.
12 Anon., *The Volvo Group*, 1972.
13 Anon., *Shipbuilders in Sweden. Facts and Figures*, The Swedish Shipbuilders' Association, Gothenburg, 1973.
14 Anon., *The Kockum Chronicle 1973*, The Kockum Group, Malmő, 1973.
15 Annual Company Reports for Volvo, Statsfőretag, Kockums, Saab, Gränges, Tändsticks, Sydkraft.
16 OECD, Annual Economic Reports on Sweden, Paris.
17 Gunnar Eliasson, *International Competitiveness – An Empirical Analysis of Swedish Manufacturing*, S.I., 1972, Stockholm.
18 Gunnar Eliasson, *Profits and Wage Determination – An Empirical Study of Swedish Manufacturing*, S.I., 1972, Stockholm.
19 Michael Drake, 'Apologia pro vita Scandinavica', *The Scandinavian Economic History Review*, pp. 84-8, Vol. XX, No. 1, 1972.
20 Assar Lindbeck, *Swedish Economic Policy*, Macmillan, London, 1974.
20a H. G. Jones, 'Sweden and Modernisation', *Futures*, London, p. 152, April 1975.

Chapter 2:

21 Roland Huntford, *The New Totalitarians*, Allen Lane, Penguin Press, 1971.
22 Anon., *Labour Market Policy 1974-75*, Labour Market Board, Broberg, 1973.
23 Anon., *The Swedish System of Investment Funds*, The Swedish Institute, January 1974.
24 Anon., *Active Manpower Policy in Sweden*, The Swedish Institute, June 1973.
25 Anon., *Statsföretag 1972 – Group Review*, 1973.
26 Anon., *Financial and Operating Statistics 1972*, Volvo 1973.

Chapter 3:

27 Simon Caulkin, 'How Kockums Bettered its Basics', *Management Today*, London, p. 102, September 1973.
28 Kurt Lekäs and Nils-Erik Norén, 'Some Fundamental Ideas in a Model for Evaluation of Industrial Projects from the Point of View of National Economy', LKAB Report, 1973.
29 A. R. Prest and R. Turvey, 'Cost-Benefit Analysis: A Survey', *The Economic Journal*, December 1965.

Chapter 4:

30 Bo Carlson, *Trade Unions in Sweden*, Tiden, 1969.
31 Anon., *Swedish Trade Union Confederation*, Tiden, 1970.
32 Anon., *SACO – The Swedish Confederation of Professional Associations*, 1974.
33 Eric Jacobs, *European Trade Unionism*, Croom Helm, London, 1973.

Chapter 5:

34 Anon., *SAF, LO and TCO Collective Agreements on Collaboration*, Andrén and Holms, 1972.
35 Anon., *SAF and LO Collective Agreements on Rationalisation*, Andrén and Holms, 1972.
36 Anon., *SAF – Swedish Employers' Confederation*, Andrén and Holms, 1970.
37 Anon., *SI – Federation of Swedish Industries*, Esper, 1973.
38 Anon., *What is the Development Council*, Kugel Offset, 1972.
39 R. W. Grubbström and Bengt Holmgren, *Ingenjörernas fördelning*, Teknisk Tidskrift, 1968.

Chapter 6:

40 Act concerning the Rights of Association and Negotiation 1936.
41 Act concerning Collective Bargaining, 1936.
42 Act concerning Employment Security, 1974.
43 F. Schmidt, *The Law of Labour Relations in Sweden*, Almqvist and Wiksell, Uppsala, 1962.

Chapter 7:

44 Anon., *Labour Relations in Sweden*, The Swedish Institute, August 1973.
45 Anon., *SFA, LO and TCO Collective Agreements on Works Councils – 1966*, Andrén and Holms, 1972.
46 Rolf Lindholm, *The Condemned Piecework*, SAF, Stockholm, 1972.
47 Håken Lundgren, *Work Organisation and Payment System*, SAF, Stockholm, 1974.
48 Jan-Peder Norstedt and Stefan Agurén, *The Saab-Scania Report*, SAF, Stockholm.
49 Scania Press Releases, 1973.
50 *The New Philosophy*, Volvo, Gothenburg, 1974.

51 Pehr G. Gyllenhammar, Speech at opening of Kalmar plant, 4 June 1974.
52 Volvo Press Releases, May 1974.
53 Anon., *Guidelines*, Kockums 1973, Malmö.
54 Nils Elvander, 'Collective Bargaining and Incomes Policy in the Nordic Countries', *British Journal of Industrial Relations*, Vol. XII, No. 3, November 1974, pp. 417-37.

Chapter 8:

55 Hans Lindestad and Jan-Peder Norstedt, *Autonomous Groups and Payment by Result*, SAF, Stockholm, 1973.
56 Jan Edgren, *With Varying Success*, SIAR, Stockholm, 1974.
57 Börje Strender, *What is a Just Wage?*, SAF, Stockholm, 1971.
58 Rolf Lindholm, *Advances in Work Organisation*, SAF, Stockholm, 1973.
59 Rolf Lindholm, *The New Style Factories*, SAF, Stockholm, 1974.

Chapter 9:

60 Act relating to Board Representation for the Employees, December 1972.
61 André Thiria, *Labour's Voice Joins the Corporate Board*, The Swedish Institute, June 1973.
62 Svante Nycander, *Industrial Relations and Workers' Participation*, The Swedish Institute, September 1974.
63 Graham Turner, 'Is German Worker Power a Success?', *Sunday Telegraph*, 22 September 1974.
64 Ian Watson, 'Testing Time for Swedish Worker Power', *Sunday Telegraph*, 2 February 1975.

Chapter 10:

65 Annual Reports of Labour Market Board, Stockholm.
66 The Swedish Economy Reports – National Institute of Economic Research, Stockholm.
67 OECD Economic Reports on Sweden and other countries.

Chapter 11:

68 Anon., *The Swedish National Pension Insurance Fund – A Survey*, Axel Abrahamsons, Karlskrona, 1972.
69 Anon., *Allmänna Pensionsfonden – Report for 1973*, Esselte Vardetryck, 1974.
70 Yngve Larsson and Lennart Fogelström, *The Long-Range Corporate Planning Model of the South Swedish Power Company*, Sydkraft, Malmö, 1969.
71 Yngve Larsson and Lennart Fogelström, 'A Model for Long-Range Financial Planning in Energy Utilities', Eighth World Energy Conference, Bucharest, July 1971.
72 Anon., *The Swedish Credit Market*, The Swedish Bankers' Association, Stockholm, 1971.
73 Martin Schitzer, *The Economy of Sweden*, Praeger, London, 1970.
74 Annual Reports of the Swedish Investment Bank, 1968 to 1974.

75 Anon., *Some Data about Sweden 1975-76*, Skandinaviska Enskilda Banken, in proof stage June 1975, Stockholm.

Chapter 12:

76 *To Choose A Future*, The Swedish Institute, Secretariat for Future Studies, 1974.
77 Data Act, 11 May 1973.
78 Anon., *Science, Growth and Society*, OECD Report, Paris, 1971.
79 Jay W. Forrester, *World Dynamics*, Wright-Allen Press, 1971.
80 Anon., 'Planning Sweden', SOU 1971:75, Stockholm, 1973.
81 Erich Jantsch, *Technological Forecasting in Perspective*, OECD Report, Paris, 1967.
82 Kurt Samuelsson, *From Great Power to Welfare State*, George Allen and Unwin Ltd., London, 1968.

INDEX